Touching the Heart

Tales for the Human Journey

Touching *the* Heart

Tales for
the Human
Journey

William J. Bausch

TWENTY
THIRD *23rd*
PUBLICATIONS

DEDICATION

To Jim Bausch
Witty, Wise, Wonderful
Brother Beyond Compare
Righteous Pilgrim
May he rest in Peace

Twenty-Third Publications
A Division of Bayard
One Montauk Avenue, Suite 200
New London, CT 06320
(860) 437-3012 or (800) 321-0411
www.23rdpublications.com

The Scripture passages contained herein are from the *New Revised Standard Version of the Bible*, copyright ©1989, by the Division of Christian Education of the National Council of Churches in the U.S.A. All rights reserved.

ISBN 978-1-58595-617-3
Library of Congress Catalog Card Number: 2006937350
Printed in the U.S.A.

CONTENTS

Acknowledgments

"Am I a Man Yet?" by Donald P. Doyle is taken from *Storytelling Magazine*, March–April 2001.

"The Story Bag" is taken from *Dancing with Wonder* by Nancy King. Belgium, WI: Champion Press, 2005.

"The Sacrifice Flower" is taken from *Stories of Awe and Abundance* by Sr. Jose Hobday. New York: Continuum International Publishing Group, 1999.

"The Tin Box" is taken from *Twelve and One-Half Keys* by Edward M. Hayes, ©1981. Used with permission of the publisher, Forest of Peace, an imprint of Ave Maria Press, Inc., Notre Dame, IN 46556. www.forestof-peace.com.

"Tommy" is taken from *Unconditional Love* by John Powell, S.J. Bethany, TX: Resources for Christian Living, 1978.

"Death Comes for the Aunt" and "Maum Jean" are from *A Touch of Wonder* by Arthur Gordon. Grand Rapids, MI: Baker Publishing Group, 1996.

"Ananias" from *BECAUSE GOD LOVES STORIES: An Anthology of Jewish Storytelling* by Steven Zeitlin. ©1997 by Steven Zeitlin. Reprinted with permission of Simon & Schuster Adult Publishing Group.

"Fortune and the Woodcutter" and "The Magic Towel" are from *In the Ever After: Fairy Tales and the Second Half of Life* by Allan B. Chinen. Reprinted by permission of Chiron Publications, New York, 1989.

"The Stolen Skin" and "The Lady of the Lake Waters" are retellings by Allison Cox. Used with permission.

"The Very Pretty Lady" is from *The Devil's Storybook* by Natalie Babbitt, published by Farrar, Straus & Giroux, 1984. Used with permission.

"St. Mungo" and "St. Alexander" are from *Sixty Saints for Boys* and *Sixty Saints for Girls*, Continuum International Book Publishing, Ltd., 1999. Used with permission.

Introduction

The earliest surviving work of literature in Western civilization is the *Epic of Gilgamesh*. For 1700 years it lay hidden beneath the earth until in 1850 archeologists found it in the collection of an Assyrian king as they were excavating the Royal Library in Nineveh, in what is now Iraq. In 1872 the first translation appeared. It told not only the basic outline of the flood story we have in the Bible, but also and mainly the story of King Gilgamesh, who lived about 2800 BC. Despite the fragmentary versions of the epic scattered over the centuries, enough of the overall plot of the story can be detected, and it goes like this.

> Gilgamesh, the son of a goddess and a human, is the sophisticated, proud, and arrogant king of the great city, Uruk. He is hard on his people, who pray for relief. The gods, who normally couldn't care less about humans, hear their pleas and create Enkidu, a wild, unkempt, uncivilized hairy man who eats grass and lives with the animals, the very opposite of Gilgamesh. Enkidu, however, becomes civilized through his encounter with a prostitute who introduces him to sex and civilization. When Gilgamesh and Enkidu meet, there is a terrible fight, but after the fight they become truly fast friends.
>
> Together they set out for adventure. In one of these adventures they come upon a great cedar forest where they kill the forest's fearsome guardian, Humbaba. The gods are angry over the killing of Humbaba and decree that either Gilgamesh or Enkidu must die, one or the other. Enkidu falls ill and dies, deeply regretting that he did not die from some great battle but was ignominiously felled by disease. Gilgamesh mourns deeply his friend's death and suddenly is filled with terror over his own mortality. He therefore sets out to find the one man

1

who had ever become immortal, Uta-napishti, to learn from him the secret of avoiding death. Uta-napishti and his wife were the only ones to survive the great flood and so the gods granted them immortality.

Gilgamesh's travels take him to the end of the world where he meets a goddess (a tavern keeper!) who tells him to give up his fruitless quest, but if he insists on continuing, he must find a ferryman to take him across the ocean to Uta-napishti. He makes the trip but, alas, it turns out that Uta-napishti cannot transfer his gift to another. It is personal. However, he does tell Gilgamesh how to find a certain plant at the bottom of the sea that will renew his youth every time he gets old. (Immortality on the installment plan.) So Gilgamesh dives into the ocean where he indeed finds the plant, but one night when he is taking a bath in a pool, a snake comes and steals the plant. (Which explains why the snake can shed its skin and renew itself each time! The thieving snake, of course, is also the forerunner of the spoiler serpent in the mythical Garden of Eden.) Gilgamesh sadly returns home but one day as he looks around his great city and its mighty walls, he finally realizes that he will live on in fame and honor, in what he has left behind. Not immortality, to be sure, but not so bad. (The very themes of the Homeric epics: the greatest achievement is to live on in fame and honor—to leave behind a good name—and mighty deeds.)

Thus our civilization's very first story. And its five-millennia-old themes are the universal ones we all relate to: the quest for fame, the fear of death, and the search for immortality. It also addresses the nagging human questions: What is life all about? Are fame and a good name sufficient compensation for death? Then, too, the story raises issues of sexuality, male bonding, and overcoming life's obstacles. So the *Epic of Gilgamesh*, as old as it is, is forever current. It is our epic, our story. And it reveals to us something else about ourselves: from the beginning we are intractably a storytelling people. Moreover, as we shall soon see in Chapter One, story themes get played over and over again, which is why novelist Willa Cather observed that there are really only two or three basic stories in the whole world. Take the *Epic of Gilgamesh*, for example. Centuries and centuries later, in the twentieth century in fact, its basic theme appears in this folktale, "The King and the Wise Woman."

He was a powerful king, loved by the queen and feared by his enemies. He had everything but he had no child (no "immortality"). "Who will carry on my work?" he cried. "Who will inherit my power, my memory? I must have an heir!" And so a reward was offered to anyone who could help the royal couple fulfill their dream and overcome their sterility. Many tried and many died as the king and queen remained bitter and childless.

One day a wise old woman came to the king and queen. Shown into the throne room, she told them then and there that a child could be theirs if the king would but do one thing. "And what is that?" the king asked anxiously, filled with hope.

The Wise One spoke, "Your Majesty, because there is no system in your kingdom for washing away human waste, there is much sickness in the land. All waters are the same. Use your army, therefore, to dig canals through the cities and villages so that the waste water may go to one place while the water for drinking and cooking will go to another."

The king was skeptical. "And this will bring me a child?"

The Wise One smiled. "It is assured, Your Majesty." It was done. The pestilence that had attacked the people for generations was eventually gone, but after many months there was still no sign of pregnancy.

So the Wise One was summoned back before the throne. "You have lied to me. I did as you said and yet no child is ours. Prepare to die."

But the Wise One spoke quickly. "Oh, my good king, but you have fulfilled only a part of the requirement. You must now parcel out the land to the serfs and peasants, allowing each a lot large enough for both sustenance and sale."

"Why," roared the king, "should I give away what is mine?"

"So that you might have one with your name to follow," she said softly.

The mention of the one spoke so deeply to the king that he did as the old woman had instructed. Every able-bodied peasant and serf was given his own lot. They could, for the first time in memory, feed their families and guests with ease. Then the king and queen waited. But still no child grew between them. The king was furious and demanded that the old woman be brought before him and he condemned her to death.

"Your Majesty may kill me, but then you will never know if the last requirement will bring fruit."

"The last?" the king asked with suspicion and hope.

"Yes, Your Majesty, one last thing will ensure you an heir. Of this I am sure."

"If it does not," said the king with menace in his quivering voice, "your heirs will be denied their mother."

"Have no fear. The last thing you must do is dismantle your army. For the last two decades our kingdom has fought war after war. Make lasting treaties with your neighbors and dissolve that force that once protected your aggression."

"But my army!" exclaimed the king.

"I give you no choice, Your Majesty." And so it was done. For the first time in the memory of many, young men remained home behind plow and anvil and children danced safely by the borders. The king, having sacrificed so much, was sure that now he would receive his heart's desire.

But the days turned into months and the months turned into a year when the king had a scaffold erected in the throne room and the old woman was sent for. "Now you will die. Do you have anything to say?"

The old woman's eyes looked toward a window and she spoke quietly. "Your Majesty, your wife was barren, as was the land. Your people died of sickness, starvation, and war, and now look at your land. You have given your people health, wealth, and the security of peace. You have given them a better life and your name is spoken with reverence. It is bestowed upon the children of your subjects and will be passed down to their children and their children's children. And it will be always a name spoken with honor. You, through acts of loving kindness, will be the father of and remembered by all the children of this land."

The king, whose eyes had followed the old woman's, gazed at the new landscape he had created. Taking her hand, he knew she was right. His children would now number with the stars and he would be remembered forever.

This is the same basic theme as in the epic. Like Gilgamesh, the king settled for immortality through the legacy he would leave behind. (In Chapter Six the identical theme will reappear in the Japanese story, "Santoro.")

The Story Behind the Story

Story is a human imperative. Story defines our humanity, lends identity to tribes and nations, asks our questions, poses our problems, cuts us down to size, and dangles mystery before our eyes. It is surely not without reason, as we shall see in this book, that the West's most influential work is the Bible, which is also a storybook, a compendium of stories gathered, reworked, retold, and reedited over the centuries. The "fictionalized history" we call the Bible gives us the stories of creation, exodus, Abraham, Moses, David, warriors, kings, fools, prophets, wonder workers, knaves, Jesus, Peter, and Judas.

To sum up, everywhere in the world at all times and in all places in every era, story is the vehicle of wonder, guidance, reflection, and wisdom. Until very recently, the oral story prevailed for most of humanity's journey. Even with the invention of writing, less than one percent of the people could read and write, so story's dominance, power, and place must be respected. It's only in modern times that story has been denigrated, much, as we shall see, to our loss.

From Word to Page

I just mentioned the oral story and here, for the sake of completeness, I must make three emphatic remarks. The first is one of common sense, that the stories were spoken (and performed) before they were written

for century after century. The second is that in the process these oral stories were endlessly reworked, redacted, and reinterpreted over the centuries before they were written. The third is that the stories were even
more reworked, emended, and edited after they were written down. In
short, what we get when we pick up the written story—*The Song of
Roland*, *The Iliad*, the Qur'an, or the Bible—is the end-product of centuries, even millennia, of vocal and literary activity. There are, then, really no single authors, even though we speak of them. We say, for instance,
that Homer wrote *The Iliad* and *The Odyssey*, but "Homer" is a code word
for the hundreds of poets and performers who spoke and gave their own
twist to the recitation, the hundreds of scribes who updated and
imposed their own agendas. We say that Moses wrote the first five books
of the Bible, the Pentateuch, but they too, are the products of many,
many hands over a very long time. Matthew, Mark, Luke, and John are
also code names for virtual committees who over many decades had
their hands in the production of the gospels. Sir Thomas Malory's *Morte
d'Arthur* is a retelling of the ancient Arthurian legends gathered from
many sources in several languages. The Grimm Brothers reworked and
reedited ancient spoken folktales.

My point is that since the great stories, epics, and folktales of Western
civilization (including the Bible) were first spoken, sung (the psalms,
The Song of Roland), or, more accurately, performed, two cautions immediately stand out. First, we must appreciate that we miss entirely the
rhythms, cadences, and puns of the original performance. We miss the
modulating tone, the facial expressions, the raising of the eyebrow sig-
naling that the sober word that has just been said might possibly be
nonsense. We miss the shouting, whispering, speeding up, or slowing
down. We miss the gestures, grimaces, smiles. Our use of punctuations,
italics, capitals, and boldface type can't really convey all of this.

This was brought home to me when in my college days I was attempting to read Shakespeare. Even with the footnotes, I wasn't getting anywhere. Then one day I bought a recording (an old 78 record, the size,
back then, of a dinner plate) by the great actor Sir John Gielgud called
"The Seven Stages of Man." It contained excerpts from Shakespeare's
plays. I was mesmerized. Gielgud's performance, his interpretations, his

voice brought all to life, and I could sense the genius of the playwright, the magic of his poetry, the seduction of his words.

As you read the written story, try to be aware of the voice(s) behind it. (The written word, to be sure, has its advantages, not the least of which is preservation.) Our worship of and reliance on the fixed written word—and now the lifeless digital word—has dulled our appreciation of a true performance, and worse, made us believe that truth in found only in factuality, a recent conceit, as we shall see. And, as I indicated above, this has robbed us of some good puns. Here's an example from the gospels. John the Baptist says, "Do not imagine you can say, 'We have Abraham for our father.' I tell you that God can make children for Abraham out of these stones." For a long time interpreters scratched their heads trying to figure out what possible connection there could be between "children" and "stones." That is, until the scholars took the Greek text and put it back in the original performing language that the Greek was translating: Aramaic, the language Jesus and John the Baptist spoke. There the word *ben* (as in, for example, Ben Sirach) means "son" or "child" and its plural is *banim*. The word *eben* means "stone" and its plural is *ebanim*. So John the Baptist was saying that God was able to make *banim* out of *ebanin*, a nice pun, an obvious play on words, and so spoken, it would have brought smiles.

Truth Claims

Thus, we finally come to the point of why I told the story of Gilgamesh and why I wrote this book: to help people see the centrality of stories, to read and hear Scripture as story and not as history, and to learn to enrich and expand their lives by looking at the "story *behind* the story." I want to break readers out of the literalism that constricts their spiritual and social lives, to give them an appreciation of metaphor and symbol, and, if you will, the "sacramentality" of the world.

Finally (and I shall mention this again at the end of the book), I want to disabuse people of something they learned in school, namely that scientific truth is the only truth. Scientific truth, it is claimed, is clear, demonstrable, and obvious. Anything else is subjective, personal, and unacceptable for public discourse or policy. That "truth" equals scientific truth is an accepted and established axiom. But this *shibboleth* is disastrously wrong. This book maintains that there exist truths of a very different order, and that truth comes in different ways and resides in other modes and at other levels. The falling apple demonstrably obeys the law of gravity. That is a truth. But so are the fictions of Jane Austen and Charles Dickens, the fables of Aesop, and the parables of Jesus. They carry truth as well. As the old saying goes, "Some stories are factual. All stories are true." This book makes a point of that.

This book is based on a series of lectures that I have given several times and reflects much of its original tone. The first eight chapters cover the ways stories can enrich our lives. Chapter Nine deals with some of the sociological realities that support the first eight chapters. The title of the book indicates that it is filled with stories. Indeed it is: some old, some new, some favorites repeated from some of my previous books.

> Many centuries ago, a rich sultan in Baghdad gave a banquet in honor of the birth of his son. All the nobility who partook of the feast brought costly gifts, except a young sage who came empty-handed. He explained to the sultan, "Today the young prince will receive many precious gifts, jewels, and rare coins. My gift is different. From the time he is old enough to listen until manhood, I will come to the palace every day and tell him stories of our Arabian heroes. When he becomes our ruler he will be just and honest."
>
> The young sage kept his word. When the prince was at last made sultan, he became famous for his wisdom and honor. To this day, an inscription on a scroll in Baghdad reads, "It was because of the seed sown by the tales."

May these tales for the human journey seed your heart.

CHAPTER ONE

The Seven Basic Plots

"I create fiction to tell the truth."

EUDORA WELTY

A woman went to see the Governor about getting her husband out of the penitentiary.

"What is he in for?" the Governor wanted to know.

"For stealing a ham."

"That doesn't sound too bad. Is he a good worker?"

"No, I wouldn't say that. He's pretty lazy."

"Oh. Well, he's good to you and the children, isn't he?"

"No, he's not. He's pretty mean to us, if you want to know the truth."

"Why would you want a man like that out of prison?"

"Well, Governor, we're out of ham."

That was to get your attention. How about these two:

Tanzan and Ekido were once traveling together down a muddy road. A heavy rain was still falling. Coming around a bend,

9

they met a lovely girl in a silk kimono and sash, unable to cross the intersection.

"Come on, girl," said Tanzan at once. Lifting her in his arms, he carried her over the mud.

Ekido did not speak again until that night when they reached a lodging temple. Then he could no longer restrain himself. "We monks don't go near females," he told Tanzan, "especially not young and lovely ones. It is dangerous. Why did you do that?"

"I left the girl there," said Tanzan. "Are you still carrying her?"

How about this one from that irreverent and crude Jewish comedian, Lenny Bruce:

You and I know what a Jew is—One Who Killed Our Lord. I don't know if we get much press on that in Illinois—we did this about two thousand years ago—two thousand years of Polack kids whacking the crap out of us coming home from school. Dear, dear, there should be a statute of limitations for that crime. Why do you keep busting our chops for this crime? Why, because you skirt the issue. You blame it on the Roman soldiers. All right. I'll clear the air once and for all, and confess. Yes, we did it. I did it. My father found a note in my basement. It said, "We killed him. Signed, Morty." And a lot people say to me, "Why did you kill Christ?" I dunno…it was one of those parties got out of hand, you know.

We killed him because he didn't want to become a doctor, that's why we killed him.

The first story usually elicits a soft "aha" kind of laughter, signifying that people catch something beneath and behind it. The second story gets an uneasy chuckle. That's because underneath the punch line, it carries a heavy burden. Bruce's monologue is weighted with a painful history. I open this book with these samples because both have their place in storytelling and both point to my main theme: good stories are about more than they are about. They are revelatory of the human condition, the human experience, the human journey. They carry truth. To support this contention, let me, in the first two chapters, build on the foundation laid by Christopher Booker in his magisterial work, *The Seven Basic Plots*. We will follow his outline and frequently use his wise words.

The More Things Change...

Booker reminds those old enough to remember, that in the mid-1970s people waited in long lines outside movie houses all over the Western world to see a breakthrough horror movie unlike anything they had ever seen. It was Steven Spielberg's *Jaws*, a name that would fall into the common vocabulary of American folklore, become enshrined in Disneyland's Universal Studios, and become a regular rerun on television to rival *The Wizard of Oz*. The story is familiar. The idyllic serenity of a little Long Island seaside resort, Amity, is suddenly shattered by the arrival offshore of a monstrous, oversized shark who violently attacks and devours a hapless girl. Other victims follow, causing great alarm and panic. The local police chief (Roy Scheider) finally convinces the mayor, anguished over all that lost summer revenue as people are scared off, that there is a terrible monster out there. He hires a shark specialist (sardonic Richard Dreyfuss) and a crusty captain (Robert Shaw) to set out to do battle with the monster. After many an encounter, false starts, and near disasters, not the least of which is the devouring of the captain, the shark is slain. The community breathes a sign of relief and there is universal jubilation. The great threat has been lifted. Life in Amity can begin again.

Few of the zillions of people who saw this gripping movie would know they were actually seeing an ancient rerun or that an unkempt bunch of animal-skinned Saxon warriors, huddled round the fire of some drafty hall twelve hundred years before, had listened to the minstrel chanting the verses of that very story. Only back then it was called *Beowulf*, not *Jaws*.

Compare. The first part of *Beowulf* tells the story of another seaside community by the name of Heorot. Its serenity is also shattered by the arrival, not of Jaws, but of a monster called Grendel, who lives in the depths of a nearby lake. The people are thrown into an absolute panic as, night after night, Grendel makes his mysterious attacks on the hall where they sleep, seizing one victim after another and tearing them to pieces. Finally, when it's all almost too much to bear, the hero Beowulf sets out to do battle. He deals first with Grendel and then with his even more terrible monster mother. There is a bloody, climactic fight in the churning waters until at last both monsters are slain. The community breathes a sigh of relief and there is universal jubilation. The great threat has been lifted. Life in Heorot can begin again.

The plot lines in both *Jaws* and *Beowulf* are the same. In fact, they seem to be telling the same story—which, in fact, they are. Do you think that the author of *Jaws*, the late Peter Benchley, copied *Beowulf*? Not likely. More likely, his story arose in his own fertile imagination. Still, the fact remains that the two stories are similar and both are similar to other versions all over the world. How do you explain this convergence? What is the explanation? That we will explore shortly.

The Prevalence of Story

But first we must take note of this phenomenon. At any given moment, right now, all over the world, hundreds of millions of people are engaged in what is one of the most common and familiar of all forms of human activity: the story. Reading stories, telling them, formally or informally, watching them on television, on DVDs, the computer, the stage, in movies, magazines, books, the newspapers. Our history books are largely made up of stories. The first historian, the Greek Herodotus, penned his work in the form of stories. The Bible is basically a story-book. Even much of our conversation is taken up with recounting the events of everyday life in the form of stories. "Did you hear about…?" "I read the other day…" "Well, Joan told Alice and she told me that…" "Have you read *The Kite Runner*? Great book." (Indeed it is.) We're daily awash in stories. So deep and so instinctive is our need for them that, as small children, we have no sooner learned to speak than we begin demanding to be told stories, evidence of an appetite likely to continue to our dying day. And we have to tell them in exactly the same way, as every parent or grandparent knows. Don't you dare condense three little pigs to two little pigs to save time!

So central a part have stories played in every society in history that we take it for granted that the great storytellers, such as Homer or Shakespeare or Jesus or Dickens or Elie Weisel, should be among the most famous people who ever lived. In our times we also take it for granted that certain men and women, such as Humphrey Bogart, Lawrence Olivier, Meryl Streep, Kathryn Hepburn, or Anthony Hopkins, are regarded as among the best known figures in the world, simply because they have acted out the characters from stories on the movie screen. Nor do we find it odd that we have named many of the most conspicuous heavenly bodies—Venus, Mars, Jupiter, Orion, Perseus, Andromeda—after characters from stories. (Nowadays, some parents, raised on television, even name their children after television story characters.) And we are unconsciously giving a nod to traditional tales when we buy a Midas muffler, shop at the Jack and Jill clothing stores, visit a Shangri-La or Humpty's restaurant, stay at the Sandman hotel, buy a Mercury, and use Apollo car washes or Mitchum aftershave. So, stories persist and are expressions of our lives, revealers of our souls, and mirrors of our culture. Here's one called "The Soul-Taker."

Once upon a time there were three sisters who lived high in the hills and they honored God alone. And one day as they were roaming through the hills looking for things to eat, and looking for some things that might be of some benefit to them, they discovered a cave. And inside the cave they found a huge, huge chest full of gold. It was so heavy it would have taken a dozen people just to lift it, let alone try to move it. They looked at it and were stunned. And finally, one of the sisters, in a moment of panic, yelled out, "It's the Soul-taker! It's the Soul-taker! Let us flee!"

And so the three sisters ran out of the cave yelling and screaming, running right into the arms of six robbers who happened to be hiding out in those very hills. They kept fighting the robbers off and saying, "No! Get away! Get away! It's the Soul-taker! We must get away!" Finally, the robbers calmed the three sisters down and said, "Now, what is this Soul-taker you're shouting about? Show us. And so the three sisters led the robbers to the gold. And when the robbers saw the gold and how much there was, all they could do was dream and fantasize that they wouldn't have to rob ever again. They had more than enough gold right here in front of them. However, while all the robbers were looking over all that gold, the three sisters slipped away and hid out.

Now, these six robbers had been in the hills for a long time and they were very hungry. And they were also very weak from running from various groups of people, and so among the six of them, they couldn't budge the huge chest full of gold. Yet, they didn't want to leave it there. They were afraid somebody else would find it. But they didn't know what to do. They sat down thinking until they finally decided that the best thing would be if three of the robbers would go into town with three of the gold pieces and buy food and provisions for everybody and the other three would stay and guard the chest. So it was decided. They took a few of the gold pieces and three of them went off into the village and the other three stayed at home to guard the treasure.

The three that stayed in the cave silently looked over the gold for a long, long time until finally they began talking to each other saying, "You know, gold splits three ways much better than it splits six, right? Why do we have to share it with everybody, especially the other three?" But they said, "Yeah, but what can we do?" They thought a while and finally said, "We'll fix an ambush. That's it! When the other three come back, we'll jump out, kill them, and then we can divide the gold just among the three of us. We'll be twice as rich."

Well, the fact is, they weren't the only ones scheming and plotting. The three that had gone into town just happened to be thinking the same thing. They said to one another, "What would it be like to have all that gold and split it just among the three of us instead of all six of us?" And they said, "Yeah, but what can we do?" They thought about it for a while on the long trip into town, and finally they said, "We won't just buy food and provisions, we'll buy some poison. We'll eat our food before we go back. We'll put the poison in the other food and then they'll eat and die. And then we can split the gold just three ways."

So it was all decided. Smiling to themselves as they came back toward the cave, they weren't expecting the ambush. The three hiding inside jumped out and slaughtered them. Then they took the provisions and the food and went inside the cave. Rejoicing at their cleverness and new-found wealth, they ate the food, got organized for their escape, but before they could do another thing, all three of the robbers lay there dead along with the other three they had killed.

It was weeks and weeks, in fact, almost a year, before the three sisters came back toward the cave. What did they see? At the outskirts of the cave they found the skeletons of three of the robbers. And inside with the gold they found the other three skeletons. They were astonished. And the sister who had originally yelled "Soul-taker" looked at the other two and said, "I told you it was a Soul-taker. We must get out of here!" And with that, they all ran out of the cave, again yelling as loud as they could, "Soul-taker! Soul-taker! Soul-taker!"

This is a timeless story of greed and it is found in many variations throughout the world and it fascinates us.

We even find everywhere the irresistible lowest form of humor story, the dreaded pun. For example:

After Quasimodo's death, word spread through the streets of Paris that a new bell ringer was needed. The bishop decided that he would conduct the interviews personally and went up into the belfry to begin the screening process. After observing several applicants demonstrate their skills, he decided to call it a day, when a lone, armless man approached him and announced that he was there to apply for the bell ringer's job. The bishop was incredulous. "You have no arms!"

"No matter," said the man, "Observe!" He then began striking the bells with his face, producing a beautiful melody on the carillon. The bishop listened in astonishment, convinced that he had finally found a suitable replacement for Quasimodo.

Suddenly, rushing forward to strike a bell, the armless man tripped and he plunged headlong out of the belfry window to his death in the street below.

The stunned bishop rushed to his side. When he reached the street, a crowd had gathered around the fallen figure, drawn by the beautiful music they had heard only moments before.

As they silently parted to let the bishop through, one of them asked, "Bishop, who was this man?"

"I don't know his name," the bishop sadly replied, "but his face rings a bell."

There's more to this story to make you groan.

The following day, despite the sadness that weighed heavily on his heart due to the unfortunate death of the armless campanologist, the bishop continued his interviews for the bell ringer of Notre Dame. The first man to approach him said, "Your Excellency, I am the brother of the poor, armless wretch who fell to his death from this very belfry yesterday. I pray that you honor his life by allowing me to replace him in his duty."

The bishop agreed to give the man an audition and, as the armless man's brother stooped to pick up a mallet to strike the first bell, he groaned, clutched at his chest and died on the spot.

Two monks, hearing the bishop's cries of grief at this second tragedy, rushed up the stairs to his side. "What has happened?" the first asked breathlessly. "Who is this man?" (Here it comes.)

"I don't know his name," sighed the distraught bishop, "but he's a dead ringer for his brother."

Stories and puns like these are found everywhere in every era and in every culture. As I noted, we are innate storytellers.

The Commonality of Stories

Yet, the question lingers: Why do we indulge in this strange form of activity? Why are we such a storytelling people? What real purpose do stories serve? Not only that, but note that wherever men and women have told stories, all over the world in any time frame, the stories emerging in their imaginations have tended to take shape in remarkably similar ways. In short, no matter where they arise, the stories are the same all over and at all times. Folktales, for example, tell the same basic story in places culturally and geographically worlds apart. It is one thing, for example, as Booker puts it, for variants of Cinderella to be found all over Europe, from Serbia to the Shetlands, from Russia to Spain; at least all these share some common cultural and linguistic traditions. But when the very same story is found in China, Africa, and among North American Indians, it becomes clear that there has to be a common source rooted deeply in human nature itself.

What's going on? Why such similar basic plots? "Is a puzzlement" as the musical King of Siam said. One current theory says that the cause for the similarities lies in the human heart, the human mind itself. The human mind is so constituted, some scholars say, that it works in certain forms or grooves and around certain basic ingrained images. Something like the water that takes the shape of the glass it's poured into. In our deeper unconsciousness, our basic genetic inheritance, our psychic configuration, is the same for all people and that sameness provides the elemental stuff for images and symbols that are the stuff of story. Theologians would say that humankind is made in the image and likeness of God and that is the common element, and that common origin is behind the common ways we tell the same stories and use the same images.

Whatever the case, we find consistent themes and consistent patterns underlying all stories. Even the same basic figures keep reappearing: witches and ogres, giants and wicked stepmothers. Personified evil comes in the guise of Stromboli in *Pinocchio*, the Wicked Witch of the West in *Oz*, Specter or Goldfinger in the James Bond movies. Personified goodness comes in the guise of wise fairies or animals: Raphael, Gabriel, Fairy godmothers, Jiminy Cricket, Gandolf. Courage is personified in such heroes as Moses, David, Dr. Jones, Frodo, and John Wayne. In fact, scholars have come up with seven basic plots that play over and over again all over the world and in every age. Again, following the schema given by Christopher Booker, we might describe these as seven basic plots of the human journey. Let's look at them—and recognize them in our own lives.

1. The Combat Myth, or Overcoming the Monster

To briefly recap from the Introduction, the earliest known version of the "overcoming the monster" theme is the ancient Sumerian *Epic of Gilgamesh*. Among its subplots is this one: the kingdom of Uruk has fallen under the terrible shadow of a monstrous figure called Humbaba who lives across the world in an underground cavern in a cedar forest. The hero Gilgamesh goes to the armorers who equip him with special weapons. He sets out to find Humbaba's lair. There is a series of taunting exchanges and finally Gilgamesh kills his opponent.

Five thousand years later, in 1962, millions gathered for the latest version of the "overcoming the monster" theme. It was the premier opening of a new movie about the Gilgamesh story. Only this time it was called *Dr. No*, starring Sean Connery as James Bond, kicking off one of the most popular series ever. But the plot, notice, is exactly the same. The Western world falls under the shadow of a great and mysterious evil, the mad and deformed Dr. No who lives halfway across the world in an underground cavern on a remote island. The hero, James Bond, goes to the armorer, Q, who equips him with special weapons. He sets out on a hazardous journey where he finally comes face to face with the monster. They engage in a series of cat-and-mouse exchanges and ultimately, as they must, enter into a gigantic struggle. Bond finally manages to kill his opponent. The Western world has been saved and Bond can return home triumphant, with, of course, his latest female conquest.

Every culture has some version of this "overcoming the monster" theme. The Greeks had tons of them, such as the famous stories of Perseus overcoming two monsters; Theseus, who kills the monstrous Minotaur; and Herecles, who slays the many-headed Hydra. The Hebrews had David and Goliath, Samson and the Philistines, Saint Michael and Satan. Christians had Saint George and the Dragon, Harker and Dracula, Aslan and the Winter Queen. In storytelling, the monster is a potent symbol, representing everything in human nature that is somehow twisted and less than perfect, threatening and fearful. Notice, too, that every monster in storyland is enormously egocentric. The monster is simply heartless, unable to feel for others. We would call them "cold-blooded killers." Cold blood. No feeling—like the hired killers of the movies or the mechanical killers like Chucky or Freddy Krueger in the slash movies.

Of course, that is also always the monster's fatal flaw, what we call the "Icarus effect." Icarus was the brilliant son in Greek mythology who wanted to fly, but ignoring his father's warning, flew too close to the sun with his wax wings and plunged to his death. So, the monster. He is so egocentric that there is always something he overlooks. Pride, in short, gives him a blind spot and that is why in the end he can be outwitted, just as the martians were in H.G. Wells's *The War of the Worlds*. They overlooked something as apparently insignificant as the destructive power of bacteria. The same theme is sounded in this variation of the story of the nasty monstrous polar bear who didn't count on the courage of a tiny gray bird, as told in "How the Robin's Breast Became Red."

> Long ago in the Far North, where it is very cold, there was only one fire. A hunter and his little son took care of this fire and kept it burning day and night. They knew that if the fire went out the people would freeze and the white bear would have the Northland all to himself.
>
> One day the hunter became ill and his son had to do all the work. For many days and nights he bravely took care of his father and kept the fire burning. The great white bear was always hiding near, watching the fire. He longed to put it out, but he did not dare, for he feared the hunter's arrows. When he saw how tired and sleepy the little boy was, he came closer to the fire and laughed wickedly to himself. Well, one night the poor boy grew so tired that he could keep awake no longer and fell fast asleep. Then the white bear ran as fast as he could and jumped upon the fire with his wet feet, and rolled upon it until he thought it was all out. Then he trotted happily away to his cave among the icebergs.
>
> But a little gray robin had been flying near, and had seen what the white bear was doing. She was greatly worried when she thought that the fire might be out, but she was so little that she could do nothing but wait until the bear was out of sight. Then she darted down swiftly and searched with her

sharp little eyes until she found a tiny live coal. This she fanned patiently with her wings for a long time. Her little breast was scorched red, but she did not stop until a fine red flame blazed up from the ashes. Then she flew off to visit every hut in the Northland. Wherever she touched the ground, a fire began to burn.

Soon, instead of one little fire, the whole North Country was lighted up, so that people far to the south wondered at the beautiful flames of red and yellow light in the northern sky. But when the white bear saw the fires, he went further back into his cave among the icebergs and growled terribly. He knew that now there was no hope that he would ever have the Northland all to himself. This is the reason that the people in the North County love the robin, and never tire of telling their children how its breast became red.

The Christian version, of course, is that the robin's breast became red when it pulled a thorn from Jesus' head.

Monsters are our worst fears appearing as concrete characters. In novels, Dickens's Nicholas Nickleby finally has to confront his monster, Uncle Ralph. In World War II dramas, the monster is the enemy: the Nazis, the Japanese. More recently, there is al-Qaeda. The Hollywood westerns are classic hero versus monsters stories. The heroes in *The Magnificent Seven* confront the cruel outlaw gang devouring a Mexican village. Gary Cooper overcomes gunmen out to get him in *High Noon*, and Luke Skywalker and Princess Leia defeat the dark lord, Darth Vader.

Monsters and overcoming them are a staple of human stories because they are a staple of human living. We all have our fears. The child fears abandonment and dark forces under the bed. The adolescent fears unacceptance, being different. The adult fears failure. The elderly fear death. No wonder "monsters" are also a staple of the stories of the spiritual journey: betrayal, temptation, the seven deadly sins (pride, avarice, lust, greed, anger, envy, gluttony). To the unredeemed, unforgiven, and unresurrected, Jesus offers acceptance, forgiveness, and eternal life. Jesus' stories promise victory.

2. Rags to Riches, or Constriction to Expansion Stories

In this category, the ordinary, insignificant person, dismissed by everyone as of little account, suddenly steps into the center of the stage.

An obscure little squire, Wort, accompanies his master to London for the solemn ceremonies surrounding the choice of a new king. A mighty stone has appeared in St. Paul's churchyard with a sword fixed in it, with the inscription that anyone who can pull out the sword shall become king. All the great men of the nation try and fail. But to everyone's astonishment the unknown squire steps forward and removes the sword effortlessly. He becomes King Arthur, the greatest king his country has ever known.

This "rags to riches" theme persists because it's our favorite fantasy: someday, perhaps, all will recognize—even without cosmetic surgery—how powerful, how great, how wonderful we are. We shall be known and loved or, in adolescent jargon, popular; no, a celebrity!

The notion of transformation is beguiling. Cinderella gets a makeover and dances with a prince. Orphaned Aladdin becomes a hero and wins the princess. Puss in Boots transforms the orphaned boy, Dick Wittington, into the Marquis of Carabas. Lowly flower girl Lisa Doolittle goes to the ball and is taken for a princess. Despised and abused Jane Eyre marries Rochester. An obscure chorus girl, Ruby Keeler, dances her way to fame in *42nd Street*; dowdy Charlotte Vale becomes a woman loved in Bette Davis' stunning movie, *Now, Voyager*. Every Christmas, the reindeer with the bright, bulbous nose who was at the bottom of the heap and wasn't allowed to play reindeer games, becomes Santa's sled leader.

Note how many are orphaned; being orphaned is a metaphor for how disconnected and bereft they are. All of these heroes go through many alternating crises, from lows to highs to new lows and final highs. It's not a smooth path. The path of spirituality is nothing if not about the lifting up of the lowly, the forgiveness of the sinner, the healing of the lame, the rising of the dead, a slow falling in love with God, as it was for Francis of Assisi. The rags to riches motif symbolizes the fulfillment of those who love God. Indeed, "the last shall be first." That's why Mary sang, "My soul magnifies the Lord and my spirit rejoices in God my Savior." Why does she sing so? "[F]or he has looked with favor on the lowliness of his servant." Miss Nobody becomes Miss Somebody!

3. The Quest

The Quest type of story abounds and has a recognizable pattern. The hero or heroine gets a call; for example, a group of government agents calls on Dr. Indiana Jones to find the Holy Grail before the Nazis do and he takes off on an amazing series of adventures. There are dastardly villains to be overcome, lovely damsels to be defended before finally attaining the goal of his quest, the Holy Grail. Dorothy Gale wonders if there is anything over the rainbow and is "called" by a knock on the head to find out. Then there are always villains. Dorothy's villain is the Wicked Witch of the West. And there are always mentors. Her mentors are the Good Witch and an unsteady trio of a scarecrow, a tin man, and a cowardly lion. Finally, there is the denouement. Dorothy returns, having found out what really matters.

Identical quest stories are *Star Trek*, *The Divine Comedy*, *The Odyssey*, *Watership Down*, *Treasure Island*, *Pinocchio*, *The Lord of the Rings*, *The Sorcerer's Stone* in the Harry Potter series, and *Peter Pan*. They have their stock heroes and villains: wicked stepmothers, Prince John, Monstro, Voldemort, Captain Hook. They have their helpers along the way: Tobias, Gandolf, Ron Beasley, Jiminy Cricket. The pattern, as I said, seldom alters. Let's recall it. There is a call. For the hero or heroine to remain quietly at home becomes impossible. The "times are out of joint" and a response must be made. Dr. Jones, Dorothy Gale, Francis of Assisi, Martin Luther King, Jr., Jesus—they are compelled to act.

Second, as we indicated, there are always companions: helpers, friends, animals, those who sometimes complement the hero or heroine's qualities and supply those he or she doesn't have, such as Raphael for Tobias, Sam Gamgee for Frodo, and Horatio for Hamlet.

Third, there is the journey itself with its trials and ordeals and fears. There are the familiar journey tales of *Alice in Wonderland*, the Indiana Jones series, *The Lord of the Rings*, *Huckleberry Finn*, and *Star Trek*.

Here's a Mideast story of some spiritual journeyers. It stings a bit.

I'm a beggar. And you know what? I like being a beggar. You know what else? I'm good at it. Over the years I've really learned how to get you to part with your money. Now, in the beginning, when I found out that the Almighty, the Compassionate One, had chosen a path for me, it was begging. I wasn't overjoyed. But in his mercy, he allowed me to see the world the way he does when I was faithful to my path. You see, my path in life as a beggar is to make your journey lighter, whether you want it or not. And when you pass me by on the street, God, in his mercy, now allows me to see you the way he does all the time, because no matter what you do or you don't do, I see you for what you really are.

For instance, I'll tell you about a few of the people who pass me on the street during the day, and I'm sure you'll find yourself in one of these people. I'm leaning up against the wall. I'm in the same place every day. I haven't had a bath in weeks. You can smell me half a block away. I've got my hand out. You're coming down the street. You're about to attack the world again. You've got your attaché case, your briefcase in hand. You're heading there. You're on time. You know I'm there, so what do you do? You very discreetly cross the street at the corner and you go down the other side of the street so you don't have to deal with me. And then at the corner, of course, at the light, you turn and cross the street again, and nobody knows. They just think you're getting through the crowd quicker. But I saw you, and so I pray God, in his mercy, will come as close to you in your need as you have come to me in mine.

You're a woman. You had a rough morning. You were screaming and yelling at your kids, your husband. You couldn't decide who was going to pick up the kids at school. Everything was going wrong. You couldn't find the keys in your purse. You're late for work. You're running down the street. You forget I'm there. You're on me before you even know it. You smell me first. Your nose wrinkles up and your eyes scrunch up and you mumble something. And I stick out my hand, and you grab your purse and say, "Uh, uh, uh, I'll catch you on the way back. It's too hard to get anything right now. I'm late." Off you go. I saw you too. And so I pray God, in his mercy, may deal with you as quickly as you have dealt with me. He'll catch you on the way back.

Or you're coming down the street; you're feeling pretty good, you have a few coins, a couple quarters. You see me. You see me every day. And you know you shouldn't give the coins to me because I'm just going to buy a bottle of booze. But you drop the coins into my hand or my cup or in my basket and you say, "Now get yourself a cup of coffee or a sandwich. Don't buy booze." Off you go. And I give thanks that God will be as gracious to you as you have been with me, but that he will always make conditions with the gift.

You're coming down the street. You're feeling pretty good. You've got a couple extra bucks. You buy a lottery ticket. Then you think, "Why not give it to the poor?" So you give me your lottery ticket. You give me a buck or two. "God bless you," you say. And I say, well, there's still a little generosity left in the world. At least he talked to me, you know, and he said God bless me. So I watch you go down the street and I pray God, in his mercy, will give at least a hundredfold to you as you have given to me and a quick blessing as you go.

Now, you come down the street. You've got a lot of money. You're feeling good. It was a good day. You've seen me day in and day out. You stop. You give me five or six dollars. You tell me where the shelter is—as if I didn't know already. You tell me where to go get a cup of coffee. You tell me to go get a shower, clean myself up, and you wish me well. And I watch you go off and I pray God, in his mercy, will heap blessing on your head, running over in the fold of your garment, for your simple kindness to me, because there is still generosity left in the world. And then if you should happen to pass me on the street and you should happen to give to me what I need before I have to beg for it, then it is me who backs away from you and wonder who you are.

Because even all of you, who have everything you want practically, you know what it's like in your deepest need for someone to give you that before you have to beg for it. And it is only God who comes to visit in every generation, in every religion, who gives before we have to beg. And it's me, then, who wonders who you are, and whether or not God has come to visit me in my misery as he is wont to do.

So, you see, no matter what you do when you pass me on the street, I know you for who you really are. I see you in that moment the way God sees you every moment of your life. He has given me that great gift. And the next time you see one of me on the street, and there are a lot of us these days, be careful. Make sure you know who it is you're dealing with when you pass me by. And every time you see one of us, I want you to just think about this question. I know what my journey in life is. I'm here to make your way lighter. Do you know what your journey is?

This is the human journey—with its trials, temptations, challenges, and fears.

Obstacles

The fourth element in the pattern is the fearsome obstacles. There are, for example, the monsters. The Cyclops threaten Odysseus and his men; the Harpies plague Aeneas and later the Argonauts; Professor Moriarty tries to kill Sherlock Holmes; the Winter Queen contends with the children from the wardrobe. Like the Sirens or the Lorelei who bewitch sailors and lure them to their deaths, there are the women who try to seduce Sir Percival, and the fox who lures Pinocchio to Pleasure Island. In movieland, Lola tries to seduce Joe in *Damn Yankees*, and married Miles Fairley tries to seduce the widow Lucy Muir in *The Ghost and Mrs. Muir*. Again, the same cast of characters accompanies the spiritual journey: dark figures like greed, materialism, pornography, ambition, infidelities, addictions, consumerism, and so on, and the bright figures in the biblical stories and lives-of-saints stories provide us with a pattern for coping.

4. Voyage and Return

Easy examples of this type are *The Iliad, The Odyssey, The Time Machine, Alice's Adventures in Wonderland, Peter Pan, Robinson Crusoe, The Lord of the Flies, The Third Man,* and the movie *Brief Encounter.*

The latter, a 1946 film written by Noël Coward and directed by David Lean, is a gem that will break your heart. The "normal" world is represented by the humdrum home life of the heroine Laura (played by Celia Johnson), married to Fred, her kindly, unimaginative, boring husband who likes nothing better than to sit by the fire doing a crossword puzzle. In interior monologue, with a romantic Rachmaninoff piano concerto blasting out of the gramophone, she unhappily reconstructs how, some weeks before, in a train station refreshment room in a nearby town, she had unexpectedly "fallen into another world" by meeting a handsome, sensitive doctor named Alec (played by Trevor Howard), also married. She recalls how they fell in love, snatching several more surreptitious meetings, visits to the movies, drinking champagne in a restaurant, walking in the country.

Their affair goes through the familiar cycle of the dream stage, frustration stage (as she feels growing guilt, lying to her husband, is spotted by friends in the restaurant), and nightmare stage (their attempt to make love in a friend's flat is aborted when the friend unexpectedly returns; Laura and Alec both realize the affair cannot last and he tells Laura he is about to leave with his family for a new job in South Africa). After they have made their final farewells on the station platform, she returns miserably home to the "normal" world of Fred and his crossword puzzles, puts on the Rachimaninoff, and relives in her mind the whole sad story.

The voyage and return motif is found in those who have left the church or abandoned religion and returned. Examples include the prodigal son, C.S. Lewis, and Dorothy Day.

5. Comedy

This category comes easiest to us. Right away we think of *The Marriage of Figaro*. No? Too high brow? How about *A Night at the Opera, The Importance of Being Ernest, A Night in Casablanca,* changing room numbers in *Some Like It Hot,* Laurel and Hardy, Martin and Lewis, the

Smothers Brothers, Shakespeare's *Comedy of Errors*, and a million jokes? Or, if you're old enough, you might remember the Burma Shave signs along the highway:

> Cattle crossing
> Means go slow
> That old bull
> Is some
> Cow's beau

> My job is
> Keeping faces clean
> And nobody knows
> De stubble
> I've seen

> Pedro walked
> Back home by golly
> His bristly chin
> Was hot-to-Molly.

Of course, today the signs along the road have been replaced by the bumper sticker: "Out of my mind. Be back in 5 minutes." "There are three kinds of people: those who can count and those who can't." Then there is the elderly priest, speaking to the younger priest.

> The older priest said, "It was a good idea to replace the first four pews with plush bucket theater seats. It worked like a charm. The front of the church fills first."
> The younger priest nodded, and the old priest continued, "And you told me a little more beat to the music would bring the young people back to church, so I supported you when you brought in that rock 'n roll band. We're packed to the balcony."
> "Thank you, Father," answered the young priest. "I am pleased that you are open to new ideas."
> "Well," said the elderly priest, "I'm afraid you've gone too far with the drive-thru confessional."
> "But, Father," protested the young priest, "my confessions have nearly doubled since I began that!"

"I know, son," replied the elderly priest, "but that flashing sign on the church roof that says 'Toot 'n Tell or Go to Hell' can't stay."

The usual source of comedy is misunderstanding: characters donning disguises or swapping identities, men dressing up like women or vice versa (the comedy *Some Like It Hot*), secret meetings when the wrong person shows up, scenes in which characters hastily hide. To that degree we might say that the essence of comedy is always that some redeeming truth has to be brought out of the shadows and into the light.

We might also say that the function of humor is to provide us with a more or less harmless way of diffusing the social strains created by egotism. This is why comedy focuses on people who take themselves too seriously, giving the rest of us a chance to see how foolish this makes them look. So if a poor little old lady walks down the street and slips on a banana peel, we do not see this as funny. We offer sympathy. If the same thing happens to a pompous lady cocooned in self-importance, we find it comical precisely because we like to see her bubble burst.

We laugh at people who think they are self-made and have everything under control, when in fact they do not. So we laugh at the officious Laurel and Hardy trying to get the grand piano down the stairs and see it constantly slipping out of their hands. Or John Cleese in *Fawlty Towers*, with his persona as a cool, efficient hotel proprietor wallowing in chaos behind the scenes. The "inferior" butler, Jeeves, constantly redeems the mess of the upper class.

One-liners turn around our expectations. Some Henny Youngman classics:

I've been in love with the same woman for forty-nine years. If my wife ever finds out, she'll kill me!

The wife and I have the secret to making a marriage last. Two times a week we go to a nice restaurant, a little wine, good food. She goes Tuesdays; I go Fridays.

We always hold hands. If I let go, she shops.

She was at the beauty parlor for two hours. That was only for the estimate.

I just got back from a pleasure trip. I took my mother-in-law to the airport.

There was a girl knocking on my hotel room door all night! Finally, I let her out.

A drunk was in front of a judge. The judge says, "You've been brought here for drinking." The drunk says, "Okay, let's get started."

A car hit a Jewish man. The paramedic says, "Are you comfortable?" The man says, "I make a good living."

Comedy is rooted in tragedy. It flourishes in hard times. Humor says in jest what you can't say out loud. For instance, the doggerel, "Froggie Went a-Courting" allowed the English to poke fun at the queen, which they couldn't do openly for fear of losing their heads. The Queen of England, you see, was being courted by a Frenchman.

Humor is at the heart of the Christian faith. In a homily I gave one Easter I began by telling jokes, and after the people had stopped laughing I said that in telling these jokes I was imitating the ancient tradition of telling jokes on Easter Sunday to imitate God's cosmic last laugh on Satan who thought he had won with the death of Jesus, only to be upstaged by the resurrection (storified, you may recall, in Aslan's "resurrection" in *The Lion, the Witch, and the Wardrobe*). All laughed at his discomfiture and comeuppance.

6. Tragedy

Who better to introduce this category than Shakespeare? Listen to Richard III on the eve of his death:

> Have mercy, Jesu! Soft! I did but dream.
> O coward conscience, how thou dost afflict me!
> The lights burn blue. It is now dead midnight.
> Cold tearful drops do stand upon my trembling flesh...
> All several sins, all us'd in each degree
> Throng to the bar, crying all "Guilty! Guilty!"
> I shall despair. There is no creature loves me.

Two endings to stories seem the most dominant in tragedies. Either the story ends with a man and woman united in love or in death—and a death that is violent and premature. The usual scenario in tragedy develops like this: the hero, or protagonist, somehow frustrated or incomplete, divided within himself or herself, is in need of change. He or she is being tempted into a course of action that is in some ways dark and forbidden. Examples are Voldemort, Faust, Anna Karenina, Madame Bovary, Dr. Jekyll, Hamlet, Lex Luther, Carmen, Bonnie and Clyde, and Judas.

They all ultimately "answer the call," as it were, to evil. In the quest stories there is also a call, remember—like Jesus calling Francis of Assisi—but we know it is a call to do right and we have no doubt it should be answered. In tragedy, however, there is unease. The call is more akin to temptation. It's a call to an appetite, an obsession: the obsession for power or sex or conquest, sensation (extreme television), all of which violate some convention or duty or standard of normality. And we know—and the protagonists know—something is out of sync and we see them wavering or struggling with the decision to keep their dark impulses out of the light, until, at one fateful moment, the bounds are overstepped. Soon they are into obsession and it blinds them, and this blindness is their weak spot and eventual undoing.

There are predictable steps to the story pattern of tragedy. At first there is exhilaration and things go remarkably well for the hero, like Faust's joy at signing a pact with the devil or Joe Boyd in *Damn Yankees* (Faust retold musically on Broadway) who gets to the World Series. Then there is Humbert Humbert finding his Lolita; Macbeth getting royal power; Dr. Jekyll being able to escape at night to indulge in nameless wicked-ness; married Anna Karenina seducing Count Vronsky; Bonnie and Clyde knocking over one store and bank after another and getting rich; John Foster Kane at his apex in *Citizen Kane*.

Then, inevitably, after a time, things begin to go wrong. The hero, such as Dorian Gray, for example, cannot find contentment and goes deeper into evil, until things slip out of control and the forces of opposition or fate close in. The dwarfs and animals hunt down Snow White's wicked stepmother; Holmes closes in on Moriarty; the hapless

Don Jose stabs Carmen to death; the police riddle the bodies of Bonnie and Clyde; and the once powerful John Foster Kane dies alone whispering "Rosebud."

Basically, these protagonists have been taken over by a fantasy (I am invincible) that inevitably spins them out of control. At first, there is elation and a sense of power and control, and then a loss of both, a capitulation to addiction. The perfect metaphor of this loss of control is the sorcerer's apprentice from a tale by the second-century Roman poet, Lucian. It was the subject of a poem by Goethe in 1797, transferred to a musical version by Paul Dukas in 1897, and, of course, animated in Disney's *Fantasia* in 1940. You know the story.

> An old sorcerer has to go on a trip and he leaves his apprentice to fetch water from the well. The boy eventually tires of this grunt work. Then he remembers the spell used by the master to command a magic broomstick. He uses the spell to order the stick to do the work. For a while all goes well and he takes it easy. But by and by, enough water has been brought in, in fact, more than enough. The boy suddenly realizes with horror that he doesn't know how to turn it off. As more buckets pile up the water, he takes an ax to the stick. (A dark deed piled on the previous dark deed: a common pattern.) All that this accomplishes is to split the stick in two. So now he has two sticks bringing in twice as much water. Just as the whole house is about to be washed away, the sorcerer returns and orders the broomstick to stop. The day is saved, and the boy is sadder but wiser.

The story is an allegory of an out-of-control addiction. The addictions of sex, alcohol, drugs, gambling, and pornography, including internet porn, have the same elements of tragedy.

7. Rebirth

This last category of the seven basic plots concern stories of new beginnings and inner transformation, rebirth. In the Bible there is Zacchaeus the tax collector, the woman at the well, the good thief. In popular culture there are the films *Overboard*, *It's a Wonderful Life*, and *The Sound of Music*.

In fairy tales, for example, *Snow White* and *Sleeping Beauty*, the hero-
ines fall under a dark spell, some wintry physical or spiritual imprison-
ment, until liberated by the hero, in this case, the prince. In *The Frog
Prince* and *Beauty and the Beast*, it is the heroine who liberates the hero.
In literature there is *A Christmas Carol*, the story of Scrooge's rebirth. In
Crime and Punishment, Rodion Raskolnokov, the murderer, is redeemed
by Sonia. *The Secret Garden* shows us three characters who are imprisoned: Mary Lennox, the snobbish, sour-tempered heroine; morose and
bent Mr. Craven; and his sickly son Colin. They are all reborn. In real
life there are the conversion stories of Saint Paul, C.S. Lewis, Thomas
Merton, Dorothy Day, recovering alcoholics and drug addicts, and millions of others who have found forgiveness, redemption, and second
chances. We celebrate such people in the nearest thing we have to a
national religious anthem, "Amazing Grace," which sings out, "I once
was lost, but now am found / Was blind but now I see."

Conclusion

In summary we might put it this way: all classic stories have the same
psychological and spiritual patterns and images. There are always basic
figures and situations, basic plots around which the stories take shape.
Some stories have just one plot, others have several, and rare ones, like
The Lord of the Rings, contain all seven plots. In any case, this is why we
resonate with stories, because there are elemental human needs and
yearnings at stake for all people: the need to grow, to mature, to find our
way to God. Saint Augustine said it well when he wrote that our hearts
are meant for God and that they are restless until they rest in God.
Therefore, life is a journey, however uneven and however perilous,
toward that fulfillment. Quest, tragedy, comedy, rebirth, and the rest are
subplots of that journey.

Now, as a link to the next chapter, here is a story to think over. Ask
yourself the critical question of this and every story, including eventually the biblical ones: not "What does it say?" but "What does it mean?"

> There once lived a poor woman who faithfully visited the
> shrine of her guardian spirit each morning. She was so devot-

ed that one day the guardian spirit left a gift for her in the shape of a small green cap. She put the cap on and, to her great surprise, was able to understand what the birds, animals, and plants of the forest were saying. "It's a listening cap!" she cried happily.

Just then two robins landed on a nearby branch and began to converse: "It's so sad about the maple tree," said one.

"How true," replied the other. "I heard it crying again last night. Do you know the story behind the tree's sadness?"

"Yes," said the first robin. "I was there the day it happened. The town mayor chopped down the maple in order to make room for a teahouse in his garden. Unfortunately, he didn't dig up the roots, and that's why the tree still cries out in pain. It isn't dead, nor is it alive. It just remains under the teahouse."

"Is that why the mayor is so weak and sickly?" asked the other bird.

"Yes," said the first. "The maple has put a dark spell on him. On the day the tree finally dies, the mayor, too, will be carried to his grave."

Upon hearing all of this, the poor woman rushed home and made herself up to look like a wandering doctor. With the listening cap still on her head, she walked up to the door of the mayor's grand house. The wife of the mayor gladly welcomed the doctor. She asked her to examine her husband, adding that she had already tried all the known remedies without success.

"When did your husband have the teahouse built in the garden?" asked the doctor. "Just last year," said the mayor's wife.

"And has your husband been sick ever since?"

"Yes," she said. "How did you know?"

"It's a special talent of mine," answered the doctor. "Before I examine your husband, I would like to have a cup of tea in the garden."

"Of course," she replied. "I'll fill the pot."

The phony doctor went into the teahouse and sat quietly. Soon she heard a low moan coming from beneath the floor. "Is that you, poor maple tree?" asked a butterfly floating into the room. "Are you feeling any better today?"

"No, I feel much worse. In fact, I'm going to die soon, and when I do, so will the mayor. I'll see to that."

"Please don't die," said the butterfly.

"No, don't die, don't die," echoed the garden roses.

The doctor rushed to the mayor's bedside and said, "If you want to live, have the teahouse torn down at once! Then tend to the maple whose roots still rest beneath it. Help the tree to grow strong again."

He agreed and told his servants to demolish the teahouse. The sickly mayor cared for the maple himself. Soon it began to send healthy green shoots into the air.

"I will live!" cried the tree at last.

"The maple lives!" shouted the garden.

Within a few days the mayor was feeling much better, and after only two weeks he was well and strong again. The wandering doctor was given a large bag of gold, and with the listening cap still on her head, the once poor woman went on her way with a gentle smile upon her lips.

1 Overcoming the monster

2 Rags to Riches

3 Quest

4 Voyage & Return

5 Comedy

6 Tragedy

7 Rebirth

CHAPTER TWO

Tellers, Types, and Techniques

*The folktale is the primer
of the picture-language of the soul.*

JOSEPH CAMPBELL

Says the mountaineer:

I used to date a girl named Beumadean Skelvidge, and she had to be the ugliest girl in the world. She went to see the psychiatrist, and he made her lay face down on the couch!

One time she was taking a little white duck to the county fair. She stopped at the Blue Bird Cafe to get a soda, and the waiter hollered at her, "Hey, where are you going with that pig?" She said, "This ain't no pig, it's a duck!" "Shut up," he said, "I'm talking to the duck!"

When Beumadean was just a little thing she got separated from her parents out there at Jackson State Park. When she found a policeman, she said, "Do you think we'll ever find my mommy and daddy?" The policeman said, "I don't know, honey…there's lots of places out here for them to hide!"

She was undressing, and this Peeping Tom was watching. He reached in and pulled down the shade!

Storytellers, types, and language—how they captivate us! They make us laugh, cry, and ponder. Storytellers create tales that change or structure the world in which they live and so give us hope and fire the imagination. Because of that, storytellers have been venerated in oral cultures all over the earth. So, as Booker reminds us, except in times of war, the Irish *shanachies* (storytellers) were second only to the king. In Siberia, skilled taletellers were hired by cartels of lumbermen, fishermen, and hunters to tell stories to wile away the leisure hours. Ivan the Terrible required three blind old men to tell him folktales before he fell asleep. The African griot, a key member of his society, chanted genealogies, advised rulers, and told stories that recorded history. (Remember *Roots*?) Even today, Hungarian soldiers, by a centuries-old custom, can be required to tell stories after lights out or pay the penalty of shouting into the stove, "Oh, Mother, have you brought me up to be a big brute of an ass who hasn't even been taught to tell a tale?" And what kinds of tales did these tellers recite? Wonder tales, tales of transformations, noodlehead and numbskull stories, jocular tales, and put-down tales such as this one:

> "Well," snarled the tough old Navy chief to the bewildered seaman, "I suppose after you get discharged from the Navy, you'll just be waiting for me to die so you can come and pee on my grave."
>
> "Not me, Chief!" the seaman replied. "Once I get out of the Navy, I'm never going to stand in line again!"

As Booker puts it:

> There are cautionary stories to keep children in line, stories of ghosts to make the listener shiver, long adventures of heroes and heroines, amusing exploits of animals who could talk and had interesting things to say, touching accounts of love lost or

won, frightening tales of rape and murder, horrifying stories of cannibal kings and ogres on mountaintops, and trolls under bridges who cracked bone and sucked marrow. There were stories that seemed almost straightforward recordings of battles or of matters of belief, teaching tales that enabled marginal peoples to survive, and stories that detailed in fascinating ways the proper method for propitiating the local gods.

These tales could be as short as the English ghost story reported by the venerable English collector Katharine Briggs:

> He woke up frightened and reached for the matches, and the matches were put into his hand.

Or they could be days-long recitations that were part devotion, part history, part mystery, and part entertainment, like the tales told about Gilgamesh, Hercules, or Frodo Baggins in *The Lord of the Rings*. In the very center of these stories, of course, is human truth served up in different guises.

Versions of Stories

A good story is simply one that lasts and resonates because the listeners or readers like it and demand it again. A good story is told and retold or read and reread, just like the stories of Scripture. No two listeners, of course, hear exactly the same tale the same way. Each brings something to the story and the story is then re-created between the teller and the listener, between the writer and the reader. Sometimes we can actually hear tales being changed by different tellers. Occasionally a particular transcriber is so able, so effective, so inventive, that the story itself is changed forever and that version perdures. For example, Charles Perrault, a very famous collector and author of tales, was such a reworker of stories. He reinvented, among others, the Cinderella story in such a potent form that it is *his* telling and not the five hundred European variants that remains the standard version of the tale. One of them, to show you how earthy they can get, tells about the tree on Cinderella's mother's grave, the stepsisters cutting off their heels and toes to fit into the slipper, or the doves pecking out the stepsisters' eyes at the wedding. In his seventeenth-century retelling, Perrault did something of a makeover. He gave Cinderella a fairy godmother and a midnight warning, two things up to that time she did not possess. And then someone, Perrault or perhaps the English translator of his book, made a brilliant mistake. The heroine's fur (*vair*) slipper was misread as glass (*verre*) and that's how we got that. In stories, all mistakes are made true by the telling.

There is no argument: stories are powerful and the people who told and listened to stories knew it. Stories were pressed into civilizing society. Tales that warned about speaking out of turn or talking too much or hanging around with bad companions or finding common ground about one's strengths and weaknesses were common.

Story is also history, for each tale carries with it, over the miles and through the generations, the bruises and blandishments of the societies in which it dwelt. Cinderella can be traced back to China, where noblewomen had their feet bound as infants. This emphasis on the lotus foot in the tiny slipper that defines the nobility of its wearer can still be seen in a number of the variants. *Little Red Riding Hood*, according to some, began as a tale to warn French girls about sexual experimentation. It was so effective that, even when the ending of the story has been changed, the moral is set: Do not go to bed with wolves!

Types of Stories

Now if, as we saw in Chapter One, there are seven basic story plots, there are also basic stock figures: the hero, the dark figure or villain, the braggart, the fool, the nitwit, and so on. They all embody a truth about human nature. Let's take a quick look at some of these, because that will appear in all our stories and in our lives.

The figure of the conniver or trickster can be found in every folklore tradition. The trickster as hero or as god plays an important role in tweaking society's pretenses: Anansi in Africa is sometimes heroic, sometimes foolish, with definite supernatural powers. Likewise his famous Native American counterparts, Coyote and Rabbit, act as both fooler and fooled. The trickster as wise person is found in Mideastern tradition, especially in the Jewish stories of resourceful rabbis and the Turkish tales of the Hodja. In Mexico, the trickster supreme is Quevedo. The German Till Eulenspiegel, a popular peasant jester, actually lived in the fourteenth century, but within another two centuries had become a legend around whose name had accumulated volumes of anecdotes and jests. Many of the stories told about these particular tricksters hark back to other tales and other times. Whether tricksters are animals like Brer Rabbit, Raven, or the wily fox, or supremely human like the German master thief, they play their tricks out to the end. And sometimes they entail bloody and awful endings. The point of these tricksters is to represent chaos in the ordered life and poke fun at our illusions.

Sometimes the tricksters themselves are tricked, but win or lose, the stories always make us smile at their ingenuity or shake our heads fondly at their chutzpah, that sly gustiness that outwits us all in the end. "The Wily Dachshund" is a case in point.

> A wealthy man decided to go on a safari in Africa. He took his faithful pet dachshund along for company. One day, the dachshund starts chasing butterflies and before long the dachshund discovers that he is lost. So, wandering about, he notices a leopard heading rapidly in his direction with the obvious intention of having lunch. The dachshund thinks, "OK, I'm in deep trouble now!"
>
> Then he notices some bones on the ground close by and immediately settles down to chew on the bones with his back to the approaching cat. Just as the leopard is about to leap, the dachshund exclaims loudly, "Boy, that was one delicious leopard. I wonder if there are any more around here?" Hearing this, the leopard halts his attack in mid-stride, as a look of terror comes over him, and he slinks away into the trees. "Whew," says the leopard. "That was close. That dachshund nearly had me."
>
> Meanwhile, a monkey who had been watching the whole scene from a nearby tree, figures he can put this knowledge to good use and trade it for protection from the leopard. So, off

he goes. But the dachshund sees him heading after the leopard with great speed and figures that something must be up. The monkey soon catches up with the leopard, spills the beans, and strikes a deal for himself with the leopard.

The leopard is furious at being made a fool of and says, "Here, monkey, hop on my back and see what's going to happen to that conniving canine." Now the dachshund sees the leopard coming with the monkey on his back, and thinks, "What am I going to do now?" But instead of running, the dog sits down with his back to his attackers, pretending he hasn't seen them yet…and just when they get close enough to hear, the dachshund says, "Where is that monkey? I sent him off half an hour ago to bring me another leopard."

Then there are riddles, which are among the earliest and most universal of pre-story components that eventually transformed into full-blown stories. Some are highly elaborated tales, and some are just a tiny step up from the bare-boned riddle.

But the tradition of riddling is very old and popular in folklore. Remember Samson's famous riddle: "Out of the eater came forth meat, and out of the strong came forth sweetness"? Recall Oedipus' contest with the Sphinx who asks this riddle:

"At dawn it creeps on four legs. At noon it strides on two. At sunset and evening it totters on three. What is this thing, never the same, yet not many, but one?"

And, as you know, Oedipus gives the answer.

"What can this creature be but man, O Sphinx? For, helpless as a babe at the dawn of life, he crawls on his hands and feet. At noontime he walks erect in the strength of his youth. And at evening he supports his tottering with a staff, the prop and stay of old age. Have I not guessed the answer to your famous riddle?" With a loud cry of despair and answering him never a word, the great beast sprang from its seat on the rock and hurled himself over the precipice into the yawning gulf below.

Of course, there are the ones we heard as kids:

What has hands but no arms
A face but no head? (a clock)

Riddle me, riddle me, what is that
Over the head and under the hat? (hair)

Plutarch wrote of Homer that he died of chagrin when he could not solve a riddle. Here's one for you:

There once lived a wealthy merchant in Kasimir whose son was as lazy as he was foolish. No matter what the merchant said, his son did the opposite. If, that is, he did anything at all. The merchant finally had all he could take.

"I want you to go to the marketplace," he told his son, "and buy something for us to eat, something for us to drink, something for the cow to eat, and something for us to plant in the garden. And you may spend only this one small coin. If you can do it, come back home. If you can't, don't come home."

As the boy walked toward the marketplace, he began to cry. He could not think of any way to buy those things with the coin his father had given him. He'd never be able to go back home. He was crying so loud that a girl working in the field heard him and asked what was wrong. When he told her about his father's orders and all he had to buy with one small coin, the girl shook her head and told him not to worry. She said he could easily do what his father wanted and told him how.

That night the boy went home with a smile on his face as well as something to eat, something to drink, something to feed the cow, and something to plant in the garden. His father was very surprised and very impressed. How did he do it?

He bought a watermelon: its flesh to eat, its juice to drink, the rind for the cow to eat, and its seeds to plant in the garden!

A more modern riddle goes like this:

You're driving in your car on a wild stormy night. You pass by a bus stop and you see three people waiting for the bus. One is an old person who looks about to die. The second is your

best friend who once saved your life, and the third is the perfect person you have been dreaming about all your life. There
can only be one passenger in your car and you can't return to
the bus stop once you have left it. To which one would you
offer a ride?

Think. You could pick up the old person who is going to die
and thus you would save that person (but forfeit your best
friend), or you could take your best friend because he or she
once saved your life; this would be the perfect chance to return
the favor (but leave the old person to die). You may never be
able to find your perfect dream person again. What would you
do? Answer: give the car keys to your best friend and let him
or her take the old person to the hospital. You could stay
behind and wait for the bus with the person of your dreams.

Then there are the "liar" stories. They are about deceivers and lying
contests. Baron von Munchausen is the master here. In Scripture, Satan
is the deceiver and the Father of Lies.

A few years back, advice columnist Ann Landers challenged her readers to come up with the world's third-biggest lie, right after "The check
is in the mail" and "I'm from the government and I'm here to help you."
Here is a sampling from the thousands she received:

"Five pounds is nothing on a person of your height."

"You made it yourself? I never would have guessed."

"You don't look a day over forty."

"Of course I'll respect you in the morning."

"Dad, I need to move out of the dorm and into an apartment
of my own so I can have some peace and quiet when I study."

"It's delicious, but I can't eat another bite."

"The new ownership won't affect you. The company will
remain the same."

"The puppy won't be any trouble, Mom. I promise I'll take care
of it myself."

"Your hair looks just fine."

"Put away the map. I know exactly how to get there."

"You don't need it in writing. You have my personal guarantee."

Then there are the shape-shifters, stories about people who morph into other creatures. They can be sorcerers or witches and learn the ability to change at will, like Snow White's wicked stepmother or the Greek gods. Or they can be enchanted or put under a spell by a magic-maker, perhaps by eating or touching something that causes them to change, such as in the familiar "frog and princess" or "beauty and the beast" stories. Or they can be born shape-shifters and be transformed, sometimes unwittingly, by natural forces: the pull of the moon, the turn of the tide, or the sloughing off of the skin.

The most feared shape-shifter in the world was the werewolf—remember Lon Chaney and the werewolf movies? However, such person-to-animal transformations, in stories around the globe, concerned more than wolves. In Japan and Korea, tales were told about were-foxes. In China, there were stories about were-bullfrogs; in Russia, were-snakes; in India, were-leopards and were-tigers.

Here's a marathon story about changing shapes; it's called "The Doctor and His Apprentice."

> Once there was a poor man who had a young son. The father had barely enough to subsist on so he was forced to send the lad out into the world to find work. The boy departed wearing a reversible jacket that was red on one side and green on the other. As he shuffled along in his red jacket he passed in front of a castle that was the residence of a doctor who happened to be standing at the window. He spotted the boy, thought a minute, then called out, "Boy, what are you looking for in these parts?"
>
> "Since I'd like to make a living," the boy replied, "I'm looking for work."
>
> The doctor who was in sore need of a servant asked, "Boy, do you know how to read?"
>
> "Yes," replied the boy, "I've been to school for six months."
>
> "Then you won't do."

The boy went away; but being a clever lad, in a few days he came back showing the green side of his jacket. Once more he passed in front of the castle and once more the doctor was at his window. Not recognizing the boy in his green jacket, he called out, "Boy, what are you looking for in these parts?"

"I'd like to make a living; I'm looking for work."

"Do you know how to read?"

This time the boy was ready and said, "No, for I've never been to school."

The doctor smiled and said, "Well, then, come in. I'll hire you. I'll give you one hundred marks a year and board."

So the boy entered and his master gave him something to eat. Then he took him by the hand and showed him his giant Book of Secrets and handed him a duster. He said, "Your duty will be to dust my book carefully every single day. That's all you'll have to do. Nothing else."

Then the doctor left on a trip. As he was gone the whole year, the curious boy took advantage of this absence to open the giant Book of Secrets and read it. Soon the bright lad was well acquainted with the doctor's skills. The physician returned. All seemed well. He was pleased with his young servant so he departed for another year. Now during this second absence, the boy learned half of the book by heart. The doctor returned. Again he was happy with his servant and departed for another year. During this absence, the boy learned the other half of the book by heart. Now, finally, his master returned for good, so the boy, not needed any longer, returned home to his parents who, alas, were as poor as ever.

Now it so happened that it was the eve of the village fair. The young lad said to his father, "Father, tomorrow go into the stable; there you will find a beautiful horse. Take it to the fair and there sell him. But remember this, Father. Whatever you do, be sure to keep the halter."

So the next day the father went to the stable and sure enough found a magnificent horse. He took it to the fair and buyers hastened around to admire the handsome animal. The father had no trouble in selling it for a good price, but, as instructed, he kept the halter and put it in his pocket. He set out on the road to his village, when suddenly he heard footsteps behind him and they were not the sounds of a horse. He looked around and it was his son! The son explained that he had transformed himself into a horse and then retransformed himself back into his natural shape while the unsuspecting buyer of the horse was celebrating his purchase in the tavern. Both father and son were delighted with the fine deal they had made.

But, as happens, after a time the money ran out.

"Don't worry about it, Father," said the boy. "I'll see that you get more. Go in the stable tomorrow and this time you will find a steer that you can take to the fair. But a reminder: when you sell it you must be sure to keep the rope that you are leading it with." The father did as the son bid and all took place exactly as before. The father was delighted with this seemingly easy and endless source of money, so he proposed to take his son again to the next fair in the form of a horse.

But meanwhile the doctor, back at his castle, was getting suspicious. He had heard of the family's new-found wealth and by consulting his book became aware of what his former servant was doing. So the doctor went to the fair. There he easily recognized the horse and he bought it. But craftily he took the father to the inn to conclude the bargain and there made him so drunk that he forgot to keep the halter. The doctor then spirited the horse quickly away to a blacksmith. "Give him a good shoeing," he advised. The horse was tied to the blacksmith's door.

Now children were coming out of school and a half dozen of them decided to hang around the blacksmith shop. While they were leaning on the fence, the horse extended its muzzle toward a one of the children and whispered to him: "Untie me!" The child was startled and started to run away but the horse repeated a little louder, "Son, untie me!" The schoolboy cautiously approached and untied him and immediately the horse transformed itself into a hare and ran away. The doctor happened to see this and quickly turned the six boys into hunting dogs who chased the hare. The hare luckily came to the edge of a stream, jumped in, and turned itself into a carp. The doctor arrived, uttered an incantation, and all the water dried up leaving the fish exposed. He recognized the carp and was about to grab it when it turned into a lark. So in turn he turned into an eagle and chased the lark, which flew over a castle and plunged down the chimney, where it turned into a grain of wheat, which rolled under the table in the bedroom of the girl of the castle.

The day passed in silence. But in the evening when it was dark and the girl had gone to bed, the young man, transformed from the grain of wheat, said: "Miss, if you wish…"

The girl, hearing a strange voice in her bedroom, cried out to her parents, who came running at once. "What's the matter?" they asked, alarmed. She replied, "There's someone talking in here! There's someone in my room!" But the young man had turned back into a grain of wheat and rolled under the table. The girl's parents turned on the lights, searched everywhere, and, finding nothing, departed. With them gone, the young man once more took his own shape and made more advances. Once more the girl cried out and her parents returned.

"There's been more talking in the room."

"There's no one here. You're imagining things," said her father and went away.

The young man once more reappeared and the girl ended up accepting him. He said to her, "Nights I shall sleep with you and days you may wear me as an engagement ring on your finger."

But by and by the determined doctor found out all that was going on by consulting his giant Book of Secrets. So he caused the girl's father to become ill and then appeared at the castle door as a doctor.

"Heal me and I will pay you well," said her father.

"All I want," replied the doctor humbly, "is the ring on your daughter's finger."

"Of course," her father promised.

But the young man was aware of what was going on and said to the girl, "The doctor attending your father is going to ask you for your ring. Whatever you do, don't give it to him. Instead, as you take it off, let it fall on the floor."

The father was cured in no time. He then called his daughter and commanded her to give the ring to the doctor as payment. She slowly took it off and, as instructed, let it fall to the floor. The ring immediately turned into grains of wheat bouncing on the floorboards. Quick as a flash, the doctor turned himself into a rooster to pick them up, but just as quickly the young man turned into a fox and ate the rooster!

Heroes, villains, noodleheads, shape-shifters, sages, tricksters—all are on the human journey. What they and their stories have in common is the language of metaphor.

Metaphor

"Metaphor" comes from a Greek word meaning literally to place things side by side: placing something "like" beside something "unlike" to draw out a vivid comparison. "God is my rock and my salvation" is an easy example. God, of course, is not hard and gritty and made out of silicon. Only the most benighted literalist would say so. On the other hand, God is like a rock: strong, reliable, and faithful. Metaphors draw comparisons and sift out the applicable from the inapplicable. "He's a regular Fred Astaire." The meaning depends on how you say it: approvingly, meaning he's a pretty good dancer, or sarcastically, meaning he's a klutz. He is unlike Astaire in that he isn't tall or thin or balding. He is like Astaire in his dancing abilities or lack thereof. It's a metaphor.

Metaphors are our daily language even though we never advert to them. They enliven our speech and our stories in ways no other figures of speech can. But they have two deadly enemies. The first is missing or overlooking them altogether, a tragedy we'll explore later. The second is taking metaphors literally, on the surface only. This is the blind spot, for example, of the fundamentalist Bible reader. Literal readings of the books of Daniel and Revelation, for example, which supposedly predict timetables for the end of the world, have caused untold harm and may yet kick off another world war.

Some metaphors, like those found in ancient literature, from the Bible to Shakespeare, from poetry to fairy tales, need decoding because they come from different times, places, and cultures. Jeff Daniel Marion, the east Tennessee poet, captures the old Appalachia culture by citing a response to someone asking for directions:

> It's just over the knob there—you know the place, the one up there next to Beulah Justice, your mother's second cousin on her daddy's side. Or if you go in by the back road it's the farm across the way from Jesse's old barn that burned down last June with them two fine mules of his. Why, hell, son, you can't miss it.

These directions make no sense whatever to anyone outside that terrain and culture, and an outsider would have to be "schooled" to understand them.

Other more modern metaphors are easily understood in our culture. We might, for example, declare the members of Congress "a bunch of clowns" or a play as "a real turkey" or some newspapers as "pawns" in the hands of some corporations. "Clowns," "turkeys," "pawns" are all significant metaphors. We don't take them literally, but we get what they mean.

Examples of Metaphor

Metaphors are common and powerful and we often take them for granted. Consider the concept of argument and notice how we have attached the metaphors of war to it.

> Your claims are *indefensible*.
>
> She *attacked* every weak point in my argument.
>
> His criticisms were right on *target*.
>
> I *demolished* her argument.
>
> I've never *won* an argument with him.
>
> You disagree? Okay, *shoot*!
>
> If you use that strategy, she'll *wipe you out*.
>
> He *shot down* all of my arguments.

See, we actually "win" or "lose" arguments! We see those we are arguing with as opponents. We attack their positions and we defend our own. We gain and lose ground. We plan and use strategies. If we find a position indefensible, we can abandon it and take a new line of attack. In other words, many of the things we do in arguing are partially structured by the metaphor of war. The war metaphor is one that we live by in this culture and we don't even realize it.

Let us consider another metaphorical concept we use all the time. Notice how we have taken the concept of time and attached to it the metaphors of money.

> This gadget will *save* you hours.
>
> I don't have the *time* to give you.
>
> How do you *spend* your time these days?
>
> That flat tire *cost* me an hour.
>
> I've *invested* a lot of time in her.
>
> You need to *budget* your time.
>
> He's living on *borrowed* time.
>
> I *lost* a lot of time when I was sick.

Then we have the orientation metaphors. That is: up-down, in-out, front-back, on-off, deep-shallow, central-peripheral.

> That *boosted* my spirits.
>
> My spirits *rose*.
>
> You're in *high* spirits.
>
> Thinking about her always gives me a *lift*.
>
> I'm feeling *down*.
>
> My spirits *sank*.

There are also the physical metaphors. A drooping posture typically goes along with sadness and depression, an erect posture with a positive emotional state.

> He *rises* early in the morning.
>
> She *fell* asleep.

He *dropped* off to sleep.

She *sank* into a coma.

He's at the *peak* of health.

She's *sinking* fast.

He *came down* with the flu.

She *dropped* dead.

He's at the *height* of his powers.

She's in the *upper echelon*.

He is *low* man on the totem pole.

Things are looking *up*.

We hit a *peak* last year, but it's been *downhill* ever since.

Things are at an *all-time low*.

That was a *low* trick.

I wouldn't *stoop* to that.

Not to belabor the point, but metaphors—words or phrases that point to striking comparisons—are commonplace, and the modern ones are understood by all, and no one takes them literally. The meaning and the comparison are obvious.

Jokes are funny and they usually are also metaphors for universal experiences.

A man is at work one day when he notices that his coworker is wearing an earring. This man knows his coworker to be normally a conservative fellow and is curious about this sudden change in fashion sense. The man walks up to his friend and says, "I didn't know you were into earrings."

"Don't make such a big deal, it's only an earring," he replies sheepishly.

His friend falls silent for a few minutes, but then his curiosity prods him to ask, "So, how long have you been wearing it?"

"Ever since my wife found it in my truck."

But there are many cases where the metaphors are not easily spotted or understood and one must know the context to understand them.

Here is a celebrated one: "Please sit in the apple-juice seat." In isolation this sentence has no meaning at all, since the expression "apple-juice seat" is not a conventional way of referring to any kind of object. But the sentence makes perfect sense in the context in which it was uttered: an overnight guest came down to breakfast. There were four place settings—three with orange juice and one with apple juice. It was clear what the apple-juice seat was. And even the next morning, when there was no apple juice, it was still clear which seat was the apple-juice seat.

Much of past literature, for example, the Bible, carries metaphors to which we don't have the key or to which we are not sensitive. So we hear or read the stories and take them as simple narratives, a good read perhaps, but hearing nothing more than the surface level of the words.

The ancients, however, were incapable of telling or writing a story in this way. In their world, everything solicited the reader's or hearer's minds and hearts to something deeper. No one at the time, for example, took literally Matthew's account of the Magi and the star or Luke's account of the shepherds. They knew rather that these were symbols and metaphors that pointed to vastly deeper truths. Jesus' invented story of the good Samaritan resonated uncomfortably with his listeners and itself became a metaphor for kindness.

No one takes Aesop's talking animals literally. No one reads *Puss in the Boots*, Mark Twain's *Huckleberry Finn*, Charles Dickens's *Oliver Twist*, or John Steinbeck's *Grapes of Wrath* only for their entertainment value. They contain deeper messages. Everyone is delighted with the double meanings of Jesus' Simon-to-Peter naming, Oscar Wilde's Mrs. Malaprope, Dickens's Uriah Heep, Gilbert and Sullivan's Lord High Executioner, and *Bewitched*'s befuddled Aunt Clara (whose name means clear but who is laughingly anything but clear).

In other words, we moderns—raised in a so-called objective, digital world where the imagination is denigrated and fairy tales are relegated to children; where legal briefs, dissertations, records, and the printed word are considered "objective" truth—have lost our ability to hear or read stories and their metaphors and hidden meanings, and this includes the Bible, which is more or less a centuries-old collection of stories.

We are the first culture in history to identify truth with factuality, the first culture in history to declare that stories can be true only if they are factually verified and validated. Only then, we say, can we believe them. But stories are not about belief. Stories are about seeing, not believing. We see there is truth in the metaphors used. In Arabia, traditional story-tellers begin their stories with, "This was, and this was not." In the country of Georgia, near Russia, they say, "There was, there was, and yet there was not"; and Native Americans begin, "Now I don't know if it happened this way or not, but I know this story is true."

> Once a samurai came to the master Hakuin and asked, "Master, tell me, is there really such a thing as heaven and hell?" The master was quiet for quite some time while gazing at the man. "Who are you?" he asked at last. The man pulled himself up and answered, "Who am I? I am a samurai swordsman and a member of the emperor's personal guard."
>
> "You're a samurai!" said Hakuin doubtfully. "What kind of emperor would have you for a guard? You look more like a beggar!" "What?" the samurai stammered, growing red in the face and reaching for his sword. "Oho!" said Hakuin. "So you have a sword, do you? I'll bet it's much too dull to cut off my head!"
>
> The samurai could no longer contain himself. He drew his sword and readied to strike the master. Hakuin responded quickly, "*That* is hell!" The samurai, understanding the truth in the master's words and the risk he had taken, sheathed his sword and bowed. "Now," said the master, "*that* is heaven."

This story is not a literal one, but obviously one with deeper meaning. Its metaphors of samurai and master are symbols for pride and humility. Hell and heaven are well described. You don't hear this as if you were hearing a news report. You hear it with the heart.

So, too, at the end of Chapter One is a story I challenged you to think about, the story about the mayor who chopped down a maple tree to make room for a teahouse. He didn't dig up the roots and so the tree still cries out in pain. The maple tree put a dark spell on the mayor and he is desperately ill. An old woman hears about it, disguises herself as a doctor, and tells the mayor that if he wanted to live he must tear down the teahouse at once and then tend to the roots of the maple tree. He does this and soon he is well, for the "maple lives," the garden cried.

Think about this story. It's about losing one's roots, about separating from one's environment, distancing oneself from nature and becoming soul sick. Just remember, as someone nicely put it, "The past is a foreign country; they do things differently there."

Stories are indeed "foreign countries" to most of us. I must here remind you of how we have difficulty seeing them as symbols and conveyers of deeper, hidden meanings, or to appreciate the fact that story, for all generations till now, has been the repository of truth. People learned and lived by their national or sacred stories. Stories launched religion, nations, and science. They were preserved, passed down, and enshrined. The ancients knew that story involved the whole person and that it wrapped around the imagination to provoke deeper understanding and deeper mystery. Stories won't let us down; they resonate truth in our souls. In short, with their metaphors and symbols, stories are subversive, as you will see in "The Lost Goat."

Long ago there was an old patriarch who wandered about the desert with his kinfolk and their flocks of sheep and their herds of goats. They led a simple life, but God always provided for them. They would graze in one place while the grass was green, and then they would move on to new pastures.

Now it happened that the old patriarch had many children. But he had a favorite son who tended a certain herd of prized goats. And among all those goats, the son himself had a favorite goat. That goat was dearest to the boy's heart. It had black and white markings and big floppy ears.

The old patriarch loved to see his son enjoying the favorite goat, but the goat was always running away from the rest of the herd. The old man would often say, "My son, that wicked goat is forever getting lost, scampering among rocks and leaping across crevices. Watch yourself when you go searching for the goat." And then he sighed as he added, "For what would I do if any thing ever happened to you?" But the boy dearly loved the little goat and paid no heed to his father's warnings. He searched for the goat whenever it was lost.

One day it was decided to break camp and set out for fresh new pastures. The flocks and herds were gathered in by the kinsmen and the other children of the old patriarch. The tents were taken down and folded away. The entire clan was ready to leave when someone noticed that the boy, his father's favorite, was not there. The old patriarch searched among his son's herd, and saw that the black and white goat with the big floppy ears was missing. He frowned and angrily shook his head. "No, my son has gone looking for that worthless goat. We shall wait here until my son returns."

They waited one day and then they waited two days. The old patriarch stood vigil the entire time, standing at the edge of the camp always scanning the hillsides. By day he watched by the light of the sun, and by night by the light of the full moon. On the third morning, the old man heard the bleating of a goat. Looking up, he saw his son's favorite goat leaping from rock to rock and descending toward him. But the old man did not watch the goat. He squinted. His searching eyes kept looking toward the distance. He kept shouting out his son's name, louder and louder. But there was no sign of the boy.

The goat came down to the old man, stopped, and bleated. The old patriarch cast his glance down at the goat, and then cursed the goat. "You have led my son to his death. He has fallen into a crevice, or been devoured by wild beasts! You have brought sorrow into my life. You are a wicked goat." And with that, the old patriarch pulled his sharp dagger from his belt and slit the goat's throat. The goat tumbled to the ground. As the little goat hit the ground, one of its floppy ears fell back revealing a tiny scroll tucked underneath the ear.

The old patriarch dropped his dagger. He reached down with trembling hands, and pulled the small scroll open. Tears filled his eyes, and he held his breath. He recognized his son's writing. The scroll with its small cramped letters read:

"Father, I have followed the goat into a remote cave high in the hills. I came out the other side where I have found the land of milk and honey. I have found the Promised Land we have been looking for. I cannot leave here, but will await your arrival with all of our people. Then we will laugh and dance! My little goat knows the way. For now, dear Father, all you need to do is: Follow the Goat."

Is this just a story, or does it tell us something else beyond a sad irony? Might it suggest that sometimes we have the answer but we often kill it; or that we tend to destroy what will save us, for example, the environment?

I want to make clear an important point. What I'm trying to do in these pages—and I hope it will become more apparent as we go along— is enable you to see that story, with all of its literary metaphors, symbols, images, and figures of speech, is the first and the best expression of the inexpressible. Story uses every art at its disposal to say the unsayable. In story, it's not what the words say—those wild images and metaphors— but what they *symbolize*. What's percolating underneath the words is what counts. People tell stories because that's the closest they can come to indicating mystery and uncovering truth. Story is truth's natural home.

That is why, for example, when something stupendous happens, we helplessly and extravagantly resort to mumbling, poetry, dance, gesture, metaphor, image, and symbol. It's fruitless, for example, to expect a straight declarative answer when you ask, "Ah, poor, smitten Romeo, I see you're in love. What's it like?" You won't get a neurological chart or a legal brief for an answer. What you will get as Romeo first sees Juliet is this:

Oh, she doth teach the torches to burn bright!
It seems she hangs upon the cheek of night
Like a rich jewel in an Ethiope's ear:
Beauty too rich for use, for earth too dear!
She shows a snowy dove trooping with crows.
As yonder lady o'er her fellows shows.
The measure done, I'll watch her place of stand,
And, touching hers, make blessed my rude hand.
Did not my heart love till now? Forswear it, sight!
For I ne'er saw true beauty till this night.

So, Juliet is brighter than burning torches; she is like a brilliant ear-ring against the night sky, too lovely for this world, veritably a white dove making others look like black crows by comparison. Ah, her smooth hand would make my rough hand blessed. I thought I was in love before, but forget it.

Note the multiple metaphors. They are not literal renderings of Juliet, but they surely reveal the truth of how she impacted Romeo.

The same is true when one encounters God, whether in nature, soli-tude, trauma, beauty, or life. Like Romeo, we stumble to express the experience with the artist's brush, with sculpture, the movement of dance, and, most spontaneously of all, the story. The story, everyone understands, isn't literal any more than Romeo's words are; it is filled with desperate metaphors about thunder and lightning on the moun-taintop, or angels or deep tunnels, smoke, clouds, or a mere whisper of a breeze. Story is the first primitive accounting of the experience of the divine and comes long before theology. We should understand that the-ology is only a latecomer parsing the ancient stories, and so it necessar-ily loses something in the translation. Theology is like explaining a joke: it often kills the message.

Therefore, theology, helpful as it is, is not the "source" of spirituality. It is but a mental unpacking for the purpose of discussing the divine encounter. You won't encounter the divine through theology, however. This encounter comes through inhaling the images of the original story and letting its metaphors and symbols course through your being. In short, it's not the intellect but the imagination that counts, that reveals the divine, that savors and touches it.

Techniques

Scholars make all kinds of divisions and distinctions sorting out leg-ends, myths, folktales, and so on. We'll quickly mention only three cat-egories: myth, parable, and fairly tale. Myth tries to explain life's myster-ies. Why is there evil in the world? Easy: some girl named Pandora opened a box and let evil out. Thank you. We are now reassured about how it all happened. Parables, on the other hand, have the opposite effect. They upset us. "What do you mean by that story? I'm not sure I like it." Think of the folks hearing Jesus' parable of the good Samaritan ("A *good* Samaritan? You're kidding!"), or the parable of Dives and Lazarus ("A *bum* in heaven?"). The parables prod us into thought and they challenge us to change our worldview. "You have built a lovely home, myth assures us; but, whispers parable, you are right above an earthquake fault."

Fairy tales are a different breed. They are symbolic stories with noble and wicked figures, magic spells and talking animals, but in their use of metaphors they carry deeper meanings. Fairy tales, in short, are a classic example of the use of metaphoric, figurative language. They have always been enormously popular, and even when printing was introduced, they flourished. The Grimm Brothers' collections soon became classics followed by others.

But in the mid-nineteenth century, storytelling and storytellers fell out of use. The Industrial Revolution brought about rapid changes in the structure of the family (father or grandfather were not around to tell stories; they were in the factories) and in the way people earned their living. Universal education brought widespread literacy. The development of the nuclear family, the disappearance of workshops, the spread of newspapers and magazines all reduced the need and the opportunity for storytelling. The oral folktale tradition lost its place in the life of the community.

Needless to say, in our own time the media have taken over as our impersonal commercially laden storytellers, and sophisticated high-tech visuals have replaced the allure and seduction of the spoken word.

But formerly those words, those stories, those fairy tales were the community vehicle of entertainment and wisdom. Moreover—and this may surprise you—fairy tales started out as tales for adults, not children. They became children's fare only when adults lost their ability to grasp metaphors or use their imaginations. But originally they were tales for adults to help them cope with the hardships of life: floods, the Black Death, sickness, disease, thunderstorms, earthquakes, eclipses, starvation, exploitation, the whole array of the forces of nature and human betrayals. By using figures of speech and metaphors, people could find explanation or at least find ways to cope with issues of survival.

Fairy tales also became potent disguises to comment, in a feudal, monarchist, and patriarchal society, on the inequalities of life and poke fun at the upper-class oppressors. In other words, people could satirize their oppressors and fantasize on their fall as they rose.

Consider the story of Zev Ben Shmuel, the Hebrew court jester for a Babylonian king. On feast days and holidays he made the rulers laugh. He told jokes and was merry. Still, Zev Ben Shmuel remained proud of his religion and heritage. He believed in one God and would not bow before the king's idols or before anyone.

> Once, the king's chief military commander, who hated Jews, insulted Zev Ben Shmuel in the hallway of the palace. "Swine!" the soldier called out. Without missing a beat, the jester held out his hand. "Pleased to meet you, Mr. Swine. Zev Ben Shmuel at your service." This infuriated the commander, who reported the mischief to the king. He demanded the immediate execution of Zev Ben Shmuel. Reluctantly the king agreed.
>
> "But is that fair?" exclaimed Zev Ben Shmuel. "After all those belly laughs I have given you? One bad joke and I'm doomed?"
>
> The king was determined to put through his sentence. "But for all the laughter you have brought to me and my court, I shall grant you one favor: I shall let you choose the manner of your death. Hanging, poisoning, being devoured by wild beasts—anything you wish, we shall carry it out."
>
> The jester contemplated his bitter fate. He thought and thought. He returned to the king and said very simply, "Old age."

Fairy tales strike a blow at oppression and offer hope for social change. Bottom-of-the-barrel Cinderella will rise to the top and become a princess while her stepsisters will fall to the bottom. (Notice the spatial metaphor.) Alice levels the Queen of Hearts and the crazy trial minions with her withering declaration, "Why you're nothing but a pack of cards!" Prisoner Colonel Hogan constantly befuddles his captor, Colonel Klink, in *Hogan's Heroes*.

Stories are filled with metaphors for deeper meaning and sometimes we can figure them out; at other times we have lost the key and need help finding it. Stories and metaphors, remember, work on the unconscious level. That is why, as we shall see in Chapter Four: Stories and the Moral Lives of Children, the right stories are critical. Stories, in other words, have a hook in them. They catch you at a deeper level than the surface words themselves. In that sense, while some stories are factual, all stories are true. They have something to say beyond what they say. With that in mind, we approach the end of this chapter with this wonderful story. It's of Persian origin, I believe: "The King in Search of a Bride."

One day a young king decided that it was time for him to find a bride. Now he was different. He did not care if she was tall or thin, blonde or dark, but he did want her to be intelligent. So he decided to travel throughout his kingdom to find the most intelligent woman in the realm. He took off his royal garments and put on the clothes of a peasant. Suitably disguised, he wandered up and down the roads and paths and through the villages and towns of his kingdom.

As he was walking down a dusty road, the king met an old man, and since they were going in the same direction he asked, "Grandfather, where are you going?" The old man gave the name of a town and, since that was the king's destination too, he asked if he could walk along with him. This was fine with the old man. They had not walked too far when the king turned to the old man and asked, "Grandfather, should I carry you or should you carry me?"

"My, what a strange question," thought the old man. "He must be crazy. I'm not going to answer him!" And he didn't; he just walked faster. The king did not say anything else either for a while until the two men came to a large field in which the heads of ripening grain were beckoning them.

"Grandfather." The king stopped and looked at the field. "Do you think that grain is already eaten or not?"

"Already eaten or not? What kind of a question is that? This man is truly crazy. I'm not going to answer him." The older man pursed his lips together tightly, lengthened his stride, and continued down the road.

The king followed silently behind him. At long last they reached the walls of the city but could not enter until a funeral procession went by. "Grandfather, do you think the man inside the coffin is alive or dead?"

"He truly is mad! I am not going to bother with him any longer!" thought the old man. Turning to the younger man, he said, "Thank you for your hospitality. This is my town and I am going home now."

"Thank you for your hospitality," replied the king, "and don't forget to knock on your front door before you enter your home."

"Knock on my front door! Knock on my front door!" fumed the older man. "No one should tell me that. I do not need to knock on my own front door!"

By the time he reached the house he was so upset that he threw open his front door and stormed through the doorway, knocking his daughter down to the floor.

"Oh, daughter, I am so sorry. I should have listened to what that young man said, but everything he said was such nonsense. I am so sorry."

"Father, slow down, calm yourself. What young man? What nonsense?"

"The young man I traveled with on the road. You will never believe the ridiculous questions he asked."

"Tell me, Father."

"First he asked, 'Grandfather, should I carry you or should you carry me?' Now, what kind of a question is that? I am not so old that he had to carry me, nor he so young that I needed to carry him!"

"Oh, Father. That is not what he meant at all. He wanted to ask you if he should tell you a story or you should tell him one. The journey is much shorter when you are listening to stories. It is as if the storyteller is carrying the listener."

"Perhaps that is what he meant," responded the old man grudgingly, "but that doesn't explain his next question. We walked past a field of grain and he asked me if I thought the grain was already eaten or not! What kind of question is that?"

"Oh, Father, what he was asking you was whether you thought the owner of the field had already sold the crop or not. If he had sold it and spent the money, it would be as if the grain was already eaten."

"Oh, daughter, but you cannot explain his last question. We waited as a funeral passed by and he wanted to know if the man in the coffin was alive or dead. Is that not nonsense?"

"Father, what he was asking you was whether or not the man inside the coffin had children. If the man had children, then his line would live on; but if he had no children, then he was truly dead."

"Oh, daughter, I have been so foolish, I must find that young man and apologize." The old man went back through the town and found the king, still in his disguise.

"I am so sorry. I understand now what you were asking me. Please come and have dinner with me."

"Who helped you understand?"

"My daughter. Please, come this way."

The men arrived home just as the meal was ready. The young man sat at the table with the older man and his wife while their daughter brought a platter filled with a roasted chicken. Because the young man was a guest, she put the platter in front of him and asked him to carve the chicken. This he did, giving the wife the drumstick, the daughter the wings, and the old man the head and neck.

When the old man looked at his plate and saw the scrawny neck and head of the chicken, he became extremely angry. His face turned bright red, and as he stood up to start yelling, his daughter gently put her hand on his shoulder.

"Father, it's all right. The young man carved the chicken well. He gave the drumsticks to Mother because she is always standing and working. He gave me the wings for one day soon I will marry and fly away from home. He gave you the head and neck because you are the head of the household. The rest he kept for himself because there was no one else to share with."

When the king heard this, he realized he had found the very clever woman he had been searching for. He asked the father if he could marry her. The father looked to his daughter and, seeing her nod, he said yes. It was then the king threw off his disguise and the daughter discovered she was to become the queen.

We Westerners find this story quite charming, but our minds are a million miles away from the mentality that birthed it. We are quite like the grandfather who took everything literally. We find it hard to appreciate the culture of another time and place that readily accepts symbols, metaphors, images, and hidden meanings. The thought that language might say more than it says, signify more than its surface words, eludes us. But such is the stuff of our cultural, emotional, and religious heritage, and we must learn how to be more like the daughter with the ability to read or listen to stories in a new and deeper way.

Let me end this chapter with a quick dialogue between Lucy, Susan, and the Beavers in C.S. Lewis's *The Chronicles of Narnia*. The Beavers are hoping for the appearance of Aslan, the Christ figure.

> Susan asked, "Is he...quite safe? I shall feel nervous about meeting a lion."
> "That you will, dearie, and make no mistake," said Mrs. Beaver. "If there's anyone who can appear before Aslan without their knees knocking, they're either braver than most or else just silly."
> "Then he isn't safe?" said Lucy.
> "Safe?" said Mr. Beaver. "Course he isn't safe. But he's good."

Stories definitively aren't safe. They are stubbornly subversive. But they're good. In fact, they're better and deeper than you think!

CHAPTER THREE

The Healing Power of Stories

The truth of a myth is not literally true, only eternally so.

WILLIAM SLOANE COFFIN

John went to visit his ninety-year-old grandfather in a very secluded, rural area of Georgia. After spending a great evening chatting the night away, John's grandfather prepared breakfast of bacon, eggs, and toast. However, John noticed a filmlike substance on his plate and questioned his grandfather, "Are these plates clean?" His grandfather replied, "They're as clean as cold water can get them. Just you go ahead and finish your meal, Sonny!"

For lunch the old man made hamburgers. Again, John was concerned about the plates, since his appeared to have tiny specks around the edge that looked like dried egg and asked, "Are you sure these plates are clean?" Without looking up the old man said, "I told you before, Sonny, those dishes are as

63

clean as cold water can get them. Now don't you fret. I don't want to hear another word about it!"

Later that afternoon, John was on his way to a nearby town and as he was leaving, his grandfather's dog started to growl and wouldn't let him pass. John yelled and said, "Grandfather, your dog won't let me get to my car." Without diverting his attention from the football game he was watching on TV, the old man shouted, "Coldwater, leave that boy alone and go lay down!"

We start this chapter with humor as a cushion because we have come to the point where we turn more serious, or at least more challenging, as we consider the healing power of stories.

Martin Buber tells the story of his paralyzed grandfather who was asked to tell a story about his great teacher, the famous and holy Baal Shem Tov. The grandfather replied by telling him how the Holy Man used to jump up and down and dance when he was praying. And while he was reciting the story, the grandfather stood up and the story carried him away so much that he too had to jump and dance to show how the Master had done it. From that moment he was healed. This is not as far-fetched as it might seem. Modern psychology uses storytelling to bring healing to people, especially the healing of deep hurts from the past. Here is a story about that great rabbi, the Baal Shem Tov.

On the day the Baal Shem Tov was dying, he assigned each of his disciples a task to carry on in his name, to do some of his work. When he finished with all of them, he had one more task. He called the last disciple and gave him this task: go all over Europe to retell the stories he remembered from the Master. The disciple was very disappointed. This was hardly a prestigious job. But the Baal Shem Tov told him that he would not have to do this forever; he would receive a sign when he should stop, and then he could live out the rest of his life in ease.

So off the disciple went, and days and months turned into years and years of telling stories until he felt he had told them in every part of the world. Then he heard of a man in Italy, a nobleman in fact, who would pay a gold ducat for each new story told. So the disciple went to Italy to the nobleman's castle. But, to his absolute horror, he discovered that he had forgotten all the Baal Shem Tov stories! He couldn't remember a single story. He was mortified. But the nobleman was kind and urged him to stay a few days anyway, in the hope that he would eventually remember something.

But the next day and the next, he remembered nothing. Finally, on the third day the disciple protested that he must go, out of sheer embarrassment. But as he was about to leave, oh yes, suddenly he remembered one story, and this would prove that he indeed did know the great Baal Shem Tov, for he was the only one there when his Master told this story. And this is the story he remembered.

Once the Baal Shem Tov told him to harness the horses, for they were about to take a trip to Turkey where at this time of the year the streets were decorated for the Christians' Easter festival. The disciple was upset, for it was well known that Jews were not safe during the Christian Holy Week and Easter. They were fair game for the Christians shouting "God-killer!" And, in fact, it was then the custom during the Easter festival to kill one Jew in reparation.

Still, they went. They went into the city and then into the Jewish quarter where the Jews were all huddled behind their shutters out of fear. They were secluded, waiting till the festival was over and they could go out on the streets again in safety. So imagine how startled and surprised they were when the Baal Shem Tov stood up and opened all the windows of the house where they were staying. And furthermore, he stood there in full view! And looking through the window, he saw the bishop leading the procession. The bishop was arrayed like a prince with gold vestments, silver miter, and a diamond-studded staff. The Baal Shem Tov told his disciple, "Go tell the bishop I want to see him." Was he out of his mind? Did he want to die? But nothing could deter this order, so the disciple went out and went up to the bishop to tell him that the Baal Shem Tov wanted to see him. The bishop seemed frightened and agitated. But he went. He went and was secluded for three hours with the Baal Shem Tov. Then the Master came out and without saying anything else, told his disciples that they were ready to go back home.

As the disciple finished the story, he was about to apologize to the nobleman for the insignificance of the story when he suddenly noticed the enormous impact the story had on the nobleman. He had dissolved into tears, and finally, when he could speak, he said, "Oh, disciple, your story has just saved my soul! You see, I was there that day. I was that bishop. I had descended from a long line of distinguished rabbis but one day during a period of great persecution, I had abandoned the faith and converted to Christianity. The Christians, of course, were so pleased that in time they even made me a bishop. And I had accepted everything and I even went along with the killing of the Jews each year—until that one year. The night before the festival I had a terrible dream of the Day of Judgment and the danger to my soul. So until you called the very next day with a message from the Baal Shem Tov, I knew that I had to go with you. For three hours he and I talked. He told me that there still might be hope for my soul. He told me to sell my goods and retire on what was left and live a life of good deeds and holiness. There might still be hope. And his last words to me were these: 'When a man comes to you and tells you your own story, you will know that your sins are forgiven.'

"So I have been asking everyone I knew for stories from the Baal Shem Tov. And I recognized you immediately when you came and I was happy. But when I saw that all the stories had been taken from you, I recognized God's judgment. Yet now you have remembered one story, my story, and I know now that the Baal Shem Tov has interceded on my behalf and that God has forgiven me."

When a man comes to you and tells you your own story, you know that your sins are forgiven. And when you are forgiven, you are healed.

Stories provide the subconscious symbols and metaphors to deal with what we cannot consciously claim. A classic example of this kind of story-forgiveness is the famous tale of King David.

David, even with his large harem, committed adultery with Bathsheba, the wife of Uriah, the Hittite soldier, and then to cover up his sin when Bathsheba became pregnant, had her husband put in the front line of battle where he was certain to be killed, which he was.

The prophet Nathan came to the court and confronted David—with a story. Nathan told David the story of a very rich farmer who had hundreds and hundreds of sheep in contrast to a very poor farmer who had but one little lamb to his name. And this lamb was very dear to the man and lived with him in his own house. Indeed it was "like a daughter to him." Well, one day the rich man had a sudden and very important visitor, and so naturally he was bound to give him hospitality. But he was unwilling to kill one of his own numerous sheep for a feast, so he simply went over and by force took the poor man's one lamb, who was less a pet than a family member, and killed and cooked it for his guest.

David was incensed on hearing the story. His indignation rose. He vowed destruction to the wretch who would do a thing like that. Who was the man? He, David, would exact vengeance. Nathan shot back with his famous sentence, "Thou art the man!" And then he proceeded to unfold his story—his parable—indicating that this is exactly what David did to Uriah. And David repented, and his story has in turn been a source of repentance for others.

Therapy groups, prayer groups, groups of all kinds have found that telling one's story helps healing. That's because of the great symbolic power of stories and how their images can go down deep and promote healing. Remember the striking films *The Color Purple* and *Fried Green Tomatoes*? Both stories provide images and role models for women who are in abusive relationships. Here are some stories from other cultures that carry similar images. The first is "Am I a Man Yet?"

One of the traditional fall outings for our family in Iowa, writes this man, was to go into the country armed with gunny-sacks in search of black walnuts. Sometimes the nuts, encased in thick green and black hulls, could be found under trees beside country roads or in the open fields. The walnuts were taken home, spread out on the dirt floor of the garage, and run over several times by the car to crack open the hulls. After drying out for two weeks or so, my dad, grandfather, and I put on old work gloves to keep the black stain from our hands, and sat on the floor of the garage. One by one, we peeled off and separated the dried hulls from the nuts.

As we did this, we shared memories of past outings, of rich "Lazy-Daisy" walnut cake and the black walnut taffy that would be made at holiday time. The buckets of hulled walnuts were then taken to the furnace room in the basement to dry out further before cracking. It was on such an anticipated journey that, unknown to me. I would be tested to see if I was a man yet. My dad always brought his shotgun along in case monster rabbits, squirrels, tigers, or bears attacked us.

I must interject here that the reason my grandmother had such a difficult time in childbirth was because my dad may have been born with a BB gun in his hands. He was born hunting. Every hunting season was on his calendar. He hunted pheasant, quail, duck, rabbit, squirrel, deer, elk, and even raccoons with coon hounds. Since he had grown up hunting, he was disappointed and confused when I didn't jump with joy to go with him to see animals destroyed. It was my dad's nature to hunt. I can't condemn him for that, but somehow I was born wearing an actor's costume and asking for a little more stage light. Killing animals and birds was not and is not my nature.

On that day, my gunnysack was getting heavy to pull as I found new sources of treasures. Then I heard my dad say, "Well, looky there, way up in the top of that tree there's a big squirrel's nest. I'll just go to the car and get my gun. We'll see if you're a man today, Donnie." I knew what he meant. I guess I wanted to be a man, but I was afraid to shoot the gun, and I sure didn't want to kill any squirrels. I fed them nuts from my hand on our back porch!

When Dad returned with the shotgun he placed it in my arms. "I'll show you how to hold it and help you aim. Be careful now," he said, "it's loaded."

Dad crouched behind me, helping me hold up the heavy gun. "We're going to aim right at that big nest and see if there's anything in it."

I didn't want to cry. I wanted to be a man, but the tears were running down my cheeks. "I don't want to do it," I said. "I don't want to kill the squirrels."

"Oh, come on, Donnie," he said, "you can do it. Be a man today."

Then my mother said, "Don't make him do it, Phil."

"He needs to!" my dad shouted. "Now come on, Donnie, point the end of the barrel right on that nest. That's it, and when you're ready, pull the trigger slowly. Now, it's going to kick a bit, but I've got you."

"Kick a bit." Never heard that before. There's another reason not to pull the trigger, I thought. "I don't want it to kick," I said.

"Well, it won't hurt you if you hold it tight against your shoulder."

I felt terrible. I wanted to be a man in my father's eyes, but I didn't want to shoot that gun. Is that what you had to do to be a man? I cocked my head to the right so that I could see the tip on the end of the barrel in the middle of the sight, and with my dad's help holding up the gun, I resigned myself to the task of becoming a man. I pulled the trigger. Bam! Kick it did. Knocked me back into my dad's chest and we both fell backward. It really hurt. Tears were coming. I couldn't do anything about it. My dad said, "Good job, look what you did." Most of the nest was blown out of the tree and there were two squealing, squirming squirrels on the ground.

I was crying hard by that time. I didn't care if I was a man or not. My dad took my hand and we walked over to look at the bloody squirrels on the ground.

"Now you need to finish them off, son," my dad said. "Put them out of their misery."

I knew they would never have been in any misery if I hadn't pulled that trigger. Through my tears I shouted, "I don't want to do it. I won't do it!"

"Come on now," my dad said, "take the gun and be a man."

My mother was there with us by that time, also crying, "Phil, stop it for pity's sake. He's only six years old."

I broke away and ran back to the car and jumped onto the back seat and covered my ears with my hands. I heard it anyway. Bam! I knew those little squirrels were blown to pieces, and it was all my fault. If only I hadn't pulled that trigger!

With the sacks of walnuts and the gun secured in the trunk, we began the long, excruciatingly uncomfortable ride home. No one said a word. Everyone was thinking.

My dad's thoughts probably were: "Is my only son ever going to be a man and want to go hunting with me?" My mother's thoughts probably were: "Why did I let that go so far? He's too young to kill." And me, well, I had many thoughts and questions: I want to run away and never see my dad again. Do I have to kill to be a man? Are guns what make us men?

I hated my dad with a six-year-old vengeance. However, with the passage of time and a somewhat more "grown up" point of view, I began to understand his passion for the hunt and his need to initiate me into his world, for his own sake, as well as for his image with his friends.

That was the last time I remember gathering black walnuts with my parents. Many years later when I was teaching at a university in Illinois, I took my own family hunting…for black walnuts. Now in the autumn of my own life, I have a loving wife, four sons, two daughters-in-law, two beautiful grandchildren, a gratifying, successful career in theater, education, and storytelling, and many loving friends whom I treasure greatly.

Sometimes when I feel especially happy with my life, I want to say to my dad, who may be looking down on me, "Am I…in your eyes, Dad, am I a man yet?"

A story of conflict, of two good people who could not make each other into their own image. Notice the boy's development: from hating his father, he moved to understanding and then to acceptance. I recall telling that story on a men's retreat and seeing several men tear up. I don't know whether they identified with the father or the son, but the story awakened things in them and surely opened the door to healing.

Here now are two deep folktales that resonate with women: "The Stolen Skin" and "The Lady of the Lake Waters."

There once lived on the northern shores a lonely man. He had always lived near the ocean bluffs, overlooking the descending levels of seastacks, those great flat-topped islands of rock, carved out of the land from centuries of pounding waves. His days were spent fishing the ocean. His only companions were the sea gulls wheeling overhead or an occasional seal that would surface among the seaweed.

One midsummer evening, the fisherman was returning from the sea. As he approached the first and shortest of the seastacks that marked his way to home shores, the man caught sight of movement on its surface. As the boat drifted toward the rocks, he heard singing that was sweet, yet wild. After tying his boat to a scrub of a tree, the man slowly climbed up the side of the rock. Upon reaching the surface, the man saw shining naked figures dancing in the moonlight. As they whirled about, the beings laughed and called to each other between the verses of their song. They were beautiful women with skin that shimmered like starlight. Their lilting voices reached deep inside the man. There appeared to be dark shadows on the ground lying near him. As his eyes adjusted to the surroundings, the shadows appeared to have substance.

The man reached out toward one. It was soft fur. Seal fur. Without thinking, he quickly stuffed the sealskin into his shirt and in doing so, lost his footing momentarily, sending rocks and pebbles cascading over the cliff. The dancers stopped suddenly, each one dashing toward the sealskins. As the women draped the skins about themselves, they transformed into the shape of seals and plunged off the cliff into the sea. That is, all but one, for there was still one woman searching desperately along the cliff edge of the great rock for her skin. The fisherman crept out of the shadows and approached the seal woman. As he first drew near, she appeared terrified. He feared that she would turn and leap into the ocean after the others. He couldn't bear for her to go. She was the most beautiful creature he had ever seen.

The woman drew a breath and stepped forward. "Please, sir," she pleaded in a voice that sounded like the rippling of waves on the sands, "give back to me what is mine."

The man could speak only of his own need. "Come home with me. Live with me. Be my wife."

The woman continued as though she had not heard him. "Without my skin, I can never go home to my family or my life beneath the waters." She began to weep again. "I will remain captive in the upper lands of the sun."

But the seal woman seemed so lovely to the man, even in tears. He refused to consider letting her go. "The others have gone. You are part of my world now."

The man took off his coat and bundled it around her. The woman appealed to him, begged him, but the man simply answered, "Come now, we'll go home."

He led her down to his boat and after lifting her in, headed toward the shore. The woman never stopped turning to gaze off toward the distant waters until the door of the man's home closed, shutting her inside. The two lived together many years. The woman gave birth to three children, with whom she would spend most of her time. She avoided the people of the village, not wanting to answer their questioning stares or hear them whisper that she seemed as distant to the fisherman as she was to the villagers. As time passed, the woman's skin became ghostly pale. Her long dark hair lost its luster, as did her once shining eyes. The woman cared for her family, but would, at times, slip down to the sea. There they would find her, standing out on the rocks, calling in a mournful voice to the seals that slipped about in the water.

One night the children were awakened by angry words. Their father's gruff voice whispered fiercely, "When will you stop talking about this? It's been years now."

"Life is ebbing away from me. I need my skin back," the woman begged.

But the man had never admitted to having locked away the sealskin. Instead he answered, "And if you had this sealskin, would you just abandon your family? What kind of mother are you? A bad one, I daresay."

The women's gaze fell to stare at the floor of the cottage. "I don't know. I only know that I cannot go on living as someone other than who I am. I need my skin back. It is a part of me."

The man yelled, "You care only for yourself! What of me?"

Then he stormed out, slamming the door, leaving the woman to weep alone.

The three children climbed down from the sleeping loft and wrapped their arms around their mother.

"Don't cry, Mother," said the oldest, "Father will be back. We will make you smile till then."

And then, at the urging of the oldest, the children began to sing a song their mother had taught them about the sea and danced about the room. The woman could not help but smile, which only encouraged her young to sing louder and dance with abandon. The two younger children careened into each other and the wall all at once, sending a high shelf crashing down on top of them. Their mother leaped to their aid.

"Are you all right?"

"We're fine," they answered laughing, shaking years of dust off of themselves.

The oldest stepped around the others and over the board that had fallen to get a look at what had toppled down off the high shelf.

"What's in this old wooden box?" The boy knelt down on the floor, fingering the overturned object. "There's a lock on it."

"I don't know," answered his mother. "I have never been able to reach up to that shelf, not even from the chair."

The woman bent down, reaching out to upright what appeared to be a long shallow wooden chest. As she lifted it, bottom side up, the lid broke off and the contents fell out to the floor.

"Oh, look!" cried the youngest. "It's a fur."

The three children fell upon the pelt, stroking the hide and guessing what it was from.

"It's from a bear," said one.

"No, it's a seal," said the other.

The youngest buried her face in the fur and said, "It smells like mother."

Three small heads turned to look up at their mother, questioning.

The woman stood, silent, barely breathing. She could not hear the children just now. Instead, she heard the crashing of waves and the singing of whales. She reached out toward the sealskin, and the children all lifted up the fur to their mother.

"Ohhh," she sighed, clutching her sealskin to her chest.

Then the woman held the pelt up to her face and breathed in the scent of the ocean air. She no longer saw the cottage before her, but rather saw images of sunlight filtering through waving seaweed, dolphins leaping in ocean spray. The children interrupted her reverie.

"Mother, what is it?"

"It is time for me to go home, dear ones," she said.

"You *are* home," insisted the eldest.

"No, I must leave."

The three children became still. She knelt down and spoke gently to them.

"If I stay, I cannot thrive. I am a prisoner on the land. You know I have told you that my real home is in the sea. I love you…and I will always be with you in my heart."

The woman turned and headed toward the door.

The children cried, "Mother, don't go!"

She paused and turned in the open doorway. "When you need me, listen for my voice at the edge of the sea." And then the woman fled into the night, clutching her sealskin.

Moments later, the fisherman returned home. He was met by his three children, standing in the doorway of the cottage in their night clothes.

"Mother has gone," they cried.

Their father looked past them and seeing the broken chest on the floor, yelled, "Wait inside!" and he ran off toward the bluff's edge.

The man reached the cliff overlooking the ocean just in time to see a seal dive off a rock into the sea. He shouted to her, yelling over and over into the night, but his voice could not be heard over the crashing of the great waves breaking against the rocks.

The fisherman never saw the seal woman again. But it is said by the villagers in that area that the fisherman's children could often be seen sitting on the rocks at the shore's edge. It seemed that the three of them would be seen laughing and singing with what appeared to be a female seal. In time this seal became known as a guardian of the bay and no one would harm her. They could always tell which one she was, for she had lustrous dark fur and shining eyes.

This is a powerful story about emotional abuse. It echoes the painful choices some women have to make to reconstruct their shattered lives. It can awaken in some the realization of their hurts and unfulfilled longings and the need to take action. Here's the second story, "The Lady of the Lake Waters."

There once was a young man who drove his sheep up into the hills, seeking greener pastures by the shore of a mountain lake. One day, after walking the flock to the lakeside, the shepherd was astonished to see a beautiful woman dressed in satin robes, sitting on the calm surface of the water. She was the most lovely woman his eyes had ever seen. The woman, unaware of being watched, was combing her long hair, using the glassy surface of the lake as her mirror. The man gasped and moved closer to the shore to see her. Whether it was the sound or the movement that startled the woman, I cannot say. She looked up and seeing the man standing there with his arms beckoning toward her, the woman quickly dove under the water and disappeared.

The shepherd called to her, "Wait! Stay with me. Be my wife."

But she did not reappear that day. The shepherd began to visit the lake daily. He would leave gifts for the woman by the shore. He would find his offerings gone the next day, but still no sign of the woman. Eventually the man could think of nothing else. He began to neglect his flock. He became obsessed. He started to visit the mountain lake at night as well as during the day. He would call out his love to the woman, "Lady of the lake waters, I love you. Please come with me and be my wife." He was certain that he could see, at times, a faint glimmering in the water at the spot where he had once seen her.

Months passed, and the shepherd persisted, consumed with his desire for what he could not have. By and by, some of his sheep wandered off and become lost, but he did not search for them. His thoughts were only for his unfulfilled longing. Finally one evening, when the moon was full, he sang out, again, over the lake, "Lady of the lake waters, I love you and I will never be happy until you are my wife. Please…"

But then he stopped, for there, rising from the lake, was the woman he had sought. She glided over the surface of the water toward him, her shining satin robes and long hair flowing with the soft breeze. The lady gently placed her hand on the shepherd's extended palm and stepped ashore.

"Shepherd, I consent to be your wife," she said and then held up her other hand to prevent him from speaking yet. "First, you must agree to this one condition. If ever you were to lay a rough hand on me three times, then I would vanish from your life, never to be seen again."

"Dear Lady," cried the man, "never would I ever think of harming you!"

He grasped her hand and began to lead the beautiful woman home when he heard sounds coming from behind them and stopped to turn and see. There, climbing out of the lake after the woman, were flocks of sheep and herds of cattle. The man was overjoyed. Now he possessed the woman of his dreams and wealth as well!

The couple married and for several years seemed happy. The shepherd was now raised in status to that of a farmer because of the flocks and herds that his wife had brought him. Because of this, they were often invited to attend the social events of the local villagers. One day, the shepherd and his wife were invited to a christening, where, to the surprise of all present, the spirit woman began weeping. Her husband gave her an angry glance and asked her, "Why are you making such a fool of yourself?"

His lady, having the ability to see into other's souls, answered her husband between sobs, "The poor baby has entered a family where it is not wanted. His mother is worn from too many children and has scant enough food or time for yet another. The man of this house beats them all. Misery lies ahead for the child. Why should I rejoice?"

He shoved her to keep her quiet and to stop her from embarrassing him in front of the others. The lady lifted her head, looked him steady in the eye, and said, "That's one."

Time passed and the farmer and his lady were invited to the funeral of the mother of the very child whose christening they had attended the year before. At the memorial service, the lady now laughed and danced and sang. Her husband angrily asked her, "Why are you making such a fool of yourself?"

The lady said happily, "The woman's sorrow is over. No longer will she struggle with being poor or mistreated. She is at peace now. Why, then, should I weep?"

The husband shoved her to keep her quiet and to stop her from embarrassing him in front of the other villagers. The lady lifted her head, looked him steady in the eye, and said, "That's two."

Life went on and the farmer and his lady appeared to live happily together, as before. At length, they were invited to attend a wedding where the bride was young and the groom was an older man of money. In the midst of the mirth and celebration of guests who had gathered from all the neighboring countryside, the lake lady burst into tears. Her husband grabbed her by the wrist and pulled her to him, whispering fiercely, "Is there nowhere we can go that you do not embarrass me by making a fool of yourself? What is wrong with you?"

"I weep because youth is married to age for the purpose of riches. It is a bad bargain, and I see misery beginning here for both of them."

The lady wrenched her wrist out of her husband's grasp and added, "Just as I see it beginning here for you, my husband. You have been rough with me for the third and last time. Farewell."

With that said, she left the wedding banquet. Her husband hurried after her shouting, "I'm sorry. Forgive me! Please, come back."

But the lake lady moved at such a pace that she was quickly out of sight and beyond hearing. The man reached their farm to find it empty. His wife as well as the flocks and herds were gone. He ran into the hills to the lake where he had first found her. He reached the top of the hill that overlooked the lake just in time to see the woman disappear beneath the surface of the waters, followed by all the flocks and herds.

Moments later, there was no trace of their passing. The water's surface was calm and the hillside empty. The only sound that could be heard in that mountain valley was the weeping of a man, a man who knew that he would never again see that which he had once prized above all else, but had forgotten to love.

These are how people in the past, unable to openly voice their needs, would tell such stories, offering possibilities of healing or expressing their frustration. In them you can see the healing power of story. It often expresses things in code and symbol and metaphor that we cannot verbalize. Reading such stories and, even more important, telling them can be very liberating—and encouraging.

Those last two stories were a bit heavy, so here's a lighter one.

A man dressed as Napoleon went to see a psychiatrist at the urging of his wife. "What's your problem?" asked the doctor.

"I have no problem," replied the man. "I'm one of the most famous people in the world. I have a great army behind me. I have all the money I'll ever need and I live in great luxury."

"Then why are you here?"

"It's because of my wife," said the man. "She thinks she's Mrs. Levine."

The following two tales will further bring out the healing quality of stories. The first is a gracious one that should speak to all of us, "Ananias." It's a retelling of a Scripture story: the conversion of Paul.

Along a cobblestoned alley of ancient Damascus, there once lived a shoemaker named Ananias. Like others of his scattered nation, the little cobbler went to his synagogue each week to pray for the birth of the Messiah. "How long, Adonai? How long is a little while?"

But then one Shabbat evening, some Galileans arrived at the synagogue door. Though dusty and tired from their long desert journey, the newcomers lifted their hands high above their heads: "Brothers! We bring glad news! God has raised Jesus of Nazareth from the dead that we might return to God!"

There was an ugly silence. One of the scribes murmured: "The chief priests of Jerusalem have sent word: 'Beware of rabble-rousers who claim that a poor crucified carpenter is the Messiah!'"

Then an old man stood up: "You are a disgrace to the people of Israel!"

Ananias sat on his crowded workbench and watched the porters throw the men outside. A great sadness crept over the little shoemaker: when would the Messiah come? He slipped out the back door and found the Galileans lying in a nearby gutter, laughing. Ananias suggested timidly: "If I were you, I might not be so happy to be tossed into a gutter."

One of the men wiped a gash on his forehead and smiled. "Now that the Messiah has come, I wouldn't mind being tossed headfirst into a manure pile."

There was something about these men that the poor shoemaker liked. "Tell me more about this Messiah...."

And so, after he had listened, Ananias became one of the followers.

What an exciting time to live—the news of the empty tomb still rang freshly in the ears of men and women! With each passing day, new miracles broke through: "Did you hear? Joseph the weaver has believed in the Messiah, and his whole family has received the Holy Spirit!" "Incredible news! The blind man who begs by the old stone well—he can see!" Yet miracles never visited Ananias. He stitched strips of leather on his workbench and mused: "After all, I'm only a simple cobbler who can hardly read the alphabet. A shoemaker must be content to sew sandals for the glory of God."

Ananias' times of prayer were also very ordinary. There were no startling revelations, only a quiet gentle Presence. But then one noontime, just as he put down his awl, something very unusual happened. A whisper rose within his heart: "Ananias!" The startled shoemaker tripped over his workbench. Then he remained still on the clay floor and listened to the silence, but the only sound was the wild pounding of his heart. But just as its beat began to calm, the voice called again: "Ananias!"

This time the little cobbler knew who had spoken. He glanced upward: "Here I am, Lord."

The voice came with a deep quiet authority: "Arise and go to Straight Street, and at the house of Judas ask for a man from Tarsus named Saul. He will be praying. In a vision he has seen a man named Ananias. You are to place your hands on him so that he may see again."

Ananias winced. Forgetting to whom he spoke, the poor cobbler scrambled to his feet: "Lord! Many people have told me about this man, about all the terrible things he has done to your people in Jerusalem. And now he has come to Damascus to arrest anyone who even calls upon your name!"

There was a long silence. Ananias looked upward: "Lord?" Silence. The shoemaker awkwardly shuffled his feet and cleared his throat: "Ahem…Lord?" Ananias sighed and bowed his head.

Then the voice spoke again: "Go, because I have chosen him to be my servant, to carry my name to Gentiles and kings, and to the people of Israel. I myself will show him all that he must suffer for my sake."

Ananias stumbled down his dirty alleyway. As in a dream, he wandered toward the wealthiest quarter of Damascus. Then the shoemaker knocked timidly on the door of Judas and waited until the huge gate opened a crack. A skeptical servant peered out. Ananias pushed past him with a clumsy dive: "Please, sir! I must see a man by the name of Saul!"

At first the servant was startled by the frantic little shoemaker, but he quickly recovered: "See here! The servants' entrance is around the back...of all the nerve!" He planted his palm squarely in Ananias's face and pushed the poor man out toward the street.

The struggling cobbler screamed. "No! I must splee a man by the nab of Salb...Pleeb, I must splee..." (It is difficult to be articulate when someone has a hand on your face.)

Just as the servant slammed the door, Ananias swung his leg into its path. This actually worked in the shoemaker's favor, since the volume of his screams markedly increased. They echoed throughout the neighborhood: "Ahhhhhhhhggrrrr! My leg!"

Then there came a deep, troubled voice from the inner courtyard: "Wait! I had a vision about that man!"

Ananias panicked and forgot everything: "Oh, no! He had a vision about me! Now I'm really in trouble...."

The angry servant grabbed the shoemaker's belt and jerked him back into the courtyard. There, under an aging olive tree, a sightless man lay on a mat. The shoemaker's fear quietly melted away: "Saul, I have been sent by the Lord Jesus whom you met along the way. He sent me here that you might see again and be filled with the Holy Spirit."

Ananias reached out for the sightless eyes. For a quiet moment, human history rested beneath the hands of a cobbler. When it was finished, a man named Saul had become Paul.

Some time passed before Paul began his ministry, and many more years fled by before the world realized its tremendous impact. And so, the little shoemaker never knew what came of the day when he stretched out his hands beneath that aging olive tree.

At the very end of his life, Ananias lay on his deathbed. He looked upward to the desert skies and whispered: "I haven't done much, Lord. A few shoes sewn, a few sandals stitched. But what more could be expected of a poor cobbler?"

But then, once again, that same voice rose quietly within his heart:

"Don't worry, Ananias, about how much you have done—or how little. You were there when I wanted you to be there. And that, my little shoemaker of a saint, is all that really matters."

And so with us. Stories like that can heal our sense of a meaningless or uneventful life, especially when our lives are compared to those of our adored celebrities. We may feel that miracles never visit us. But, as this story suggests, if we were there for someone when they needed us, that's all that matters.

G.K. Chesterton has a unique take on this theme in "The Donkey."

When fishes flew and forests walked
And figs grew upon a thorn,
Some moment when the moon was blood
Then surely I was born.

With monstrous head and sickening cry
And ears like errant wings,
The devil's walking parody
On all four-footed things.

The tattered outlaw of the earth,
Of ancient crooked will;
Starve, scourge, deride me: I am dumb,
I keep my secret still.

Fools! For I also had my hour;
One far fierce hour and sweet:
There was a shout about my ears,
And palms before my feet.

A physician tells this story. It's called "Let in the Light."

"I had a young man come into my practice with bone cancer. His leg was removed at the hip to save his life.

"He was twenty-four years old when I started working with him, and he was a very angry young man with a lot of bitterness. He felt a deep sense of injustice and a very deep hatred for all well people because it seemed so unfair to him that he had suffered this terrible loss so early in life. I worked with this man through his grief and rage and pain, using painting, imagery, and deep psychotherapy. After working with him for more than two years, there came a profound shift. He began 'coming out of himself.' Later he started to visit other people who had suffered severe physical losses.

"Once he visited a young woman who was almost his own age. It was a hot day in Palo Alto and he was in running shorts so his artificial leg showed when he came into her hospital room. The woman was so depressed. She had lost both her breasts and she wouldn't even look at him, wouldn't pay attention to him. The nurses had left her radio playing, probably in order to cheer her up. So, desperate to get her attention, he unstrapped his leg and began dancing around the room on one leg snapping his fingers to the music. She looked at him in amazement and then burst out laughing and said, 'Man, if you can dance, I can sing.'"

The doctor continues: "It was a year following this that we sat down to review our work together. He talked about what was significant to him and then I shared what was significant in our progress. As we were reviewing our two years of work together, I opened his file and there discovered several drawings he had made early on. I handed them to him. He looked at them and said, 'Oh, look at this.' He showed me one of his earliest drawings. I had suggested to him that he draw a picture of his body. He had drawn a picture of a vase and running through the vase was a deep black crack. This was the image of his body and he had taken a black crayon and had drawn the crack over and over again. He was grinding his teeth with rage at the time. It was very, very painful because it seemed to him that this vase could never function as a vase again. It could never hold water.

"Now, several years later, he came to this picture and looked at it and said, 'Oh, this one isn't finished.'

"And I said, extending the box of crayons, 'Why don't you finish it?'

"He picked up a yellow crayon and putting his finger on the crack he said, 'You see, here—where it is broken—this is where the light comes through.' And with the yellow crayon he drew light streaming through the crack in his body."

It's a healing story, a story that tells us we can grow strong at the broken places. The light of grace, renewal, and depth can come through the cracks in our lives.

Humor as Healing

Humor is a great healer. Garrison Keillor writes:

Laughter is what proves our humanity, and the ability to give a terrific party is a sign of true class. When Moses came down from the mountain with the clay tablets, he said, "Folks, I was able to talk God down to ten. Unfortunately, we had to leave adultery in there, but you will notice that solemnity was taken out." And that night the Israelites killed the fatted calf and drank wine and told Bible jokes in celebration.

He mentioned Moses. The Jews, so long persecuted, have developed a wonderful tradition of self-deprecating humor. It's one way they could cope. Here are some of their delights.

A young Jewish man excitedly tells his mother he's fallen in love and that he is going to get married. He says, "Just for fun, Ma, I'm going to bring over three women and you try to guess which one I'm going to marry." The mother agrees.

The next day, he brings three beautiful women into the house and sits them down on the couch and they chat for a while. He then says, "Okay, Ma, guess which one I'm going to marry."

She immediately replies, "The one on the right."

"That's amazing, Ma. You're right. How did you know?"

The Jewish mother replies, "I don't like her."

Q: Why don't Jewish mothers drink?
A: Alcohol interferes with their suffering.

Q: Why do Jewish mothers make great parole officers?
A: They never let anyone finish a sentence.

Q: What's a Jewish American Princess's favorite position?
A: Facing Bloomingdale's.

A Jewish boy comes home from school and tells his mother he's been given a part in the school play. "Wonderful! What part is it?" asks his mother. The boy says, "I play the part of the Jewish husband." The mother scowls and says, "Go back and tell the teacher you want a speaking part."

Did you hear about the bum who walked up to the Jewish mother on the street and said, "Lady, I haven't eaten in three days."
     "Force yourself," she replied.

Abe Goldberg was hurrying along Fifth Avenue late for work, but there was this humongous crowd surging along the street. They were a bunch of RCIA candidates going for the final stage of entry into the church at St. Patrick's Cathedral. Abe tried to sidestep them but they were like a stampede and before he realized it he was being swept along right in front of the cathedral, up the stairs, down the aisle, right into the sanctuary where he was baptized.
     Bewildered, he staggered out of the cathedral and decided to go back home. He ran into the house and told his wife, "Sarah, you won't believe what happened to me today!"
     "Not now, Abe," she says, "Can't you see I'm playing Mahjong?"
     So he goes down the hall and sees his daughter. "Becky, Becky," he shouts, "you wouldn't believe what happened to me today."
     Becky says, "Not now, Pops, I'm getting ready for the dance tonight."
     So Abe leaves and find his son Irving in his bedroom. "Irving, Irving, let me tell you something. You wouldn't believe what happened to me today!"
     Irving says, "Later, Pop, I'm cramming for my exam."

Dejected, Abe leaves and goes to the kitchen, leans against the stove, and says to himself, "I've been a Catholic for only three hours and already I hate these people!"

Our laughter at these stories makes us forget ourselves for a while. It is restorative—and healing.

Half Stories

The rest of this chapter deals with deep stuff. The stories of Ananias and the young amputee are "half stories," that is, they contain both joy and sorrow, opposite tensions, contradictions. The young man lost a leg and yet could wind up dancing. His story offers possibilities of healing—not necessarily curing. Cure refers to the body, healing refers to the soul.

Ananias was a nobody, a cobbler, not near the status of Paul who went on to fame. His leg caught in a door, a fist in his face, what could he claim? His nothingness became something when God needed him. He was where he was called to be. And it was enough. And his story heals those who wonder what they did in life. The point is that healing comes from pulling two opposites together: victim and survivor, sinner and saint, commingled until it all comes together. Maybe this will become clearer as you carefully read the words of a rabbi.

Let me tell you half a story. This is a story that starts when the Jews are at the Red Sea, with the Egyptian army at their back and the sea in front of them. The sea splits. The Jews go through, and what emerges is an enormously powerful praise poem called *Shirat Ha-Yam*, A Song of the Sea. Later, the rabbis tell the following midrashic story about that occasion: "The Angels sought to give forth in song," celebrating their victory. When God heard the angels, he turned to them and said, "Quiet. My handiwork is drowning in the sea, and you want to sing a song of praise?"

Now, it's half a story because at the very same time that God is quieting the angels down below, the Jewish people are indeed singing that song; while the angels are quieted from singing, the Jewish people are praising God for their miraculous redemption at the Red Sea. So how come the angels don't get to sing and people do?

I first understood this story many years ago, thanks to Rabbi Chaim Tsvi Hollander, who in an offhand comment explained its meaning in the clearest way. He said angels are the kind of beings that do only one thing, and they do it one hundred percent. Whatever their task is, they're one hundred percent focused and that's it, whereas human beings are just a little bit more complex. People can entertain at least two and sometimes three or four contradictory and conflicting views and feelings all at once.

So for God to allow the angels to recite *Shirat Ha-Yam*, to sing his praises while people were drowning, would be to allow unconditional celebration at a time when people were dying. On the other hand, the Jews could at one and the same time rejoice that they were saved and redeemed and also suffer that it cost the lives of those Egyptians. That's why on the Passover seder, when we recite the ten plagues, we dip ten times into the cup of wine and take out a drop to say that our joy can never be complete if the price of human redemption is the death of others.

Now the reason I'm interested in that half story is the fact that human beings are complex, and we keep our concerns that are at odds with each other all floating around within the same human being—we are not angels! This is the center of how stories and rituals are able to heal people. For when we are wounded, parts of ourselves are at odds with other parts of ourselves. Something that belongs in this corner is not connected to something that belongs in another corner. When you are wounded, when you get hurt, when you get separated, you find that the wholeness of yourself is for a moment fragmented and shattered.

And if you start with the notion that human wholeness is our ultimate goal, then symbols and stories enable us to take the various parts of ourselves, of our society, of our history, of our people, and of the wider consciousness of the entire human race, and get a hold of them, bring them together, and make them present in ways that find a harmony and a wholeness together. When that process is complete for a moment, there is a kind of healing that takes place. If you figure that the Jewish people could tell the story of enslavement in Egypt in such a way that, with all the bitterness of that event, it still turns out that ninety-four percent of the Jewish people run to a seder every year to retell that story and to gobble down that bitter herb, and then say, "Wow, that was great!"—then you have to figure that stories create symbolic contexts that make even the most bitter enslavements and pains tolerable.

Only a story can make slavery in Egypt into a symbol for redemption. To accomplish that, we have to go back to Abraham, talk about a promise and a prediction of that enslavement, and tell about Moses and Mount Sinai, and then, when we've told the whole story, all of a sudden it doesn't feel like the same pain that it was before.

Some stories tell about wounds and about pain that cannot be cured, but can only be endured. Here's a story from my family:

My father-in-law was one of the most successful pediatricians in the New York area. This is a story that's still told about him in the hospital and in the family. My father-in-law was a pediatric anesthesiologist working with a boy who had continually recurring cancer. The treatments were very painful, but, in this boy's case, my father-in-law could usually alleviate that pain. One day the boy caught a cold, but he had to have the treatment. His name was Brian, eleven-year-old Brian. And my father-in-law can't give him the anesthesia because, with a cold, it can be extremely dangerous. So my father-in-law sits the boy down and he says, "You know, Brian, I love you very much, and I have to give you this treatment. But I can't give you the anesthetic this time. I can't take the pain away. But every time I apply the treatment, I'm going to hold you. I'm going to hold you through the whole thing. And each time the pain comes, I'm going to be there and hold you, and you'll feel better." And sure enough, it worked.

Now that story is important. It shows what you can do when you can't do anything more to stop the pain. Because, you know, life is like that. Nobody can have all the pain taken away. There are times when there's nothing to do but say to someone, "I can hold you when the pain is there, but this time I can't take it away."

But in the family the story plays another important role. It says to all the kids, You have a father who's a pediatrician. There are times when you want him. Do you want to know where he is? He's at Montefiore Hospital holding Brian, that's where he is. The story serves as a symbol of a father's love, which transcends the limits of what human beings can do, not by erasing those limits, but by suggesting a way of transcending them. It's a story that accepts the limitations of human life and the need to endure through compassion and love.

Stories heal because they can pull together the polar pieces, the contradictions, the evil and the good, the lost and found, the blindness and sight, and offer a pattern of hope, meaning, and restoration.

Let's conclude this chapter with a story by Father John Powell about a young man named Tommy who was not cured but who was healed.

> Some years ago I stood watching my university students file into the classroom for our first session of Theology of Faith. That was the day I first saw Tommy. My eyes and my mind both blinked. He was combing his long hair, which hung all the way down to his shoulders. It was the first time I had ever seen a boy with hair that long. I guess it was just coming into fashion then. I know in my mind that it isn't what's on your head but what's in it that counts, but on that day, I was unprepared and my emotions flipped. I immediately filed Tommy under "S" for strange...very strange.
>
> Tommy turned out to be the "atheist in residence" in my Theology of Faith course. He constantly objected to, smirked at, or whined about the possibility of an unconditionally loving Father God. We lived with each other in relative peace for one semester, although I admit he was at times a pain in the back pew. When he came up at the end of the course to turn in his final exam, he asked in a slightly cynical tone: "Do you think I'll ever find God?"
>
> I decided on a little shock therapy. "No!" I said emphatically.

"Oh," he responded, "I thought that was the product you were pushing."

I let him get five steps from the classroom door and then called out: "Tommy! I don't think you'll ever find him, but I'm absolutely certain he will find you!"

He shrugged a little and left my class and my life. I was a bit disappointed that he had missed my clever line.

Later, I heard that Tom had graduated and I was duly grateful. Then a sad report. Tommy had terminal cancer. Before I could search him out, he came to see me. When he walked into my office, his body was badly wasted, and the long hair had all fallen out as a result of chemotherapy. But his eyes were bright and his voice was firm, for the first time I think.

"Tommy, I've thought about you so often. I hear you are sick!" I blurted out.

"Oh yes, very sick. I have cancer in both lungs. It's a matter of weeks."

"Can you talk about it, Tom?"

"Sure. What would you like to know?"

"What's it like to be only twenty-four and dying?"

"Well, it could be worse."

"Like what?"

"Well, like being fifty and having no values or ideals, like being fifty and thinking that booze, seducing women, and making money are the real 'biggies' in life."

I began to go through my mental file cabinet under "S" where I had filed Tom. (It seems everybody I try to reject by classification God sends back into my life to educate me.)

"But what I really came to see you about," Tom said, "is something you said to me on the last day of class. I asked you if you thought I would ever find God and you said, 'No!' which surprised me. Then you said, 'But he will find you.' I thought about that a lot, even though my search for God was not at all intense…at that time.

"But when the doctors removed a lump from my groin and told me it was malignant, I got serious about locating God. And when the malignancy spread to my vital organs, I really began banging bloody fists against the bronze doors of heaven. But God did not come out. In fact, nothing happened. Did you ever try anything for a long time with great effort and with no success? You get psychologically glutted, fed up with trying. And then you quit.

"Well, one day I woke up, and instead of throwing a few more futile appeals over that high brick wall to a God who may or may not be there, I just quit. I decided that I didn't really care…about God, about an afterlife, or anything like that.

"I decided to spend what time I had left doing something more profitable. I thought about you and your class, and I remembered something else you had said: 'The essential sadness is to go through life without loving. But it would be almost equally sad to go through life and leave this world without ever telling those you loved that you had loved them.' So I began with the hardest one, my dad.

"He was reading the newspaper when I approached him.

"'Dad?'

"'Yes, what?' he asked without lowering the newspaper.

"'Dad, I would like to talk with you.'

"'Well, talk.'

"'I mean…it's really important.'

"The newspaper came down three slow inches. 'What is it?'

"'Dad, I love you. I just wanted you to know that.'"

Tom smiled at me, and said with obvious satisfaction, as though he felt a warm and secret joy flowing inside of him: "The newspaper fluttered to the floor. Then my father did two things I could not remember him ever doing before. He cried and he hugged me. And we talked all night, even though he had to go to work the next morning. It felt so good to be close to my father, to see his tears, to feel his hug, to hear him say that he loved me.

"It was easier with my mother and little brother. They cried with me too, and we hugged each other and started saying real nice things to each other. We shared the things we had been keeping secret for so many years. I was only sorry about one thing: that I had waited so long. Here I was, in the shadow of death, and I was just beginning to open up to all the people I had actually been close to.

"Then one day I turned around, and God was there. He didn't come to me when I pleaded with him. I guess I was like an animal trainer holding out a hoop, 'C'mon, jump through. C'mon, I'll give you three days…three weeks.' Apparently God does things in his own way and at his own hour. But the important thing is that he was there. He found me. You were right. He found me even after I stopped looking for him."

"Tommy," I practically gasped, "I think you are saying something very important and much more universal than you realize. To me, at least, you are saying that the surest way to find God is not to make him a private possession, a problem-solver, or an instant consolation in time of need, but rather by opening yourself to his love.

"Tom, could I ask you a favor? Would you come into my present Theology of Faith course and tell them what you have just told me? If I told them the same thing, it wouldn't be half as effective as if you were to tell them."

"Oooh…I was ready for you, but I don't know if I'm ready for your class."

"Tom, think about it. If and when you are ready, give me a call."

In a few days Tommy called, said he was ready for the class, that he wanted to do that for God and for me. So we scheduled a date.

The day came, but he never made it.

Stories don't always cure the body, but they heal the spirit.

CHAPTER FOUR

Stories and the Moral Lives of Children

If you want your children to be brilliant,
tell them fairy tales. If you want them to be very brilliant,
tell them more fairy tales. ALBERT EINSTEIN

The pope is visiting town and all the residents are dressed up in their best Sunday clothes. Everyone lines up on Main Street hoping for a personal blessing from the pope. One local man has put on his best suit and he's sure the pope will stop and talk to him. He is standing next to an exceptionally downtrodden, seedy-looking bum who doesn't smell very good. As the pope comes walking by, he leans over and says something to the bum and then walks right by the local man.

He can't believe it. Then it hits him. The pope won't talk to him; he's concerned for the unfortunate people: the poor and feeble ones. Thinking fast, he gives the bum twenty dollars to trade clothes with him. He puts on the bum's clothing and runs down the street to line up for another chance for the pope to stop and talk to him. Sure enough, the pope walks right up to him this time, leans over close, and says, "I thought I told you to get the hell out of here!"

A woman was trying hard to get the ketchup to come out of the bottle. During her struggle the phone rang so she asked her four-year-old daughter to answer the phone. "It's Father Sullivan, Mommy," the child said to her mother. Then she added, "Mommy can't come to the phone to talk to you right now. She's hitting the bottle."

The Moral Imagination

Having had our introductory smile, we move to two major preambles to this chapter on stories and the moral lives of children. One is about the moral imagination and the other is about the kitchen table. As you will see, these preambles and the entire chapter are somewhat academic and require careful reflection.

The first is about the moral imagination. Which is to say that both children and adults are not morally formed or convinced by mere declarative statements, "Do this. Don't do that." As psychiatrist Bruno Bettleheim rightly observes, "It hardly requires emphasis at this moment in our history that children need a moral education that teaches not through abstract ethical concepts, but through that which seems tangibly right and therefore meaningful….The child finds this kind of meaning through fairy tales."

The late Jewish philosopher Martin Buber recalls how he fell into "the fatal mistake of giving instruction in ethics" by presenting ethics as formal rules and principles. Buber discovered that very little of this kind of education gets "transformed into character-building substance." He recalls what every teacher knows:

I try to explain to my pupils that envy is despicable, and at once I feel the secret resistance of those who are poorer than their comrades. I try to explain that it is wicked to bully the weak, and at once I see a suppressed smile on the lips of the strong. I try to explain that lying destroys life, and something frightful happens: the worst habitual liar of the class produces a brilliant essay on the destructive power of lying.

It's like Catholic kids who get an A in religion and never practice it. Knowledge alone is not sufficient to produce a moral person. You need the power of the images and metaphors of stories.

This relevant quote is from an educator, Thomas Lickona:

Stories, read or told, have always been among the favorite teaching instruments of the world's great moral educators. Stories teach by attraction rather than compulsion; they invite rather than impose. They capture the imagination and touch the heart. All of us have experienced the power of a good story to stir strong feelings. That's why storytelling is such a natural way to engage and develop the emotional side of a child's character.

Relativism and Diversity

The lesson: get there early and often with stories all through the child's growing up and teen years. And that is most critical because they face a deep danger ahead of them when they go to school. Let me put it to you this way: Have you noticed how young children are very concerned about good and evil, truth and falsehood? They always want to know, "Is he a good person or a bad person?" "Is she a good fairy or an evil fairy?" You can confidently answer their questions and should do it often and early. But once they go to school, any clarity, any certainty, is subverted. That is because today's educational system is captive to "diversity" and relativism, and so cannot say or teach what or who is right or wrong. The one certitude that comes across in our educational system from kindergarten to college is that there are no moral certitudes. As a Harvard valedictorian said, "At Harvard they teach you that you can believe anything you want as long as you don't believe it's true."

A few years ago, alarmed by the lying, cheating, and prejudices of children, schools introduced something called Values Clarification education. It floundered as soon as it was introduced, as it was bound to do, simply because nobody could answer the basic question: Whose values would be the standard? Since there was no agreement, the conclusion was that whatever you thought was right was right. The only requirement was that you were to respect other people's views. No one was more right or wrong than another.

The results were predictable. A few years ago the prestigious *Chronicles of Higher Education* had all kinds of anguished articles from professors bemoaning the fact that their students had no moral barometers. They cited the fact that the students could not really say Hitler was wrong. He may have done some bad things, granted, but maybe given the times and the way he saw it, who's to say he was bad? No one would—or could. Relativism had triumphed.

College professor Father Joseph Linehard, S.J., adds his dismay and speaks for his colleagues when he says, "A generation of college students has been so anesthetized by relativism that they cannot say that Shakespeare was the greatest master of the English language for fear of offending someone who thinks Danielle Steele is." And then he adds a comment tailored for this chapter: "But if they can never say 'You are wrong,' they can never say, 'I am right' either." You can only have an opinion, no better, no worse, than another's.

Diversity also has reached its logical conclusion by producing just the opposite of its intent: a monoculture. You notice that everyone is required, often under force of law, to be diverse in exactly the same way. You cannot be diverse within an officially approved diversity. At least not without penalty. You cannot deviate from the imposed norm and, for example, critique hot-button issues like homosexuality, gay marriage, radical feminism, or affirmative action, even if such critiques were in fact outrageous and wrong-headed—that's not the point—without dismissal, without being forced to attend diversity classes or, in some cases, without being imprisoned.

The Classic Stories

Classic children's stories, on the other hand, are not ambiguous. They capture the clear meaning of morality through vivid depictions of the struggle between good and evil, where characters must make difficult choices between right and wrong, or heroes and villains contest the very fate of imaginary worlds. The great stories insightfully avoid bland instruction for the mind and supply the imagination with important symbolic information about the shape of our world and appropriate responses to its inhabitants. The contemporary moral philosopher Alasdair MacIntyre has summed this up eloquently:

> It is through hearing about wicked stepmothers, lost children, good but misguided kings, wolves that suckle twin boys, youngest sons who receive no inheritance but must make their own way in the world, and eldest sons who waste their inheritance...that children learn or mislearn what a child and what a parent is, what the cast of characters may be in the drama into which they have been born and what the ways of the world are. Deprive children of stories and you leave them unscripted, anxious stutterers in their actions as in their words.

To be sure, in the moral realm most things are not wholly black or wholly white. In most of us goodness and badness are mixed and life is often gray. That's why we're neither monsters nor saints. But, on the other hand, contrary to the indoctrinations of relativism and diversity, there is no mistaking the whiteness of white or the blackness of black. The late Charles Malik, former president of Lebanon, said it well:

> There is truth, and there is falsehood. There is good, and there is evil. There is happiness, and there is misery. There is that which ennobles, and there is that which demeans. There is that which puts you in harmony with yourself, with others, with the universe and with God, and there is that which alienates you from yourself and from the world and from God. These things are different and separate and totally distinguishable from one another.

The great fairy tales and children's fantasy stories make those distinctions, no two ways about it. They attractively depict character and virtue. In these stories the virtues glimmer as if in a looking glass, and wickedness and deception are unmasked of their pretensions to goodness and truth. The stories make us face the unvarnished truth about ourselves and compel us to consider what kind of people we want to be.

I remember this simple one from my mother: "Why Tom Thumb Stands Alone."

Once five fingers stood side by side on a hand. They were all friends. Where one went, the others went. They worked together. They played together. They ate and washed and wrote and did their chores together. One day the five fingers were resting on a table together when they spied a gold ring lying nearby.

"What a shiny ring!" exclaimed the First Finger.

"It would look good on me," declared the Second Finger.

"Let's take it," suggested the Third Finger.

"Quick! While nobody's looking!" whispered the Fourth Finger.

They started to reach for the ring when the Fifth Finger, the one named Thumb, spoke up. "Wait! We shouldn't do that!" it cried.

"Why not?" demanded the other four fingers.

"Because that ring does not belong to us," said the Thumb. "It's wrong to take something that doesn't belong to you."

"But who is going to know?" asked the other fingers. "No one will see us. Come on!"

"No," said the Thumb. "It's stealing."

Then the other four fingers began to laugh and make fun of the Thumb.

"You're afraid!" said the First Finger.

"What a goody-goody," sang the Second Finger.

"You're just mad because the ring won't fit you," muttered the Third Finger.

"We thought you were more fun than that," said the Fourth Finger. "We thought you were our friend."

But the Thumb shook its head. "I don't care what you say," it answered. "I won't steal."

"Then you can't hang around with us," shouted the other four fingers. "You can't be our friend."

So they went off in a group by themselves, and left the Thumb alone. At first they thought Thumb would follow them and beg them to take it back. But Thumb knew they were wrong and stood fast.

That is why today the thumb stands apart from the other four fingers.

Fairy tales remind us of moral truths whose ultimate claims to normal conduct and permanence we would not think of questioning. Love freely given *is* better than obedience that is coerced. Courage that rescues the innocent *is* noble, whereas cowardice that betrays others for self-gain or self-preservation is worthy only of disdain. Fairy tales say plainly that virtue and vice are opposites and not just a matter of degree. They show us that the virtues fit into character and complete our world in the same way that goodness naturally fills all things. In short, stories feed into the moral imagination.

The Jewish Tradition of Story

The theme here is expressed in this quote from the introduction to *Because God Loved Stories: An Anthology of Jewish Storytelling.*

> "It was family life," Marc Kaminsky's grandmother told him, "it was *simkhes*, joyous occasions, and not such *simkhes*, but it was always a *tish mit menschen*, a table with people." Everything I remember, the events of my life, holidays and times of grief, news from the family, all the gatherings took place here at the kitchen table.

And what did they do at that table but talk. As Michael Gold writes:

> Talk has ever been the joy of the Jewish race, great torrents of boundless, exalted talk. Talk does not exhaust Jews as it does other people, nor give them brain fatigue; it refreshes them. Talk is the baseball, the golf, the poker, the love, and the war of the Jewish race. The Jews are a loquacious people, their conversations overflowing with talk....Even old Mrs. Fingerman's parrot talked more than other parrots. Mr. Fingerman's last distraction before he died was to teach the parrot to curse in Yiddish.
>
> This book, too, is a table with people. At her home in West Philadelphia, my grandmother Bella Stein housed the family's

snapshots beneath a pane of glass that covered her kitchen table. That was where I counted out the change from my ice cream route when I was in college, where my grandfather spritzed his seltzer from a bottle, and where my great-uncles all played pinochle on Saturday nights. In this book I am inviting storytellers to a mythic version of my grandmother's kitchen table.

The tales of these tellers come together to form a larger story. For Passover, my grandmother's table was pressed into service, joined to the dining room table along with a few card tables, all covered with a white tablecloth, to accommodate all the relatives for the Seder.

Similarly, the *tish mit menschen* becomes, in this book, a figurative Passover table at which a group of storytellers gathers to retell not the traditional Passover story of the Exodus from Egypt, but many stories of another exodus and another promised land; stories of *shtetlakh* (East European small towns), pogroms (organized anti-Jewish violence), and the Holocaust; coming to America from Eastern Europe as well as from Turkey and the Middle East; settling on the Lower East Side. They recount the Jewish American experience in story.

That's a profound statement. The Jews literally have survived because they told stories—stories of slavery in ancient Egypt, pogroms in Russia, the Holocaust in Germany—around the kitchen table and in the synagogue. Their stories gave them not only hope, laughter in troubled times, but, above all, identity. All kinds of Jews, believers and skeptics, practicing and non-practicing (ninety percent of Jews are secular), good and wicked, honest and dishonest, greedy and generous—makes no difference how far apart they are from one another, how virtuous or how vicious—they are all, every one of them, united by a common fund of stories, which give them a history, pride, and self-definition.

And there, in a nutshell, is our fundamental problem when dealing with stories and the moral lives of children. *Our children frequently have no kitchen table.* Having no kitchen table, they have no storytellers around it. Having no storytellers, they have no story. Having no story, they have no inner identity except what is conferred on them by a consumer society and its servant, the media.

Family Meals

Tish mit menchen. A kitchen table with people. Many families in America do not have a table with people. That is, they frequently do not eat meals together. People work long hours or are away on business, including both mother and father. Neighborhood and school activities beckon at all hours. Parents and children have exceedingly busy social schedules and so they grab a bite here or there or a quick microwaved dinner alone. Yet, hear the words of Joseph A. Califano, Jr., the former drug czar for the government:

> The odds that twelve to seventeen year olds will smoke, drink, or use marijuana rise as the number of meals they have with their parents declines. Only six percent of kids who eat dinner with their parents six or more times a week smoke, compared with twenty-four percent of those who eat dinner with their parents twice a week or less; for marijuana use, it's twelve percent, compared with thirty-five percent.
>
> Parents who eat meals with their kids know where they are after school and on weekends, and parents who are involved in their children's school activities and academics are likeliest to be parents of kids who don't smoke, drink, or use marijuana or other illegal drugs. Teens who attend religious services regularly are far less likely to use drugs, know drug dealers, or have friends who smoke, drink, or do drugs than those who attend such services less than once a month.

Recently a group of corporate executives, worried about gross corruption in business and corporations, met to wrestle with the problem of ethics. During the course of the discussion one of them made this significant comment: "You don't learn ethics in college. By then it's too late. You learn ethics around the dinner table."

In short, family mealtime is the premier story-telling, story-sharing time. *Tish mit menchen.* It should be a moral priority with strict rules of no television or phone calls during meals. All cell phones off. Friends will soon learn and respect meal times. But it's not that way. No kitchen table for most kids. No stories.

No Storytellers

Second, no kitchen table means no one's around it. Why? Too busy, as we said, for one thing. For another, children live in a divorce culture. It is commonly known that about half of all marriages end in divorce and the fact is that while experts disagree as to the extent of the damage to children, all agree there is damage. "Any kind of divorce has lasting inner conflict in children's lives," writes Elizabeth Marquardt, author of *Between Two Worlds: The Inner Lives of Children of Divorce.* She points out that children of divorce are two to three times more likely than other children to end up with very serious social and emotional problems, not to mention that children of divorce are far less likely when they grow up to say they are very or even fairly religious. That's because the very thing they needed to be whole—security and the cement of shared family stories—has been shattered. The fabric of their lives has been torn when one or other storyteller is missing from the table.

Many of our youth live in a culture without fathers. The United States leads the world in fatherless families, with roughly twenty-four million children, or thirty-four percent of all kids, living in homes where a father does not reside. Fatherless boys commit more crime than those with their father at home. Nearly forty percent of children in father-absent homes have not seen their dad during the past year. They have, in effect, half a storyteller.

The kitchen table being vacant, the natural storytellers too busy or absent, children learn their stories elsewhere and find their role models elsewhere. Long ago Aristotle wrote, "No habit is so important to acquire as the ability to delight in fine characters and noble actions." And the great philosopher, Albert North Whitehead, once said, "Moral education is impossible without the habitual vision of greatness." Yet, who supplies the vision? In the absence of parents, the media takes over. Consider the characters of the television series *The Sopranos*, whom our culture romanticizes even though they are in the business of cheating, lying, and murdering. Consider the music industry's "rappers," whom black columnist Bob Herbert of the *New York Times* chastised for their misogynist conduct, hate-mongering, salacious lyrics, and murderous songs that so influence the black community. Then we have very public sports figures who use steroids and drugs; sleazy politicians who daily march across the scandal stage; predatory priests; sex exploiting teachers; macho men; raunchy women; and the action figures of exceedingly violent movies and video games. All of these populate the media world as role models. They are the storytellers now.

Media

Children are awash in media. They live and breathe it—multitask chat rooms, music downloads, cell phones, iPods, and stereos—with no parental storytellers to add balance (not to mention the harm to their neurological system such over-wiring does). Consider the 50,000 to 60,000 commercials children see or hear each year, the long hours in front of television, the non-stop images on their ever-present cell phones and iPods, the incessant music vibrating in their ears. Today's kids are, as the experts put it, an image generation, and those images are often of searing violence, recreational sex, and endless consumption. An overloaded society is not friendly to the interior life.

A recent article in the science section of the *New York Times*, citing an article in the *Journal of Child Development*, reports how even babies can be influenced by the emotional messages delivered through a television screen. "Dr. Mumme and other researchers said that parents sometimes assumed that their very young children were oblivious to television programs, but that the study's findings suggested otherwise."

And, of course, there is porn, a ten-billion-dollar industry, much of which is from child porn. Porn, hard and soft, is very much a part of the child's and teen's daily diet, impossible to escape and a normal part of their moral landscape. Explicit come-ons, hidden messages, email, and Web sites such as MySpace abound. Studies show that the average age of a child's first exposure to pornography is eleven years old, and the largest consumers of pornography are children between the ages of twelve and seventeen. One out of every five children is solicited by pornography.

Smart, Not Heart

There is, however, one story message children do get, even in stable homes, one theme that is mandatory, one major obsession: Be smart so you can get ahead. This has become the ideal, the Holy Grail, the goal of parenthood. Parents inundate their infants with every conceivable electronic educational device. One year olds have laptops, three year olds are hustled off to nursery start schools or private tutoring. All this, even though pediatricians recommend no screen time for babies under two, fearing that screen time is replacing the human interaction so critical for brain development. Preschoolers go through rigorous training to get a leg up on the other kids so they can get into the right schools, the right college, the right university, the right job, the right six-figure salary.

Yet babies three months to three years old are spending on average an hour a day watching TV and another hour on other screen media, such as video games. Some parents really think technology rather than human contact will make the kids happier and smarter. I'm not arguing against training the child to do well. I am saying that there is no equivalent emphasis, time, or energy to train the child to do good. There is plenty of academic education to the point of obsession, but so little moral education. There is a great deal of instruction, but very little storytelling. So eventually, we will have all these Ivy League, well-heeled, mega-mansioned, degreed felons, thieves, adulterers, con men, cheats, and murderers walking the halls of corporations, congress, and TV land—social successes but moral failures.

I quote a favorite passage of mine, from Chaim Potok's celebrated novel, *The Chosen*. The father of the boy Daniel is speaking in anguish to his friend Reuven. He cries out:

> Reuven, the Master of the Universe, blessed me with a brilliant son. And he cursed me with all the problems of raising him. Ah, what it is to have a brilliant son! Not a smart son, Reuven, but a brilliant son, Daniel, a boy with a mind like a jewel. Ah, what a curse it is, what an anguish it is to have a Daniel whose mind is like a pearl, like a sun. Reuven, when my Daniel was four years old, I saw him reading a story. He swallowed it as

one swallows food or water. There was no soul in my four-year-old Daniel, there was only his mind. He was a mind in a body without a soul. It was a story in a Yiddish book about a poor Jew and his struggle to get to *Eretz Yisroel* before he died. Ah, how that man suffered! And my Daniel enjoyed the story, he enjoyed the last terrible page, because when he finished it, he realized for the first time what a memory he had. He looked at me proudly and told me the story from memory, and I cried inside my heart. I went away and cried to the Master of the Universe. "What have you done to me? A mind like this I need for a son? A heart I need for a son, a soul I need for a son. Compassion I want from my son, righteousness, mercy, strength to suffer and carry pain, that I want from my son, not a mind without a soul!"

That, I fear, is what we have produced with our obsession with grades and no equivalent passion for morals: minds without souls.

Identity Crisis

Finally, children, like adults, are without an identity because, unlike the Jews, they have no shared universal religious stories. They are famously religiously illiterate. The fact is that the link to the religious tradition has been broken. The young do not go to church to hear the larger story. They have no religious history, stories, rituals, vocabulary, or symbols. A recent study shows that Catholic children rank the lowest of all denominations on religious knowledge and practice. In short, in our context, the majority of kids do not know the Christian language, the Christian story, or the Christian heroes. We have left them bereft of a good moral religious heritage and so they are susceptible to every new-age fad. Their identity is whatever the culture dictates and the pocketbook will buy.

Roots and Wings

It has often been said that kids need "roots and wings." They must have roots planted early by stories to give them the stability they will need to withstand the buffeting of life. And they need wings to fly away, to explore, to grow. There must be balance. If they have too many roots and not enough wings, children will never grow up, will be afraid to leave home, and will not take risks. They will smother or live a contracted life. On the other hand, if they have too much freedom and not enough roots, they will grow up with no convictions, no anchor, no firm identity, no character, nothing to cling to.

Laura Richards's tale called "The Apron String" puts this in story form:

> Once upon a time, a boy played about the house, running by his mother's side, and as he was very little, his mother tied him to the string of her apron. "Now," she said, "when you stumble, you can pull yourself up by the apron-string, and so you will not fall."
>
> The boy did that, and all went well, and the mother sang at her work.
>
> By and by the boy grew so tall that his head came above the window sill; and looking through the window, he saw far away green trees waving, and a flowing river that flashed in the sun, and rising above all, blue peaks of mountains.
>
> "Oh, Mother," he said, "untie the apron-string and let me go!"
>
> But the mother said, "Not yet, my child! Only yesterday you stumbled, and would have fallen but for the apron string. Wait yet a little, till you are stronger."
>
> So the boy waited, and all went as before; and the mother sang at her work. But one day the boy found the door of the house standing open, for it was spring weather. He stood on the threshold and looked across the valley, and saw the green trees waving, and the swift-flowing river with the sun flashing on it, and the blue mountains rising beyond. And this time he heard the voice of the river calling, and it said, "Come!"
>
> Then the boy started forward, and as he started, the string of the apron broke. "Oh! how weak my mother's apron-string is!" cried the boy; and he ran out into the world, with the broken string hanging.
>
> The mother gathered up the other end of the string and put it in her bosom, and went about her work again; but she sang no more.

The wise mother gave the boy his roots that stayed with him ("with the broken string still hanging") and then let him go. The door of the house was not left open accidentally.

In the old days the danger was too many roots and no wings. Today, in the culture we have just described, the major danger is the opposite: we give our kids too much freedom and no roots. Look how busy and overscheduled kids' lives are. Parents don't want them to be left out. Imitating their pressured parents, being busy is a modern sign of importance, of going somewhere, and, of course, the required compiling of all those activities to list on one's resumé for college. Kids are given every experience, every movement, every sensation, and they hanker for more. As a result, they spend a considerable amount of their time away from home, out of the house, and seldom eat meals with their families at the kitchen table. Thus they are exposed to stories and role models that are as far from gospel values as you can get.

Looking Ahead

It's not an easy world for kids or parents. Children are open, generous, eager, waiting to be fed, but we're not always feeding them. The good news is that we're there first. We get the first and lasting shot at their moral lives, especially in those first formative years. We have to be there for them, control their TV watching and videogames, and never, ever permit them to have a computer in their bedrooms but only in a public place. Take them to church and, finally and most critically, tell them stories, because stories are the foundation of the moral imagination.

Such stories, for example, are portrayed in films like *The Defiant Ones* with Tony Curtis and Sidney Poitier, a black and white who hate each other's race until prison circumstances and an escape, handcuffed together, force them together, and from that experience they learn tolerance and friendship. Or about the trenchant *In the Heat of the Night* which, in the deep south, forces the two protagonists, white Rod Steiger and black Sidney Poitier, into a psychological tug of war, but in the end, because of a shared story, their relationship ends up in mutual respect. Or how about the wonderful *Driving Miss Daisy*, which pits a haughty rich Jew and an illiterate poor black against each other until, through mutual experience, their hostility blossoms into a deep friendship. *To Kill a Mockingbird* provides a marvelous role model in Atticus Finch. The recent *Walk the Line*, the biography of Johnny Cash, is less about his music than his singing of stories that reached the hearts of people in dark places and let them know they were not alone. That was his strength. In the movie, he took his song-stories to Folsom Prison and there the prisoners recognized their own experiences and took hope.

Storytelling and Values

Throughout history, traditional peoples have recognized the role of storytelling in teaching values to children. In the 1930s, anthropologist Morris Opler recorded that among the Apache groups of southern New Mexico, a person who had acted inappropriately would often be chided with the questions, "How could you do that? Didn't you have a grandfather to tell you stories?" Such was the understanding of the power of storytelling in shaping character. So we must tell stories that portray courage and honesty as one of the most effective ways of raising moral children. And, perhaps, in these days of intensive television watching and Internet obsession, such stories are more important than ever as an alternate to the values these others display. In other words, we can get there first with the most lasting images and stories and the positive images they produce.

Our contention that storytelling shapes children (and adults) gets support from those scientists who are interested in how to change people's behavior. Usually we simply tell the stories and give them left-brain directives down the chain of command. It doesn't work, these scientists say. You need to engage the right brain, home to the imagination. Dr. Dean Ornish, founder of the Preventative Medicine Research Institute in California holds that, rather than telling a patient to change or die, therapists should tap into the emotions and "reframe" their thinking through story.

Howard Gardner, a cognitive scientist, adds: "When one is addressing a diverse or heterogeneous audience, the story must be simple and easy to identify with what is emotionally resonant and evocative of positive experience." In short, if you really want to change peoples' behavior, tell them a story.

How Storytelling Works with Children

Let's parse a favorite story, the wonderful *Velveteen Rabbit* by Margery Williams.

> One day the Velveteen Rabbit asks the old Skin Horse the question, "What is real? Does it mean having things that buzz inside you and a stick-out handle?"
>
> "Real isn't how you are made," said the Skin Horse. "It's a thing that happens to you. When a child loves you for a long, long time, not just to play with, but really loves you, then you become Real. It takes a long time. That's why it doesn't often happen to people who break easily, or have sharp edges, or who have to be carefully kept. Generally, by the time you are Real, most of your hair has been loved off, and your eyes drop out and you get loose in the joints and very shabby. But these things don't matter at all, because once you are Real you can't be ugly, except to people who don't understand."
>
> The Skin Horse tells the Velveteen Rabbit that he was made Real by the uncle of the boy who now lives in the nursery. He has lost much of his brown coat and the hairs from his tail, but he explains that looking worn out, having failing eyes and weakened limbs, and losing one's hair are the emblems of having been loved and having given oneself in love to another over a lifetime.
>
> In time the Velveteen Rabbit, too, becomes old and shabby. "The Boy loved him so hard that he loved all his whiskers off, and the pink lining to his ears turned grey, and his brown spots faded....[But] he didn't mind how he looked to other people, because the nursery magic had made him Real, and when you are Real shabbiness doesn't matter."

A good lesson for children.

The Meaning of Immortality

One day, long after the Velveteen Rabbit had become Real, the Boy becomes ill with scarlet fever and the doctor orders that everything that has come in contact with him be put into a sack and burned. That means also the Velveteen Rabbit! So he spends the night out in the garden in the death sack along with lots of old picture books and all sorts of odd rubbish. As he lays covered in darkness, the Velveteen Rabbit longingly remembers his life with the Boy, the love and the play that they had shared together in this garden, and the happiness that he had known in becoming real.

On one occasion, the Boy had left the Velveteen Rabbit in a cozy spot by the back yard. He was approached by some rabbits who moved like the mechanical toys; yet they were not mechanical at all. Evidently they were "a new kind of rabbit altogether." And they, in turn, quickly discovered that the Velveteen Rabbit had "no hind legs," and that he didn't "smell right" either. One of the rabbits had called out, "He isn't Real at all! He isn't Real!" The Velveteen Rabbit protested, "I am Real!" But he suspected that there was a difference between his realness when with the Boy and being real like these rabbits who ran free and danced in the garden. And he wanted to be like those rabbits.

As the Velveteen Rabbit lies in a heap in the garden that last night, he thinks sadly, "Of what use was it to be loved and lose one's beauty and become Real if it all ended like this?" During the night, the Velveteen Rabbit crawls out of his death sack to seek the comfort of the garden he loved. "A tear, a real tear trickled down his little shabby velvet nose and fell to the ground. Where this real tear falls a flower grows up unlike any other flower in the garden, and out of the blossom of that flower steps a fairy who with one kiss bestows on the Velveteen Rabbit the gift of life."

"I am the nursery Magic Fairy," she said. "I take care of all the playthings that the children have loved. When they are old and worn out and the children don't need them anymore, then I come and take them away with me and turn them into Real."

The Velveteen Rabbit asks if he wasn't Real already.

And she answers, "You were Real to the Boy because he loved you. Now you shall be Real to everyone." And so she carries him in flight to where the "real" rabbits are.

The Velveteen Rabbit becomes an allegory of how we ourselves reach perfection through love, and through love, immortality. Will the kids get all this? The story, after all, deals with primal truths: love makes one real. Love hurts and wounds. Love endures beyond the grave. The kids won't catch all this on a conscious level but they will on the unconscious level. The images, symbols, and metaphors will sink beneath the rational surface to provide material to guide their moral decisions and discover true love.

This is how stories operate. They work in symbols and metaphors to stimulate the moral imagination. They are never to be explained, only savored. They deposit, so to speak, the material of the moral life. Stories, including the lives of the saints, along with other role models, are irreplaceable shapers of the moral imagination.

Deeper Stories

For a serious segue into the final section of this chapter, we have Annie Dillard's wonderful story about the Eskimos of Canada's northern tundra. When they travel by foot across these great expanses of flat land, they mark their way by erecting six-foot tall piles of stones. As they venture forward they also look backward, making sure they can see where they came from. When the pile of stones is nearly out of sight, they erect another pile, thereby assuring that no matter how far they venture forward, they can always find their way home.

Stories help us find our way back home, which is what these examples do.

Margaret Brown has written a classic children's tale called *The Runaway Bunny*. In it a little bunny decides to run away from home, but his mother counters his every move. He says he'll become a fish. She says she'll become a fisherman and troll for him. He says he'll become a rock high on a mountain and she rejoins she'll become a mountain climber. And so it goes: he becomes a crocus in a hidden garden and she becomes a gardener, a tree for his fleeing bird, a wind for his departing sailboat "to blow you where I want you to go," a tightrope walker for his flying trapeze, and finally a mother to catch and hug him in her arms if he becomes a little boy and tries to hide in the house. Sensing the futility of trying to run away from his mother's love, he sighs, "Oh shucks, I might just as well stay where I am and be your little bunny." To which his savvy mother rejoins, "Have a carrot."

This lovely child's tale triggers thoughts of Francis Thompson's *Hound of Heaven*, where Jesus is portrayed as an insistent hound pursuing the sinner at his every turn:

> I fled Him, down the nights and down the days;
> I fled Him, down the arches of the years;
> I fled Him, down the labyrinthine ways
> Of my own mind; and in the mist of tears
> I hid from Him, and under running laughter
>> Up vistaed hopes I sped;
>> And shot, precipitated,
> Adown Titanic glooms of chasmed fears,
> From his strong Feet that followed, followed after.
>> But with unhurrying chase,
>> And unperturbed pace
> Deliberate speed, majestic instancy,
>> They beat—and a voice beat
>> More instant than the Feet—
> "All things betray thee, who betrayest Me."

And at the end of the poem, after the Hound of Heaven has pursued him down every shameful vice and folly, he, exhausted and crumpled, hears the Voice say:

> Whom wilt thou find to love ignoble thee,
>> Save Me, save only Me?
> All which I took from thee I did but take,
>> Not for thy harms,
> But just that thou might'st seek it in my arms.

This story is but a variation on Psalm 139:

> Where can I go from your spirit?
>   Or where can I flee from your presence?
> If I ascend to heaven, you are there;
>   if I make my bed in Sheol, you are there.
> If I take the wings of the morning
>   and settle at the farthest limits of the sea,
>   even there your hand shall lead me....

This story, "The Teacup," is a variation on the popular story, "The Ugly Duckling."

> Once upon a time, some grandparents were in a little gift shop looking for something to give their granddaughter on her birthday. Suddenly, the grandmother sees a precious teacup. "Look at this lovely teacup, Harry. Just the thing!"
>
> Granddad picks it up, looks at it, and says, "You're right. It's one of the nicest teacups I've ever seen. We must get it."
>
> At this point the teacup startled the grandparents by saying, "Well, thank you for the compliment, but, you know, I wasn't always so beautiful."
>
> The grandparents, still surprised, said, "What do you mean, you weren't always so beautiful?"
>
> "It's true," said the teacup. "Once I was just an ugly, soggy lump of clay. But one day a man with dirty and wet hands threw me on a wheel and started turning me around and around till I got so dizzy that I cried, 'Stop! Stop!' But the man with the wet hands said, 'Not yet.'
>
> "Then he started to poke me and punch me until I hurt all over. 'Stop! Stop!' I cried, but he said, 'Not yet.'
>
> "Finally he did stop but then he did something worse. He put me in a furnace and I got hotter and hotter until I couldn't stand it any longer and I cried, 'Stop! Stop!' But the man said, 'Not yet.'
>
> "And finally, when I thought I was going to get burned up, the man took me out of the furnace. Then, some short lady began to paint me and the fumes were so bad that they made

me sick to my stomach and I cried, 'Stop! Stop!' But the lady said, 'Not yet.'

"Finally she did stop and gave me back to the man again and he put me back in that awful furnace.

"I cried out, 'Stop! Stop!' But he only said, 'Not yet.'

"Finally he took me out and let me cool. And when I was cool a very pretty lady put me on a shelf, right next to the mirror. And when I looked into the mirror, I was amazed! I could not believe what I saw. I was no longer ugly, soggy, and dirty. I was beautiful and firm and clean. And I cried for joy!"

Children who feel bad about themselves or their limitations and troubles can take heart because God is working on them. Stories convey this truth better than any reassuring words. Jesus' story about the lost sheep says the same thing.

For those inevitable moments of selfishness, here's one from Sr. Jose Hobday:

My mother loved older people. When we were children, she used to send us off with gifts for them: a plate of cookies, freshly baked bread, Easter eggs in a basket. She was always looking out for older people. One day she sent me to visit an old woman named Mrs. Casey. It was a very difficult mission for a child because Mrs. Casey had cancer, and as a result she had no nose. Her face was bandaged from her eyes to her mouth. Her disease also caused a very bad odor.

Visiting Mrs. Casey was a real ordeal, particularly since my mother expected me to sit and talk and spend some time with her. After a couple of visits I told my mother to have one of my brothers visit Mrs. Casey. I didn't want to see her anymore. That was all my mother needed to make sure I kept going over to see Mrs. Casey. I dreaded it every time, but I always sat down and visited as my mother wanted.

One day in November, my mother announced she was inviting Mrs. Casey over for Thanksgiving dinner. I objected, saying that her smell would ruin my dinner. My mother told me I was going to have to adjust, because Mrs. Casey didn't have any place to go. I thought about the baked turkey and the pumpkin pies and my all-time Thanksgiving favorite, sweet potatoes. Not wanting to miss any of it, I told my mother I would sit at the other end of the table. But on Thanksgiving Day my mother sat me directly across from Mrs. Casey. I kept my eyes down and tried to be polite, but it was difficult, especially when the sweet potatoes started coming around. They were filled with marsh-mallows and brown sugar, just the way I like them.

But as the sweet potatoes came to my brother, he took two. That was against the rule in our house. You took one of any-thing until you were sure everyone else had one. But he thought he was being smart. He could see I was the last one being served and wouldn't get any if he took two. He also knew that with all the company present, I couldn't object as I surely would have done otherwise. When the sweet potato platter got to Mrs. Casey, she counted the number of people and passed it on without taking any. When it got to me, there was still one left. I felt terrible. I took it. And I'm glad to say I had the good grace to cut it in half and offer a portion to Mrs. Casey. When I did that, a strange thing happened. She didn't smell any more. She looked like a lovely person. She smiled back at me, took the potato, and we had a great Thanksgiving dinner.

Later, when I learned about the life of Saint Francis, I came to see this Thanksgiving encounter as similar to the conversion experience he had when he embraced the leper. I learned never to let a scar on someone's outside, no matter how ugly, keep me from seeing the beauty on the inside.

There's a constant temptation from the media, from those who have little or no guidance, to flirt with drugs and alcohol. Here is one story, "The Quest," that is potent both for youth and adults:

Long ago, Indian youths would go away in solitude on what is called a vision quest to prepare for manhood. One such youth hiked into a beautiful valley, green with trees, bright with flowers. There he fasted and prayed. But on the third day, as he looked up at the surrounding mountains, he noticed one tall rugged peak, capped with dazzling snow. "I will test myself against the mountain," he thought. He put on his buckskin shirt, threw his blanket over his shoulder, and set off to climb the peak. When he reached the summit, he gazed out from the rim of the world. He could see forever, and his heart swelled with pride. Then he heard the rustle of leaves at his feet and looking down, he saw a rattlesnake.

"I'm about to die," croaked the snake. "It's too cold for me up here and I'm freezing. Put me under your shirt where I'll be warm and take me down to the valley."

"No," said the youth, "I am forewarned. I know your kind. You are a rattlesnake. If I pick you up, you'll bite and your bite will kill me."

"Not so," whispered the snake. "I will treat you differently. If you do this for me, you will be special to me and I will not harm you."

The youth resisted a while but this was a very persuasive snake with beautiful markings. At last the youth tucked the snake under his shirt and carried it down to the valley. There he placed it gently on the grass. When, suddenly, the snake coiled, rattled, and struck, biting the youth on the leg.

"But you promised…" cried the dying youth.

"Hah! You knew what I was when you picked me up," said the snake as it slithered away.

The flirtation with alcohol, drugs, pornography…we know what they are when we pick them up.

Lessons

There's a wonderful lesson here and we'll remember this more than any mere statement. As William Bennett remarked when he was Secretary of Education:

> Do we want our children to know what honesty means? Then we might teach them about Abe Lincoln walking three miles to return six cents and, conversely, about Aesop's shepherd boy who cried wolf. Do we want our children to know what courage means? Then we might teach them about Joan of Arc, Horatio at the bridge, Harriet Tubman and the Underground

Railroad. Do we want them to know about kindness and compassion, and their opposites? Then they should read *A Christmas Carol* and *The Diary of Anne Frank* and, later on, *King Lear*....

Stories can create an emotional attachment to goodness, a desire to do the right thing. Stories provide a wealth of good examples, the kind of examples that are often missing from a child's day-to-day environment. Stories familiarize youngsters with the codes of conduct they need to know. Stories help to make sense out of life, help us to cast our own lives as stories. And unless this sense of meaning is acquired at an early age and reinforced as we grow older, there simply is no moral growth.

The thesis of this chapter is to underscore both the power of and the need for stories to shape the minds and hearts of children. But I do not want to give the impression that all children's stories should have a "moral" to them and hit children over the head with it. Not at all. Take, for example, the following story from China called "The Magic Pot."

Once a poor but hardworking woodcutter was walking home from the forest, with an ax strapped to his back. Suddenly he came upon a large old pot made of brass. It was the biggest pot he had ever seen. "What a fine pot!" he exclaimed. "But how will I get it home? It's too heavy to carry. Wait, I know!" He untied his shoulder strap and dropped the heavy ax into the pot. He proceeded to tie one end of the strap through one of the pot's handles and the other end around his waist. Then he began the hard work of dragging the clumsy pot down the path to his small house.

The woodcutter's wife was most pleased to see the pot and said, "What a fortunate day, husband. You found a wonderful old pot and another ax."

"No, wife, I just found the pot. I had the ax before."

"But there are two axes in the pot," she said. The woodcutter looked inside and was speechless. Two identical axes sat side by side. As he leaned down to pull them out, his straw hat fell from his head and into the pot. Now two hats rested near the axes. "Wife! The pot is haunted!"

"Or it's magical!" she said happily. "Let's put tonight's dinner inside and see what happens."

One dinner became two. "Quickly," said the wife. "Get our savings from the jar on the shelf!" The handful of coins doubled.

"It is magical!" cried the woodcutter. "What shall we put in next?"

"The money, of course," said his practical wife. "Let's get rich while we can."

They placed the coins inside repeatedly, and the amount doubled each time. An hour later every jar, pan, basket, pocket, chest, shelf, and shoe they owned was filled with money. They were, indeed, rich!

"Dear wife," said the woodcutter, "we can build a fine house and have a big vegetable garden, and I won't have to work so hard from now on. I'm so happy that I could dance!"

Then he grabbed her around the waist and began to dance around and around the small room. Suddenly he slipped on some loose coins and accidentally dropped his wife into the pot! He tried to pull her back out but it was too late. He now had two wives. They stepped out of the pot and looked closely at each other. It was impossible to tell them apart.

"What have I done?" cried the woodcutter. "Can a man live with two wives at the same time?"

"Not in my house," said the first wife. "Not in my house," said the second wife.

Both women smiled and grabbed the woodcutter and made him get into the pot. Two woodcutters climbed back out. "Can two families live in the same house?" asked both of the men.

"No," said the first wife. "No," echoed the second wife.

Half the money was given to the second couple and they built an elegant house. It was right next to the first couple's fine, new house. Ever since that time, the people of the village have remarked on the strong resemblance of the woodcutter and his wife's new relatives, the ones who must have brought them all that money!

Children (and adults) can enjoy that story just for the sheer delight of it. The same way with nonsense rhymes. The point is to engage the imagination, to stimulate a humility (we might call it) that suggests there are possibilities we haven't thought of, to escape the idolatry of the "rational" world.

With that being said, let's conclude with this instructive story from Korea, "The Story Bag."

"Tell me a story," said the little boy to his servants, parents, aunts, uncles, and cousins. No matter how short or long the story, he listened attentively and when it was over, he asked for another story, from someone else even after his parents died, and as he grew from a child to a youth, every night before he went to sleep, he made sure that someone, usually his faithful old servant, told him a story. Yet when anyone asked him to tell a story, he refused.

Time passed and the boy grew into a fine young man. His uncle arranged for him to marry a young woman from a neighboring village. The night before the procession to the bride's home, the old servant heard angry voices coming from the young man's room.

"This is our last chance!"

"He deserves to die for what he's done to us."

"We have no choice."

"It's his fault."

The servant looked all around the room but found no one. Just as he was about to leave, he noticed an old bag hanging from the ceiling. Whatever was inside was tied tightly, bumping around, trying with no success to escape. He curled up, making himself as small as he could, and listened carefully.

"Tomorrow, when the young man passes the strawberry field he will feel hungry and ask for a strawberry. I will be inside it and when he eats the strawberry, he will die!"

"Good. Good," said a high-pitched voice. "But, what if he isn't hungry?"

"Further on there is a well, known for the purity of its water. I will be in the ladle and when he drinks from me, he will die from my poison," said a gravelly voice.

"Yes," shouted the voices.

But then a worried voice asked, "But what if he isn't thirsty? Have we then lost our opportunity?"

"No," said a deep voice. "When he arrives at the young woman's house, a bag of straw will be put next to his horse. I will be a red hot poker and when he steps on me, he will burst into flames and die!"

The voices cheered until a syrupy voice asked, "But what if he is helped down on the other side? Then what?"

"I have the perfect solution," offered a sweet-sounding voice. "I will be a poisonous snake and lie under the bridal bed. When the two are asleep, I will bite the young man. He will certainly die."

The voices cheered, congratulating themselves, sure they would succeed and be liberated, no matter what happened.

The old servant listened, horrified. He knew if he told what he had heard, no one would believe him. He had to think of a plan to save the young man. In the morning, he went to the uncle. "I have cared for your nephew since his birth. This is the last time I will be able to be of service to him; may I not be the one to lead the procession to the home of his betrothed?"

Moved by the old man's devotion, the uncle gave his permission and the old servant took his place at the front.

As they approached the strawberry fields, the young man cried out, "Stop! I am hungry. I want to eat some strawberries."

The old servant pretended not to hear and walked more quickly. The young man was puzzled but said nothing. Soon they came to the well and the young man yelled, "Stop! I am thirsty. I want to drink a cup of water."

The old servant walked even faster. The young man was annoyed and complained to his uncle.

"Do not worry," he said. "We are almost there. I will take care of his insubordination when we arrive."

The old servant heard the uncle's words, but all he could think about was the bag of straw with the hot poker. As the young man prepared to dismount, the old man smacked the horse and it ran a few feet before throwing his rider into the dust, unharmed. The old servant ran to the young man, helped him to his feet, and dusted off his clothes. The young man was so upset at looking foolish he could not speak. Grateful there was only one more danger to be faced, the old servant listened to the uncle's angry words, all the time wondering how he would kill the snake.

After the wedding festivities, the bride and groom retired to their bedchamber, unaware of the danger that lurked beneath their bed. The old servant quietly crept into the room, sword in hand, and waited until they were asleep. Then he threw back the rug and with one blow, cut off the head of the snake. The couple screamed. The uncle and in-laws and servants rushed into the room.

"You shall be whipped within an inch of your life," yelled the uncle.

"Please, sir," said the old servant, "before you punish me, may I explain why I have behaved so strangely?"

Knowing how much the old man loved his nephew, the uncle nodded. After the old servant told how he had heard the angry voices in the bag in the young man's room and how they plotted to kill him, he showed them the burned edges of the wheat in the bag and the remains of the poisonous snake. "If all else failed, they were sure the snake would kill your nephew."

"Why?" asked the young man. "I have never harmed them."

"Not intentionally, that is true. But every time you refused to tell a story, one more story spirit was imprisoned in the bag for all time. This was their last chance to free themselves."

"Oh, no. What can I do?"

"Tell stories to anyone who asks for one."

And he did.

Let parents, grandparents, and teachers do likewise!

CHAPTER FIVE

Stories for the Second Half of Life

*The ability to make a discovery is the ability
to see what lies beyond the common sense of the day.*

Daniel Boorsten

A man was telling his neighbor, "I just bought a new hearing aid. It cost me $4000, but it's state of the art."

"Really?" answered the neighbor. "What kind is it?"

"Twelve thirty."

Morris, an eighty-two-year-old man, went to the doctor to get a physical. A few days later the doctor saw Morris walking down the street with a gorgeous young lady on his arm. A couple days later the doctor spoke to the man and said, "You're really doing great, aren't you?"

Morris replied, "Just doing what you said, Doctor. 'Get a hot mamma and be cheerful.'"

The doctor said, "I didn't say that. I said you that you got a heart murmur. Be careful."

You know you're getting older when everything hurts and what doesn't hurt, doesn't work. Your knees buckle and your belt won't. You can only burn the midnight oil till nine o'clock. And the twinkle in your eyes is the sun hitting your bifocals.

You're getting old when you stoop down to tie your shoe and ask yourself, as long as I'm down here, what else can I do? Or when you bend down to straighten out the wrinkles in your socks only to discover you're not wearing any. Or when you stroll down memory lane and get lost. Or when you find yourself before the open refrigerator door and ask yourself life's most profoundly theological question, "What am I here for?"

Disconnect

We laugh, as we good-naturedly should, but behind the laughter we have to be alert to the tragedy, namely, the devaluation of older age. As with children, society is not favorable to elders (my preferred word), prejudice connected with growing older is rampant. Unfair generalizations run wild: "All elderly people are forgetful." "All elderly are ill tempered." "Mental impairment goes with aging." "Most elderly people are not interested in sex and cannot enjoy it." All these statements are ageist.

Paternalism, which denies even capable people of making decisions for themselves, abounds. Family members and doctors are prone to this. At times they even talk baby talk to elders and assume that they are wholly or partially deaf. Then there is age rationing, denying potentially life-saving health care to the elderly, care not denied to the young. Why squander resources on those soon to die anyway? There are deep social reasons for why the aging and aged are dishonored and disconnected. Let me share three.

First, we live in a *capitalist culture* in which profit is the highest goal and the measurement of all striving and success; it is the engine that drives everything. What maximizes profits motivates our actions, decisions, and policies. Elders are devalued in a capitalist culture because they are not profit-producing. They are no longer useful for production or reproduction. They are considered drones, although drones with savings to be extracted.

Moreover, as I hinted above, elders are increasingly resented as more and more they are becoming an economic liability on society. Who will take care of them? Who will pay for them? Europe is a good example of demographic freefall. Europe is way below replacement. In most countries there are far more elderly than children and so you can understand that their economy is staggering under the burden of caring for and supporting the elderly, with no money feeding in from the bottom.

In the United States, Social Security is under heavy strain for the same reason: not enough young people to pay into it. Some maintain that in thirty years it will be gone. (It is not without coincidence, as some have pointed out, that laws which permitted the abortion of millions and millions of potential payee babies have now reappeared as euthanasia laws to subtract the paid.) In any case, more and more often, the elderly are looked upon as financial or economic enemies. As a former governor of Minnesota said, "Let them get on with their dying."

Second, we live in an *youth-obsessed culture*. Consider our frenzied focus on perfect health and the millions of products that promise it. Notice that the admired older adults in our culture are not those who gracefully accept the limits and challenges of old age, but those who imitate youth; those who swap iTunes with their grandkids, those who are surgically enhanced and painstakingly coiffed.

The message is clear: it's fine to be old as long as you don't look or act like it. Indeed, in a youth culture, old age is viewed as a problem, an affliction, an incurable disease. So, as with any diseased group, we isolate and segregate the elderly out of the mainstream and into nursing homes and into senior citizen communities—and thousands and thousands of these populate the country: Leisure Village north, south, east, west. No wonder some elderly feel lonely, abandoned, and alienated from mainstream life and from God.

The media, that great creation of a consumerist society, constantly show images of youth and vigor and gusto. Youth is idolized. Youth is celebrity. Youth is trend-setting. Youth is a huge market with billions in disposable income. A *Newsweek* cover of a sweating, gray-haired young man bears the cover line, "My God, I'm really turning 50!"—like he just discovered he had AIDS. Nursing home ads ask, "What shall we do about Mother?" She's a problem to be solved, not a person to be accepted as who and what she is.

Another ad shows a despondent man worrying about his job. His problem? He has gray hair. But through the wonderful world of chemistry he can turn it back to black by using this special formula product and—yes!—look young. In the next scene he has been promoted to vice president because he is "youthful!" Yes, aging is over the hill, the enemy, and a whole industry of cosmetic surgery, hair color, and wrinkle creams flourishes to keep it at bay. "Old is ugly. Old is shameful. Whatever you do, don't look or act old!" The point is that the word "young" conveys all that is attractive and positive, and the word "old" connotes unattractive and negative, boring, stubborn, slow, or behind the times.

Third, we live in a *utilitarian society*. Such a society craves what works and, more specifically, what works for me, not necessarily what is right or good or for the benefit of the community at large. Therefore the heavy emphasis, as we saw in the chapter on children, is on knowledge. Knowledge is power, power to control, manipulate the computer or the market, gain prestige, make money. Wisdom is how to use that power for the good of all, but it is not honored. It is not practical.

The fact is that traditional wisdom-figures, the elders, are passé. Technology forces elders out of the loop, makes them obsolete. It's inevitable. In the "olden days," when society was based on agriculture, age and experience were invaluable assets. The old farmer knew when to hasten harvesting, noting the clues that winter would come early—the squirrels had thicker fur perhaps, or the birds began migrating sooner than expected. The young farmer would not know such subtle warnings and would learn from his father. The elders passed down skills in harvesting, tanning, hunting, and so on. That's why old people appeared in folklore stories more frequently and with greater reverence.

Today, as we are all aware, there is huge technological divide between generations. Take the computer, for example: it's a whole different language. The common joke is right on: Grandma or Grandpa asking four-year-old Jimmy to work the computer. The technology (the iPods, disk burning, gigabytes, palm players) are beyond most elders. The young have to teach the elders to cope in a high-tech society. There is nothing vocationally for the elder to hand down to the youth; the elders must learn from the youth. Recently the *Asbury Park Press* featured a front page headline, "Teens Help Seniors with the Internet." That says it all.

The elderly can't even pass on cooking skills and old recipes because microwaved food packages do it faster. They can't share family histories around the table because the family seldom eats together. They can't as easily pass on carpentry or mending skills because the family can get it cheaper at Home Depot or Lowe's. They can't even always connect the generations because the grandparents have moved to Florida or are on a cruise or divorce has split the family and the generations. In gay and lesbian families you can't even pass on one half of the child's genetic heritage.

Results

These are some of the cultural aspects of our society that are not elder-friendly: we are a young country, a young market, an obsessively young culture, and this has serious emotional and spiritual fallouts. The real pity is that elders themselves accept the stereotypes, have bought into them. They really have to learn to stop using "old" in a negative context and not tolerate characterizations such as old bags, old biddies, old fogies, old-fangled, old-fashioned, old geezers, over the hill, blue hairs, golden oldies, frail, doddering, out of touch, not getting any younger. Cute, but un-Christian and untrue. Where there's life, there's hope.

> In the recreation room of a California retirement facility, four elderly women are playing bridge and chatting and keeping an eye on the flow of people in and out of the area. Soon an elderly man walks into the room. They all recognize him as a newcomer and they all perk up. One of the women says, "Hello, there. You're new here, aren't you?"
>
> He smiles and replies that indeed he is. He has just arrived this morning.

The second woman says, "And where did you live before you moved in?"

He says, "I was just released from San Quentin, where I spent the last twenty years."

A third woman perks up at this, and asks, "Oh, is that so? What were you in for?"

He says, "I murdered my wife."

The fourth woman sits up in the chair and smiles and says, "Oh, then you're single?"

Anyway, with such emphasis on youth and feeling good, we learn to dread any kind of limitation that goes with aging. We struggle with anything that makes us feel old and become alarmed at any signs of its approach.

The Christian View

All this is not the Christian view. In the scriptural narratives, growing old is a symbol of blessing and gray hair is a "crown of glory" (Prov 16:31). Moreover, the Scriptures are filled with stories of God's breaking into the individual lives of older persons to confer a particular gift or vocation. Think of Abraham and Sarah, Zachariah and Elizabeth, Anna and Simeon. The epistles speak explicitly of care for widows, honoring the elderly, and imitating their faith.

Nowhere in the biblical canon are they pitied, patronized, or treated with condescension. Nowhere is growing old itself described as a problem. Nowhere are elders described as pitiable, irrelevant, or behind the curve, as inactive or unproductive. Nowhere are they, as in so many Western dramas and narratives, lampooned as comic figures. On the contrary, they are seen as the bearers of wisdom by virtue of their age. It never seems to occur to the New Testament authors to characterize the aging process itself as an evil to be overcome.

The Christian view is that aging is also a gift from God, a time to embrace the cycle of life, assess its good and bad times, and seek opportunities for spiritual growth and spiritual witness. Elders learn that they are not being punished by God because they are sick or handicapped.

They learn to relish the role of wounded storyteller and do not forfeit the virtue of hope and their trust in Jesus who overcame death. We will see more of this later.

Moving Beyond

Elders must move *beyond the culture's negative messages*. Let's examine seven of them.

First, they must move *beyond the myths*. If there is a single myth about aging that most symbolizes what elders dread, it is the assumption that their memory will inevitably decline in old age. Yes, as their brain cells die, they have their senior moments, but in a stunning new study, psychologists have demonstrated that it is the elders' own expectation of memory loss that actually brings that fate upon them. In short, fear of aging is the single most powerful agent creating exactly what elders fear.

Using standard psychological measurements of memory, researchers studied two populations of people who hold their elders in high esteem—elderly mainland Chinese and older, deaf Americans—and compared them to a group of elderly mainstream Americans who don't. In addition, the researchers compared memory retention in the elderly with younger people in all three groups. Not only did the mainland Chinese and American deaf far outperform the mainstream Americans on four psychological memory tests, but the oldest in these two groups, especially the Chinese, performed almost as well as the youngest. They conclude that the results can be explained entirely by the fact that the Chinese have the most positive, active, and "internal" image of aging across the three cultures studied.

In another landmark study a fifteen-year longitudinal study of older people, begun in 1970 in the industrial city of Gothenburg, Sweden, there was no measurable decline in many body functions until after age seventy, and very little decline by eighty-one. Cognitive abilities were intact to at least age seventy-five, and still intact in almost all who had reached eighty-one, although speed at rote memory declined. American studies of healthy people aging in their own communities, as opposed to those shunted off to institutions, failed to show the evidence of decline in intelligence cognitive skills, and even in memory, that had appeared in all previous cross-sectional studies of aging. In short, mental decline is not inevitable and we should not buy into this myth or be like the woman one observer describes in this story, "The Cruise."

> The little cruise ship was crowded with people, many of them retired, all of them off for three days of pleasure. Ahead of me in the carpeted passageway was a tiny woman in brown polyester slacks, her shoulders hunched, her white hair cut in a short, straight bob. From the ship's intercom came a familiar tune, Begin the Beguine by Artie Shaw. And suddenly, a wonderful thing happened. The woman, unaware that anyone was behind her, began to shimmy and shake. She snapped her fingers. She swiveled her hips. She did a quick and graceful Lindy, step back, shuffle, slide. Then, as she reached the door to the dining salon, she paused, assembled her dignity, and stepped soberly through. She became a hunched old lady again.
>
> That visual fragment [the observer continues] has returned to mind many times. I think of it now as I recall another birthday and an age where most people would not believe that I still shimmy, too. Younger people think folks of my years are beyond music, romance, dancing, or dreams. They see us as age has shaped us: camouflaged by wrinkles, with thick waists and graying hair. They don't see all the other people who live inside.
>
> We present a certain face to the world because custom indicates it. We are the wise old codgers, the dignified matrons. We have no leeway to act our other selves or use our other selves.

The observer is correct. There's more to us (yes, I am an elder)—more dreams, desires, and passions, more memories, wit, and intelligence—than meets the eye. Elders should resent being categorized as formless "senior citizens" to be distracted like children, patronized, and not engaged as persons. But in a market-driven society where elders are no longer "useful," they are patronized, not revered for who they are. If the general population only knew! That's why I like this story.

> A man in his seventies went into a large toy store a week before Christmas and began looking around at the various displays.

He returned several times to a counter that featured a little train set. He was particularly fascinated by the great-sounding whistle from the engine as the train scurried around its little oval track. Finally, he said to the clerk who was demonstrating the toy, "I'll take one."

"Your grandson will love it," said the clerk.

"Then I'll take two," the man replied.

Second, elders must move *beyond their conventional roles.* Not that suddenly elders become a swinging Aunty Mame or Beau Brummel, but in the sense that they can sort their priorities and become mature enough to be indifferent to public opinion. Listen to this excerpt from Paula Darcy, from her book *Gift of the Red Bird.*

I see that in the last few years I lost myself in the roles I was playing. Mother. Author. Speaker. Friend. Counselor. Rather than these roles being channels for God to use in certain seasons of my life, they became my life. They became my security and my identity. They were how I saw myself, and who I thought I was. When I was stripped of them, I felt like nothing. Instead of being a facet of me, these roles became my worth. As they moved, changed, disappeared, I did, too.

I filled some of these roles so that others would approve of me. Now I am learning to approve of myself. It leaves room for my god to be God and not the voices and approval of others. The power of this insight is worth all the months in bed. I think about my early prayers for strength, health, and peace of mind. I wanted it to fall from the bedroom ceiling. I didn't want to work for it. I wanted an instant cure. I prayed for my body to be well as I was simultaneously misusing it. I begged to find peace while I pressed my nervous system to the bone.

Today I am making a list: "To what or whom has my life belonged?"

The telephone

My child

Appointments

My church

My friends

The television
My need for approval
My guilt

This evening I sit on my deck, enjoying the moon. I look again at my list. It would be easy to criticize myself, but that won't solve anything. Only waking up will change things. I take a sharp black marker and remake the inventory. I write God at the top, and me second. My child is third. I scratch out the television. The noise it creates is half of the reason I am seldom quiet. It pretends to fill an emptiness. But it only fills space. The emptiness doesn't go away.

And, of course, there is Jenny Joseph's famous poem "Warning," telling how she will wear purple as a warning to her friends that her sober, proper days are over and she's ready to make up for a proper life by doing scandalous things, such as running a stick along public railings and going out in the rain in her slippers. I offer my own version from the distaff side:

When I am an old man I shall wear crimson
      with an orange scarf that doesn't go,
      which doesn't quite suit me.
And I shall spend my pension on barmaids and winter trips
      and toeless footwear
      and say we have no money for coffee.
I shall sit down on park benches when I am weary
      and pilfer small samples and ring others' doorbells
      and run my nails along classroom blackboards
      and make up for the dull properness of my youth.
I shall go out in my nightwear in the rain
      and read the papers in supermarket aisles
      and learn to cuss.
You can wear terrible shorts and never shave
      and down five shots at a time
      or only dogs and mustard for a week
      and hoard dimes and fishhooks and bottle tops
          and junk in boxes.

But now we must have clothes that fit our jobs
    and pay our bills and not piss in the street
    and set a good example for the young ones.
We must have kin to dinner and read the reports.
But maybe I ought to prepare now?
So that those folks who know me
    are not too shocked and upset
when suddenly I am old and start to wear crimson.

The point is that, as we get older, there are more important issues than worrying about what other people may say or think. It's about being comfortable with the person you have become, warts and all.

So, let all elders move beyond the roles of convention. Let them think, "To heck with your children and neighbors."

Third, elders must move *beyond victimhood and role playing*. In their decades of living, elders have been wronged, betrayed, hurt, abused. Are they to be victims forever? The spiritual task of elders is to move from victims to survivors. "I am not a victim. I am a survivor." That's the powerful message of movies like *The Color Purple* and the disarming *Fried Green Tomatoes* with the wonderful Kathy Bates. Yes, elders have sinned, but have they never sung Amazing Grace? Life is not what you have done, but what you can do, can become.

Man of La Mancha is the story of the ridiculed Don Quixote, who lives with the illusion of being a knight of old, battling windmills that he imagines are dragons. Near the end of the musical, Don Quixote is dying and at his side is Aldonza, a prostitute he has idealized by calling her Dulcinea, Sweet One, much to the howling laughter of the townsfolk. But Don Quixote has loved her in a way unlike anything she has ever experienced. When Quixote breathes his last, Aldonza begins to sing The Impossible Dream. As the last echo of the song dies away, someone shouts to her, "Aldonza!" But she pulls herself up proudly and responds, "My name is Dulcinea." Aldonza was who she was. Dulcinea is who she is now. She's moved beyond Aldonza. She moved from doing (being a prostitute) to being (one loved).

Elders also are invited to move beyond what could have or should have been, but wasn't. And it is a shame. They should have married this one or that one, a theme wonderfully portrayed in the Merchant-Ivory film *The Remains of the Day*, with Anthony Hopkins and Emma Thompson. They should have taken that job or invested in that real estate. They would be wealthy today. Yes, it all could have, would have, should have been—but it isn't. That is past. Now is now and they have a sadder but wiser new identity.

That identity is that God has made us infinitely lovable. To grasp that great revelation will give elders a new sense of value and an identity beyond all social roles. In short, elders do not always have to be doing something, but can revel in just being, being beloved.

And that leads us to the fourth task: elders must move *beyond the masks of society*. That imperative is conveyed in "The Magic Towel."

> Once upon a time, an old woman lived with her son and daughter-in-law. The old mother resented the young woman's beauty and made life hard for her, ordering her to do all the heavy work in the house. The young woman was sweet and kind and made no complaint, which only infuriated the old woman more. One day the old woman told her daughter-in-law to make rice cakes, and when the young woman was finished, the old mother counted them. Then she went to the village on an errand. A traveling monk stopped by at the house, and the young woman gave him a rice cake out of kindness. After the priest left, the old mother returned, counted the cakes, and immediately noticed one was missing.
>
> "What have you done with the last cake!" she shrieked at her daughter-in-law. "You vain, greedy thing!"
>
> "I gave it to a monk," the young woman explained, trying to calm the old woman.
>
> "Well you must fetch it back!" the mother-in-law yelled.
>
> So the young wife ran after the monk, apologized profusely, and asked for the rice cake back. The monk laughed and returned the gift. Then he gave the young woman a small towel. "Use it to wash your face," he said. "I know that life is hard with your mother-in-law."
>
> From then on, the old mother noticed that her daughter-in-law became more and more beautiful. This made the old

woman ever more jealous and so she spied on her daughter-in-law one morning. She saw the young woman wipe her face with the towel, and each time she did so, her face became more radiant and lovely. "She uses a magic towel!" the old woman muttered to herself.

So the next day, the old woman sent her daughter-in-law on an errand and then stole the magic towel. She washed her face and peered at herself in the mirror. But she saw no change. "I am older," the mother-in-law thought, "so I must wash harder!" She wiped her face over and over, and then looked in the mirror. To her horror, her face became long and horse-like, and then hairy and round like a monkey's. Finally her features changed into a goblin's!

"Aie!" the old woman cried and collapsed on the floor. At that moment, her daughter-in-law returned. She saw the demon in the house and turned to flee. The old woman cried out, "Help me!" The daughter-in-law recognized the old woman's voice and felt sorry for her. "You must find a remedy!" the old woman pleaded. So the daughter-in-law ran out, looking for the monk. She found him some distance away and told him what happened. He laughed. "When a wicked person uses the towel," the monk said, "they end up looking like a demon!"

"Is there no cure?" the young woman asked.

"Yes," the monk laughed again, "just tell your mother in-law to use the other side of the towel!"

The young wife ran home and told the old woman the remedy. The mother-in-law immediately turned the towel over and wiped her face. The first time she did so, her face changed from a goblin's to a monkey's. The second time, it turned into a horse's snout, and the third time, it became her own wrinkled but human face.

The old woman embraced her daughter-in-law and wept. "Dear daughter," the old mother begged for forgiveness, "I did not see how ugly I was toward you!" And from that day on, the old mother never spoke a cross word to anyone. She became kind and generous, and worked side by side with her daughter-in-law. The old mother hoped that the monk with the magic towel would return some day, so she could thank him. But he never came back—nor did he need to.

The Meaning

Here is what we must ask ourselves: What does the story mean? In storyland, the tale is an elder story about masks. The towel wipes away outward appearances and reveals the soul. Most social situations require masks of various kinds—a happy one at cocktail parties, or an industrious one at work, for instance. Indeed, in our social and professional circles, image is more significant than substance, and the mask more important than the person. Masks are an integral part of modern life, partly because individuals must play so many different roles: parent, spouse, worker, friend, citizen, to name a few. With each role come certain conventional behaviors, and these shape the social masks individuals wear.

But if youth must master the art of wearing masks, "The Magic Towel" suggests that elders must learn to remove them and attend to inner substance rather than outward appearances. The money spent on cosmetic surgery might be better spent on a retreat or given to the poor, and then true inner beauty might be evident.

Fifth, elders must move *beyond inertia*. Have you ever noticed how often the elders in fairy tales struggle with poverty? Indeed, the theme of poverty is much more prominent for older protagonists. But however poor a youth may be, at least the future seems infinite and full of promise. Not so, however, with the older adult, confronting the specter of decline. And unlike the hero, the elder does not leave his or her dismal situation seeking better fortune. Instead, fortune comes to the elder in the middle of ordinary, everyday chores, and the elder's task is to be open to this unexpected magic. (Remember Abraham and Sarah!) If the virtues of youth are courage, perseverance, and confidence, those of the elder are alertness, openness, and curiosity. Can you find these elder qualities in "Fortune and the Woodcutter"?

Once upon a time, there lived an old woodcutter and his wife. He labored each day in the forest, from dawn to dusk, cutting wood to sell in the village. But no matter how hard he struggled, he could not succeed in life, and what he earned in the day, he and his family ate up at night. Two sons soon brightened his hearth and they worked by his side. Father and sons cut three times the wood and earned three times the money, but they ate three times the food, too, and so the woodcutter was no better off than before. Then the young men left home to seek their own fortunes.

After twenty years, the old man finally had enough. "I've worked for Fortune all my life," he exclaimed to his wife, "and she has given us little enough for it. From now on," he swore, "if Fortune wants to give us anything, she will have to come looking for us." And the woodcutter vowed to work no more.

"Good heavens!" his wife cried out. "If you don't work, we won't eat! And what are you saying? Fortune visits great sultans, not poor folk like us!" But no matter how much she tried to persuade him—and she reasoned, cried, and yelled—the old woodcutter refused to work. In fact, he decided to stay in bed.

Later that day a stranger came knocking at the door and asked if he could borrow the old man's mules for a few hours. The stranger explained that he had some work to do in the forest and that he noticed the woodcutter was not using his mules. The old man agreed, still lounging in bed. He simply asked the stranger to feed and water the two animals. The stranger then took the mules deep into the forest. He was no ordinary man, but a magician, and through his arts he had learned where a great treasure lay. So he went to the spot and dug up heaps of gold and jewels, loading the booty on the two mules. But just as he prepared to leave, gloating over his new wealth, soldiers came marching down the road. The stranger became frightened. He knew that if the soldiers found him with the treasure, they would ask questions. His sorcery would be discovered and he would be condemned to death. So the stranger fled into the forest and was never seen or heard from again.

The soldiers went along their way, noticing nothing unusual, and so the two mules waited undisturbed in the forest. After many hours, they started for home on their own, following the trails they had used with the woodcutter for many years. When they arrived at the woodcutter's home, his wife saw the poor animals. She ran upstairs. "Dear husband," she cried out, "come quickly. You must unload the mules before they collapse!"

The husband yawned and turned over in bed. "If I've told you once, I've told you a thousand times. I'm not working anymore."

The poor woman hurried downstairs, thought for a second, and then fetched a kitchen knife. She ran to the mules and slashed the bags on their backs to lighten the load. Gold and jewels poured out, flashing in the sun. "Gold!" she cired.

In a flash, her husband was downstairs, and he stared in astonishment at the treasure spilling into their yard. Then he grabbed his wife and they danced deliriously. "Fortune did come to us after all!" he exulted. And when the old man and his wife gave half their treasure to their sons and half the remainder to the poor, they were still as rich as rich could be!

This story introduces us to a man who has married, raised his children, seen the children leave (empty nest), and worked at a trade for "twenty years"—meaning he's an elder. Instead of living happily, though, the woodcutter and his wife live alone in dreadful poverty. The poverty is a figure of speech connoting loss and depression: the loss of health, loved ones, financial security, beauty, strength, agility. Some elders feel life is passing them by, has passed them by. Some are in depression with feelings of sadness and guilt. Some elders find themselves settling in, asking, "What else can I expect?" This story powerfully suggests that "the best is yet to be." Opportunity and possibility are always there.

This absolutely delightful "old Yankee" story is called "Edith and Bessie." As you read it, imagine the pluck of a banjo in the background, the scent of pine, and picture a storyteller with a distinct Yankee twang.

Years ago, when I was up Booton parts, up on the very edge of Canada, in Maine, I was doin' my student teachin' and there were two girls there I need to talk to ya about. They were sisters. Their names were Edith and Bessie. They were schoolmarms, and they'd been workin' there in that school system for about forty years. Now it turns out that Edith, who was the older sister, taught fourth graders, and her sister, Bessie, who was two years younger, well, she taught the second grade course.

Now they's been there a long time and they was just like any other schoolmarms you'd want to meet, supposedly, 'cept for one thing—they hated men. I'm here to testify that not all schoolmarms hate men. These two, however, did. And they were right scared of 'em. They didn't go out at night, didn't go out after dark. And the other strange thing about these two was that they kept one of them little Maine cats there, right there in the pantry. Never let it go out. Never let it go out smellin' out that sweet Maine air. Was kind of a sad thing. They kept it in the pantry there with one of them little boxes with a kinda scratchy stuff in it. Got kinda whiffy, but they coped.

Well, it turned out that one Friday night there come a knock on the front door. Bessie, she went scurryin' in there. She stood by the porch door and she said, "Who is it?" and the voice outside said, "It's Mr. Miller. Let me in." She said, "No, Mr. Miller, I can't letcha in. It's dark outside. It's Friday night. We're all done, and you're a man. Goodbye, go away!" He said, "Now, Bessie, we been goin' through this for forty years now, and I'm quite sick of it. So would you get your sister then and come back to the door and let me in? I want five minutes of your time, that's all. That's all!" She said, "I'll be right back." So she went to runnin' into the pantry where her sister was changing the cat box and she said, "Now, Edith, Mr. Miller, the principal, he's at the door, he's at the porch door. I don't know what to do." Edith said, "I'm comin'. For cryin' out loud!"

So she got up and the two of 'em went. There's safety in numbers, ya know, and they come standin' on the veranda door, and they both listenin' out there, and sure enough, it's Mr. Miller. He says, "Now, Edith, it's me, Mr. Miller. I got to come in and talk to ya. I'll just take up five minutes of your time. I just told Bessie that. I'll be gone in just a minute." Well, they had kind of a little tete-a-tete and they talked about it, ya know, and they decided it was fine. So they unlatched, unbolted, and unsnapped all those things up and down the door, and they opened up. They let him right in; and didn't he come right in and set right down in the middle of that plastic on the divan? Well, the two of 'em turned to him and said, "What is it? Say your piece, and then get goin'."

"Well," he said, "next Friday night, Edith and Bessie, I gotta ask ya to come to the Grange Hall 'cause we're gonna have a supper. We're gonna try to raise some money for uniforms for the boys' basketball team. Now, Edith and Bessie, I know ya don't go out at night, but I've got to have the support of all the faculty. Ya got to be there. I don't care if ya stay two minutes, just show your faces and then go home. That's all I got to say. I'm goin'. Goodbye." And Mr. Miller, he got up and he went through the door and disappeared. Well, they just went runnin' over to that door and slid and locked and bolted and turned all kinds of things until they were secure once more, and they went over and smoothed out the dimple in the divan plastic.

Now, they spent the next whole week wonderin' what on earth they were going to wear. Oh, they fretted. Finally, on Friday afternoon, Bessie, she said, "I know. I know what we're gonna do. I got it. You know them black dresses we got. You got lace on the bottom o' yours, and right on the waist. We'll take it off yours, put it on mine. And we'll take the lace offa my collar and cuffs and put it on yours. And then nobody'll know the difference. They'll think they're brand new dresses."

Well, Edith complied because she thought this was a grand idea. They'd been doin' this forever when anything come up 'cause these are the same dresses they did their interviews in for their teachin' jobs. They got their little sewin' all finished up and they went and put on their dresses. They were lookin' right sharp. And then they went down there. Sorta spooked up the old car and got down to the Grange Hall, and well, Edith, she sat down on the very end 'cause she was the head of the family—you know, them long grange tables there, and her sister didn't want to get too far away, so she set right down on the corner there, with their elbows touchin' so they'd be close and could get out quick.

There was an empty seat next to Bessie, though. I betcha ya can guess who sat there, can'tcha? A man. A stranger. A vacuum cleaner salesman. He commenced to talkin' to Bessie and he was quite chewin' on her ears, as they say, and he was just tuggin' at her, talkin' about every little thing, and she responded. Edith was right upset. Edith could not believe her sister was answerin' questions and talkin' and smilin'. Those two chatted right through the ham and beans; right through the pineapple upside-down cake and coffee. They were chattin' 'bout every little thing.

At the end of that night, Edith vowed she would never speak with her sister again. That was it. They were done. She'd been betrayed. Well, the next day Edith was just beside herself. Then there's a knock on the door about three o'clock in the afternoon. Vacuum cleaner salesman. No vacuum cleaner. He asked for Bessie. Oh, she come a-runnin'. And sure enough, he asked her out for tea, and they went. Now poor Edith didn't know what to do. She sat 'round just tearin' her hair out, wonderin' what was goin' on. Well, she locked herself up in her room. She didn't want to come out because she didn't want to see her sister's shabby face comin' through that door after she'd been out cattin' around.

Now, as I told you, the two of 'em were right close. Didn't know what to do. So Edith waited. She never heard the door slam, but she fell asleep and she thought her sister musta come in late. She didn't bother with her on Sunday neither. But Monday mornin' it was four-thirty in the mornin' and it was time to get up for breakfast, and time to get goin' to school, so she went and knocked on Bessie's door. She said, "Bessie, get up. I ain't talkin' to ya no more in this lifetime, but ya better get up. You're on your own for breakfast every mornin' from now on." But there was no noise on the other side of the door. She said, "Now get up, Bessie. I'm not gonna have it! You gotta come down, and we're gonna get ready to go to school!" She rapped on that door one more time, but sure enough, there was no answer. She flung that door wide open, and she looked at a bed that had not been mussed in some time.

And this is kind of a sad part of the story. You see, Bessie, she plumb eloped with that vacuum salesman. She never darkened the door of that house by the sea again. She never come back to Booton parts, and Edith lived out her days all by herself, right there in that little house, with the mists swirlin' around it, kinda sad, kinda wishin' she thought differently about her sister.

She never heard from Bessie again except for one kinda cryptic little postcard she got. It had a heart-shaped bathtub on the front. It was from some place called the Poconos. And it had one small phrase on it. It simply said, "Dear Edith, Let the cat out. Love, Bessie."

An elder tale, as we might call it. It's meaning: it's never too late. Possibilities loom. At any age, there's a world out there.

Sixth, elders must *re-examine the routine* that has dulled both wonder and the spiritual life and recapture both.

As we get older, we tend to get jaded. We've seen it all before. We lose sight of the wonder we had as a child. Therefore it is incumbent upon all elders to get away, not on a breathless, frantic trip (if it's Tuesday, it must be Atlantic City), but to a quiet place, a retreat of some sort, where nature abounds and re-inhale the healing power of nature and learn to wonder again.

A poem by the romantic poet William Wordsworth easily comes to mind:

I wandered lonely as a cloud
    That floats on high o'er vales and hills,
When all at at once I saw a crowd,
    A host of golden daffodils;
Beside the lake, beneath the trees,
Fluttering and dancing in the breeze.

Continuous as the stars that shine
　And twinkle on the milky way,
They stretched in never-ending line
　Along the margins of the bay:
Ten thousand I saw at a glance,
Tossing their heads in sprightly dance.

The waves beside them danced; but they
　Out-did the sparkling waves in glee:
A poet could not but be gay,
　In such a jocund company:
I gazed—and gazed—but little thought
What wealth the show to me had bought:

For oft, when on my couch I lie
　In vacant or in pensive mood,
They flash upon the inward eye
　Which is the bliss of solitude;
And then my heart with pleasure fills,
And dances with the daffodils.

Lisa Beamer was on the early morning television show *Good Morning America* some time back. She's the widow of Todd Beamer, who said "Let's roll!" and helped take down the hijacked plane that was heading for Washington, on September 11, 2001. She said it's the little things that she misses most about Todd, such as hearing the garage door open when he came home, and her children running to meet him.

Then she told about a very special teacher she had in high school many years ago whose husband died suddenly of a heart attack. About a week after his death, this teacher shared some of her insights with a classroom of students.

As the late afternoon sunlight came streaming in through the classroom windows and the class was nearly over, the teacher moved a few things aside on the edge of her desk and sat down there. With a gentle look of reflection on her face, she paused and said, "Class is over. I would like to share with all of you a thought that is unrelated to class, but which I feel is very important.

"Each of us is put here on earth," she continued, "to learn, share, love, appreciate, and give of ourselves. None of us knows when this fantastic experience will end. It can be taken away at any moment. Perhaps this is the Power's way of telling us that we must make the most out of every single day." Her eyes beginning to water, she went on, "So I would like you all to make me a promise. From now on, on your way to school, or on your way home, find something beautiful to notice. It doesn't have to be something you see, it could be a scent, perhaps of freshly baked bread wafting out of someone's house, or it could be the sound of the breeze slightly rustling the leaves in the trees, or the way the morning light catches one autumn leaf as it falls gently to the ground.

"Please look for these things and cherish them. For, although it may sound trite to some, these things are the stuff of life. The little things we are put here on earth to enjoy. The things we often take for granted. We must make it important to notice them, for at anytime it can all be taken away."

The class was completely quiet. We all picked up our books and filed out of the room silently. That afternoon I noticed more things on my way home from school than I had that whole semester. Every once in a while, I think of that teacher and remember what an impression she made on all of us, and I try to appreciate all of those things that sometimes we all overlook.

As we get older we must also review our integrity and scan for the inevitable dullness of routine that has sapped our spiritual life, as a lady of France learned in "The Bribe." (Whatever you think of the word "bribe" now—it suggests a shoddy and despicable deed—it once had a very opposite meaning. For the word originally meant "a piece of bread." In the dictionary you'll find under "bribe" precisely that definition: Old French for "a piece of bread, scraps." And a briber was one who begged for bread. Here is a story of how it got its present meaning.)

Once upon a time, hundreds of years ago in France, Antoinette was busy cleaning up her maisonette when she heard the familiar cry of a wandering holy man. "Alms...alms for the poor," he cried as he walked with effort down her narrow cobblestone street. Since, as you know, monks had no worldly goods and didn't work for a living, it was not unusual for these holy men to walk the streets begging for whatever people would give them.

Antoinette therefore went to her cupboard and cut a bribe—a piece of bread—from a fresh loaf and she sliced a wedge of cheese and dipped a cool drink from an urn down under the pantry floor. These she gave to the monk who by habit had paused at her curb in expectation of this mid-morning meal.

He was most grateful and thanked her profusely. "I will pray for you," said the holy man. "I will pray to God that your kindness will be rewarded with life everlasting. And I will pray the same for your husband and mother," he promised, as he humbled himself and took his leave. She smiled graciously and returned to the house.

But I must tell you this. The act of charity I just described wasn't what it seemed. The truth was that, for one thing, it was neither spontaneous nor unexpected, even though it may have been at one time in the past. Generosity, you see, had become a habit with the mistress and the monk, a ritual in which appearance and flattery played a larger role than the kindness it portrayed. In a word, the mistress and the monk were faking it, even though maybe neither of them realized it fully. They may not have realized that they had assumed acting roles in this small drama that they performed with regularity before a neighborhood audience, an audience whose acknowledgment the lady of the house held in high regard.

You see, the monk would come by in the mid-morning of every third day without fail, publicly announce himself while still a ways off; chanting "alms...alms for the poor" and then post himself at her dooryard for her to see—and the neighborhood as well. For her part, the mistress would expect him to come by in the mid-morning of every third day and would, without fail, have ready a refreshing drink, a wedge of cheese, and a bribe of fresh bread, given with greetings and well-wishes to the holy beggar who stood most visibly three paces past the bush nearest to her door. Neither had rehearsed this well-crafted script but each knew it by heart. Its lines and gestures had become their second nature. The mistress and the monk were faking being nice to each other and they didn't even know they were faking. They were playing to an audience.

That is, until the day Abner appeared at her door.

Now, this happened to be the mid-morning of the third day, but the voice chanting, "Alms...alms for the poor" just didn't sound right to the mistress' ear. Yet, there was the familiar robed figure in her dooryard, and at the appointed time, head bowed above his folded hands, as was usual. So the mistress could do no less than prepare her bribe and bring it to him. But when the holy man raised his hands to accept the bribe—the piece of bread—the mistress was taken aback. These were different hands. This wasn't a monk, or rather, it wasn't her monk, and instinctively she withdrew the tray with the bribe on it.

"Another holy man prays for me," she said quickly. "I don't need your prayers. Another prays for me." But the monk answered simply, "I am Abner, a name, Mistress, which means light and brightness. I wish only alms." He said this touching her wrist lightly. "Nothing more," he continued. "Please, mistress, I call upon your gentle kindness, alms for the poor."

But the mistress couldn't move. Although the hand touching her wrist had no power of grasp, it held her fast nonetheless. "I only wish alms," he had said, and was it not alms she had to offer? Why then had instinct withdrawn her bribe? This holy man was also deserving of her gentle kindness, was he not? Was it kindness, after all?

His face she never saw, downcast as it was beneath the fold of his monk's hood, but Abner of light and brightness had surely stared into her very soul in that flash of truth revealed. All the while, all these years, her bribe had not been offered freely from an overflowing grateful heart. Instead, it had been selfishly given in exchange for flattery and favor, and now she knew it. In that moment she knew it.

The touch upon her wrist had undeniably exposed her bribe for what it was, and not only her own pious pretense, but that of so many others in her village and across the land who also conspired with these wandering holy men to be seen as the "righteous" they wished others to think them.

So it was that the word that originally stood for hospitality and kindness of the highest order—giving a piece of bread in the Lord's name—lost its good name and fell into disrepute and disuse. Today, we say "a piece of bread" instead of "bribe." Once it was the symbol of open generosity and genuine good will. Now the word "bribe" stands for ill-mannered fakery and the worst kind of human insincerity.

This is an elder tale that reminds us that part of the task of our mature years is to re-examine our motives, remove the pride, and rededicate ourselves to the virtues we once aspired to. And, along the way, so we don't get too glum, we must also take a look at ourselves and laugh. This will help.

A ninety-year-old man went to his doctor for his annual check-up. The doctor asked him how he's feeling. The man says, "I've never felt better. I have an eighteen-year-old bride who is pregnant with my child. What do you think about that?"

The doctor considers his question for a minute and then begins, "I have a friend who is an avid hunter and never misses a season. One day when he was going out in a bit of a hurry, he accidentally picked up his umbrella instead of his gun. When he got to the creek, he saw a prime beaver sitting beside the stream of water. He raised his umbrella and went, 'Bang, bang' and the beaver fell over dead. What do you think of that?"

The ninety-year-old man said, "I'd say somebody else shot that beaver."

The doctor replied, "My point exactly."

Seventh, and finally, elders must move *beyond the denial and fear of death*.

First, a few enjoyable epitaphs.

Here lies Johnny Yeast.
Pardon me for not rising.

Here lies the body of Jonathan Blake.
Stepped on the gas
Instead of the brake.

Under the sod and under the trees
Lies the body of Jonathan Pease.
He is not here, there's only the pod.
Pease shelled out and went to God.

Remember, man, as you walk by,
As you are now, so once was I.
As I am now, so shall you be,
Remember this and follow me.

To which some wag replied by scribbling on the grave marker:

To follow you I'll not consent
Until I know which way you went.

But here are some serious thoughts to consider. In our therapeutic society we (who have been raised on the supremacy of feeling good, self-determination, self-enhancement, and entitlement to a sense of well-being, together with the ability to shape our body through medical or cosmetic surgery anyway we want it) have embraced the self-deception that death can be avoided if we work hard enough and trust scientific advancements, which indeed have extended life dramatically. After all, the oldest of the old is one of the fastest growing groups in the United States, with centenarians increasing from a group of about 15,000 in 1980 to 100,000 at the beginning of this century. Such a phenomenon leads to the functional denial of suffering and death.

In fact, there is a whole cadre of "academic futurists" who maintain that our biological evolution is on the verge of being superseded by our technological evolution. Soon (it's happening already with pacemakers, plastic knives, and artificial intelligence), we will rebuild our bodies from the ground up. The old Christian concept that our humanity is given (by God) will give way to our humanity as something to be achieved. We are only raw material. We can be "upgraded" to join with machines (cyborgs) and from there to transmute into superandroids. We can jettison the old DNA blueprint—a failed experiment, according to these futurists—and transcend our biological selves. In short, we no longer have to follow a genetic script. (Cosmetic surgery that makes people look like their favorite celebrities is already here.) Soon we will be able to have chips implanted in our brains and become "live" hard drives. In fact, there are no limits to what we can become: from earth-bound bodies to conjoined machines, to shucking off the material altogether to become pure consciousness. We can, in a word, become immortal. Such is technology's promise. With Saint Paul, in a new context, we can ask derisively, "Death, where is thy sting?"

This confidence that science will eventually do away with death, and with funerals becoming more and more commercialized—note the increasing use of designer coffins and the hiring of experts to plan secular funeral "celebrations"—lead to a loss of the Christian sense of mystery and passage.

As Wendell Berry sees it:

> The ancient norm or ideal seems to have been a life in which you perceived your calling, faithfully followed it, and did your work with satisfaction: married, made a home, and raised a family; associated with your neighbors; ate and drank with pleasure the produce of your local landscape; grew old seeing yourself replaced by your children or younger neighbors, but continuing to be useful; and finally died a good and holy death surrounded by loved ones. Now we seem to have lost any such thought of a completed life. We no longer imagine death as an appropriate end or as a welcome deliverance from pain or grief or weariness. Death is now apparently understood, and especially by those who have placed themselves in charge of it, as a punishment for growing old, to be delayed at any cost. We seem to be living now with the single expectation that there should be and always will be more of everything, including life expectancy.

This modern expectation is a far cry from the mind and heart of the late Cistercian Abbot, Basil Pennington, who wrote: "I do not know the day or the hour, but I have full confidence that the Lord will complete the work that God wants to do in and through my life and then take me home....I move toward the great light."

Indeed, we have moved away from any Christian sense that we are on a journey with a goal, in a cycle of sent forth and return or, perhaps better put in gospel terms, that life is a talent to be used and returned with interest to the Giver and that meanwhile, as Saint Augustine expressed it, "Our hearts are restless until they rest in Thee." No, our culture is so much about us that God and the afterlife do not fit into our cosmos.

Yet our faith speaks of Jesus' victory over death and of death as a going home where there are many rooms in God's house. Stories like the following Russian tale, "Death Comes for the Aunt," should resonate in our souls.

> A long time ago there lived a little boy whose parents had died. He was taken in by an aunt who raised him as her own child. Years later, after he had grown up and left his aunt, he received a letter from her. She was in terminal illness and, from the tone of her letter, he knew she was afraid of death. This man whom she had raised and touched wrote her a letter in which he said:
>
> It is now thirty-five years since I, a little boy of six, was left quite alone in the world. You sent me word that you would give me a home and be a mother to me. I've never forgotten the day when I made the long journey of ten miles to your house. I can still recall my disappointment when, instead of coming for me yourself, you sent your servant, Caesar, a dark man, to fetch me. I well remember my tears and my anxiety as, perched high on your horse and clinging tight to Caesar, I rode off to my new home. Night fell before we finished the journey and as it grew dark, I became even more afraid.
>
> "Do you think she'll go to bed before I get there?" I asked Caesar anxiously.
>
> "Oh, no," said Caesar, "she'll stay up for you. When we get out of these woods, you'll see her light shining in the window."

Presently, we did ride out into the clearing and there was your light. I remember that you were waiting at the door; that you put your arms tight around me; that you lifted me—a tired, frightened little boy—down from the horse. You had a fire burning on the hearth; a hot supper waiting on the stove. After supper you took me to my new room. You heard me say my prayers. Then you sat with me until I fell asleep. You probably realize why I am trying to recall this to your memory now. Very soon, God is going to send for you and take you to a new home. I'm trying to tell you that you needn't be afraid of the summons or of the strange journey or of the dark messenger of death. God can be trusted. God can be trusted to do as much for you as you did for me so many years ago. At the end of the road you'll find love and a welcome waiting. And you'll be safe in God's care. I'm going to watch and pray for you until you're out of sight. And I shall wait for the day when I make the same journey myself and find you waiting at the end of the road to greet me.

Notice the metaphors and symbols: Caesar, the dark figure, is death; the light at the end of the journey is Jesus, the light of the world. The house is the "many rooms" in my Father's house that Jesus promised. The supper is the heavenly banquet. God is the loving aunt. I've used this story several times at dying bedsides, for it is a comfort to the dying and to all of us in the second half of life.

Elder Tales

At this point we should summarize a few general remarks about stories, folktales, fairy tales, and aging. All stories, like "Snow White" and "Little Red Riding Hood," contain important insights about human psychology. Fairy tales are basically parables of the human journey through life. Note that in most familiar stories the protagonists are children, like Little Red Riding Hood or at most an adolescent, like Cinderella. Not surprisingly, therefore, interpretations of these fairy tales have emphasized the psychology of youth and focused on the tasks of growing up. In the typical fairy tale, a child or youth sometimes voluntarily leaves home, seeking better fortune in the world, as in "Tom Thumb," or is involuntarily thrown out of the house, as in "Hansel and Gretel," or snatched away, as in *Pinocchio*. In any case, in psychological and spiritual terms, the departure represents a major task of adolescence, when each individual must separate from his or her parents to begin an independent life.

The process is rarely easy in the real world, and so fairy tales depict their protagonists struggling through many ordeals, fighting witches or outwitting giants. Eventually, the young hero or heroine wins a kingdom and finds true love, symbolizing what most individuals achieve in real life: they "find themselves," take a place in society, and make commitments to spouse and career.

That's the underlying hidden spiritual and psychological message of these tales. Notice, too, that most fairy tales end at this point with the youthful dream of happiness charmingly summed up by the phrase, "and they lived happily ever after."

Real life, of course, does not end with youth or eternal happiness. So now the question naturally arises: What happens in the "ever after," when the hero and heroine have children of their own and white hair crowns the Prince and Princess? What happens when Snow White and Prince Charming become Edith and Archie?

Well, there is a distinctive group of fairy stories that provide some of the answers. There are very few American ones as you might surmise; American stories center on looking young, being active, and being sexually active. The tales found in other cultures are different. They feature protagonists who are explicitly called "old," so these stories may be called elder tales.

Deeper Tales

These elder tales symbolize the developmental tasks individuals must master in the second half of life, just as youth tales symbolize the tasks of the first half. As we have seen, elder tales like "The Magic Towel" do not speak of growing up, but of growing psychologically and spiritually. Elder tales portray a new set of virtues—wisdom, not heroism—such as "Edith and Bessie" or "The Bribe." In these tales elders are called to mediation and communication, rather than battle and conquest. The elder's role is to raise bridges, not swords. Elder tales give us hints about meeting the challenges of the second half of life.

So, for the second half of life there are stories of new beginnings, challenges to shuck off old competitions and jealousies, opportunities to find interest and fortune in other areas, wisely expecting good fortune to come to one's doorstep. Spiritually, there is the time in the elder years to go on retreats, read, pray, and to reflect, like Antoinette, on our motives and practices, and so to recover our first love, to be the wisdom figures and the contemplatives of the community.

Autumn Wisdom

Sister Margaret Dorgan, DCM, a member of the John of the Cross Monastery Hermitage of the Diocesan Carmelites of Maine in Orland, Maine, wrote this on aging:

> Added years are not a source of mourning. The term "advancing age" is appropriate because it truly is a matter of forward motion. You look at a tree and all the trees you have ever gazed at enter into your perception as you relish the wonder of this particular tree rising up before you. Your world does not become gray and colorless. Most of us may need glasses, but what we see can add a shining brilliance to our inner vision. When hearing is adversely affected, whatever our ears do convey can arouse a new canticle of praise within us. And if deafness comes, the voice of the Holy Spirit, the Comforter, speaks quietly to lift our hearts.
>
> Growing older is an adventure we have not encountered until now. We feel a greater need for God's help. Demands are high, but the return is also high. "How numerous have you made, O Lord my God, your wondrous deeds. And in your plans for us, there is none to equal you" (Psalm 40:5).
>
> Our brains can sometimes seem to leave us in the lurch. What is the word I'm trying to think of? It's gone. The short-term memory is on vacation. Then we use our creativity to substitute other phrases to convey what we want to express. I can't

think of the name of that flower in my garden. So I describe it in its budding beauty. The large red blossom, the towering height. Ah, it's a dahlia. I do not curse my forgetfulness but use the occasion to remember God who has created the beauty in every dahlia I have rejoiced in. Help me, Jesus, to transform anger at any mental lapse into praise of my Creator. This makes all that seems like loss into gain—the gain of turning my awareness to my God who is always aware of me.

At a retreat on prayer I once met a woman who usually had a friend nearby because she was moving into Alzheimer's. How much of the prayer program did she comprehend? Who could tell? She explained to us, "Some of my mental faculties are leaving me. I ask God to let me know beforehand what will be taken from me next, so I can give it to God ahead of time."

Finally, a precious story about Madame LaFarge, an unflappable, magnificent old woman who lived in the center of Paris.

Madame LaFarge was famous for her tulips, her red tulips. Some time after her husband died, she wrote a note to her grandson, Pierre, "Now that you're almost a man, why don't you come and visit me? You can come twice a year. You can come for the opening of the tulips in the spring. You can come back for the planting of the bulbs."

Pierre was delighted. He was five years old. He was put on the train at Nice and bounced all the way to Paris. The chauffeur brought him to the great house and Grandmamere said, "Pierre, did you like the train ride?"

"Oh, yes, Grandmamere, I played lots of tricks. It was a sleeper train. Everyone was at supper and I moved all the tickets. Everyone was in the wrong bed. It was a good trick."

She said, "Yes, Pierre." Her eyebrows went up and up and up. She said, "Pierre, are you ready for the opening of the tulips?"

"Yes, Grandmamere."

She nodded her head and the servant drew open the curtains, flung open the French doors and they stepped out. Pierre gasped. There was a great rectangle of four hundred red tulips. "Grandmamere!"

"Exactly, Pierre. Now, Pierre, let's have croissants and coffee."

They went in and had coffee and croissants and as Pierre reached for a croissant, he knocked over the teacup that went flying in a high arc. His Grandmamere didn't even look but she shot out an arm and caught it.

"Grandmamere! How did you catch that cup?"

"By watching, Pierre. Now I hope you have a good week."

One day while Grandmamere was out shopping Pierre pulled in this great wooden tub into the great front hall, filled it with hot, soapy water and with all of his clothes on, he went up to the top of the banister, slid all the way down—splash!— water all over. Just then his Grandmamere opened the front door. She said, "Wash behind your ears, Pierre."

Well, Pierre did have a wonderful week in Paris. He played tricks on everybody. His Grandmamere brought him every- where, but mostly he played tricks on the servants at home. One morning the chauffeur woke up and the chauffeur was in a panic. He couldn't find the car keys anywhere...until he fin- ished his oatmeal. He said to himself, "Pierre!" The next morning the gardner was putting on his boots. "Croak!"— there was a frog in one and "Croak!"—a frog in the other. He thought, "Pierre!" That very same morning, the chambermaid couldn't find her bloomers anywhere. She looked out the win- dow and there on top of the cedar tree, her bloomers. And she thought, "Pierre!"

He played a hundred tricks all week and at the end of the week he was driving off and Grandmamere was waving good- bye. There was a tear coming from her eye. The servants were waving goodbye. There was something else in their eyes. He would come twice a year and the servants would say, "Hide the cats! Hide the dogs! Hide yourself! Pierre! Pierre! Pierre!"

Well, when Pierre was nine years old, he was again bounc- ing on the train to Paris and he knew this would be a good year. He got to Paris and it was fall. It was so cold and out in the garden of the great house the gardeners were planting the red tulip bulbs. That afternoon there was a tea, two hundred people at the tea. Pierre was under the table. Two of the servants bent over to pick up an enormous tray with tea on it and one of them got one tray, one got the other while Pierre was under the table tying their shoelaces together. Everything went a-tumbling. Everyone was upset, except Grandmamere because he never played a trick on her.

But now he was thinking, "It's time. Everyone's afraid of Grandmamere but me." And Pierre thought of the perfect trick. He thought he was a genius. He ran down the next morning. "Grandmamere, I'm running around the corner."

"Yes, Pierre."

Pierre went to the florist. He bought one black tulip bulb. At four in the morning, he crept out to the garden. He reached way down into the earth. He took out a red tulip bulb and he planted a black tulip bulb.

Soon enough he was taking the train back home, and all winter long he laughed. Pierre couldn't wait! Finally, the spring came. He bounced on the train all the way to Paris. He didn't even play a trick, he was so excited. He jumped out of the train, got into the great car, and Grandmamere was in the back.

"Hello, Pierre." Pierre was so excited through the traffic. He couldn't sit still. Grandmamere finally said, "Calm down!"

"I'm excited."

"So am I."

"Grandmamere, you know, I've been thinking about you. You know, maybe this year one of your tulips will be a different color."

"What do you mean?"

"Well, things happen in life."

"Not to me, they don't."

"Because I love you, I'm willing to wager that one of the tulips will be a different color."

"I don't approve of wagering...how much?"

"I am willing to wager my gold coin."

"All right. I'll take you up this one time."

"Yes, Grandmamere."

They got to the Great House and Pierre couldn't wait. Finally Grandmamere said, "You ready for the opening of the tulips?"

"Yes, Grandmamere."

She nodded her head. The servants drew the curtains, threw open the door, and Pierre stepped out. He gasped! There was a great rectangle of four hundred black tulips! He looked up and Grandmamere seemed to be smiling.

"Nice for a change, isn't it, Pierre?"

"The gold coin….Here, the gold coin." He gave her the gold coin.

The next morning Pierre woke up and he swung his feet to the floor, and into his slippers—"Croak!"—there was a frog. "Croak"—and a toad. Pierre thought, "The gardener!" He went to brush his hair and it was turning white. There was flour in it. He thought, "The cook!" He couldn't find his trousers anywhere and then he heard "Da, da da, da dada—it was a trumpeter. He looked down into the garden and the four servants were at attention and the serving maid was hoisting, not the French flag, but Pierre's trousers to the top.

It was just then the sun was glinting on something just underneath his pillow. And it was the gold coin, put there by his very wise and very clever Grandmamere.

How else to end this chapter but with these well-known lines by Robert Browning:

> Grow old along with me!
> The best is yet to be,
> The last of life, for which the first was made:
> Our times are in His hand
> Who saith, "A whole I planned,
> Youth shows but half; trust God: see all, nor be afraid!"

CHAPTER SIX

Stories for the Spiritual Journey

Stories are to society what dreams are to individuals.
Without them we go mad. ISABEL ALLENDE

One day Rabbi Meir of Rothenberg sat at his desk studying the Holy Books.

The morning light streamed through the window, casting a golden glow on the high wooden shelves and leather-bound volumes that covered the walls of his room. As he pondered over the meaning of the words that lay before him, he heard a knock on the door. "Who is there?" he asked, and smiled when he heard the reply. It was his youngest daughter, Rachel, coming to see him for a morning visit.

Rabbi Meir held out his arms as the young girl ran to greet him. Rachel was a curious child. She was bright and quick and showed wisdom beyond her years. On her own (for it was not usual for girls to study the Torah in those days), she had learned to read in Hebrew and Aramaic. She knew all the prayers for week days, Shabbat, and the holidays and could recite whole passages in the Torah from memory. But Rachel knew, as did all the children in her family, that the most difficult challenges of all were to be found in the study of the Talmud. Most of all, Rachel wanted to join with her father in that study, but girls almost never had that chance.

Standing next to Rabbi Meir's chair, she asked him, "Father, teach me, how do you study the Talmud?" In the quiet of the study room, he answered, "Talmud is very difficult. It requires that you not only read and memorize, but also that you think."

"Please, Father," Rachel begged, "let me try!"

"Very well, my daughter. I will give you a lesson. Now, listen carefully. Two men working on a rooftop fell down through the chimney. When they landed on the floor, one had a clean face, and one had a dirty face. Which one went to wash his face?"

(The answer to this question may seem obvious, but is it? What do you think?)

Rachel puzzled for a moment to herself. The dirty one, of course. Everyone washes his face when it's dirty! Right? But then she had a second thought and said eagerly, "I know, Father. The one with the clean face went to wash!"

Rabbi Meir said, "And how do you know that is the answer?"

Confident now, Rachel replied, "Because he looked at the dirty face of his friend and thought that his must be dirty too, whereas the dirty one looked at the face of his friend and thought that his face must be clean!"

Rabbi Meir smiled at his daughter. "That is good thinking, my child," he said, "but to study Talmud you must think a little harder than that."

"Why, Father?"

"Because," said Meir, as he stroked her hair, "if two men fall down a chimney, how is it possible that only one of them would have a dirty face?" Rachel's face fell when she heard the reply but her father consoled her: "You did very well. Always look for the question behind the question. That is how we study Talmud."

And with that idea to think about, Rachel returned to her reading for the day, while her father, Rabbi Meir the scholar, went back to the difficult passage of the Talmud that lay before him, to study, to question, and to write.

The Question Behind the Question

That story itself is a good example of the "question behind the question." Good stories—not the surface ones that titillate the senses, but the deeper ones, from funny to serious, that stimulate the soul—provoke "the question behind the question."

Whether comedy or tragedy, epic or poem, history or fiction, good stories provide the memories and images that guide our actions and shape our choices and insights. So, for example: Sherwood Anderson's *Winesburg, Ohio* is surely among the most charming and poignant descriptions of life in a small town, but it is also a story that pulls us into deeper reflection when we become aware of the repression and inner violence in that place. Hemingway's *In Our Time* and Fitzgerald's *Tender Is the Night* are both, in their own ways, really about American loss of innocence: about how the Great War and the brutality of modern life permanently altered our belief system—themes presented as physical trauma in Hemingway and madness and decay in Fitzgerald. Faulkner's *Light in August* depicts the ravages of racism in the American south, but at the same time, in the "question behind the question," it presents a more elusive story of love, kinship, and redemption. Flannery O'Connor's outrageous stories challenge us to look behind her bizarre characters to discern God's spirit and grace at work. In short, underneath these stories, as it were, with their metaphors and symbols, are deeper stories about coping with and fashioning life, about ways of being human.

That great preacher, William Willimon, relates how he was attempting to enlighten a class of students on the short stories of O'Connor, patiently explaining to them all the levels of meaning, when a student objected, "What gives you the right to see all this stuff in this woman's work? Maybe she didn't mean anything other than what I read. Maybe she didn't mean for that ashtray to be a symbol of Ash Wednesday. Maybe the river is just a river and not a baptismal font. Did it ever occur to you that you're reading way too much into a really simple story?"

Willimon says he admired the student's courage but not his stupidity. He adds,

> I realize I was dealing with a bright young thing on whom we had spent years of education and a fortune in tuition, beating into him the notion that the world is flat. A tree is a tree. A mystery is be explained. A miracle is to be disproved. Everything going on out there is the result of some easily discovered material cause and everything going on in here is due to something your mother did to you when you were three.... I wish I had the wit to tell the student who challenged my read of Flannery O'Connor that it wasn't that I was reading all this stuff *into* her simple story. It was that, as a Christian, I had been trained to expect to read a whole new world *out* of such stories.

Religious Questions

We can detour a bit here and remind you that the same "question behind the question" principle holds true for the Bible. Some biblical authors even spell it out. The author of the Gospel of John, for example, is one of them. Near the beginning of the book (Chapter 3), he tells a story about a leader of the Jews named Nicodemus who completely missed the point of what Jesus was saying by taking literally Jesus' metaphorical words about being born anew. He naïvely asks: "How can anyone be born after having grown old? Can one enter a second time into the mother's womb and be born?" You can see Jesus shaking his head, thinking, "Dimwit, you don't get it, do you? You're taking me literally." Toward the end of the book (Chapter 16), the author again reminds the reader about the nature of this kind of writing by attributing to Jesus the comment, "I have said these things to you in figures of speech."

Saint Paul's letters show that he had little interest in taking the Hebrew Scriptures, his Bible, as being either historical or factual. Writing to the community in Corinth about the Exodus events, he said, "These things happened to them to serve as a warning and they were written down to instruct us" (1 Corinthians 10:11). In other words, Paul looked at the ancient stories as metaphors for life's journey. Paul told his followers in Galatia how he found guidance in the old stories. In reviewing the story of Abraham, Sarah, and Hagar, for example, he wrote: "Now this is an allegory" (Galatians 4:24). Paul does not question the historical accuracy of the stories, but on the other hand neither does he suggest that anyone could find the real meaning of the ancient texts by reading them only on the surface.

Augustine, a bright young man with a superior classical education, confessed to Bishop Ambrose that he tried to read the Bible but found it woefully inferior literature. "You young fool," replied Ambrose. "You can't get it because when you read the Bible about 'fish' you think 'fish.' When you read 'bread' you think 'bread.'" Ambrose had to explain to him levels of meaning beyond the surface appearance of things.

Modern Education

Back to our main thrust. I want to propose that this ability, this instinct to probe the question behind the question, has been dramatically undermined today. There has been a surrender to the pragmatic mind and the loss of imagination. With so many slick, digital, high-tech surface images and actions, there is no solicitation to probe deeper. As I have mentioned in a previous chapter, the media—that pervasive media: it is the air we breathe—inundates us and our children with ongoing surface images and sense-stimulating tales of gross violence, uncommitted sex, and endless consumption. Outside of the family, we get little corrective because our schools, no matter how sensitive and progressive some of them are, are ultimately captive to ideology and political correctness.

Higher education no longer offers a corrective either, for it has devolved into an institution where lucrative research, now the university's core purpose, has replaced teaching. Tenured faculties are scholars first and teachers second. According to Nicholas Leman in *Time* magazine, Harvard professors, for example, the highest paid in the country, teach only twenty-eight weeks a year. The teaching loads are borne by graduate assistants and part-time faculty who handle full loads for a third or less of the salaries of full professors. Furthermore, higher education has, by and large, abandoned the large classical stories and the liberal arts. Which is why Peter Beinart, writing in the *New Republic*, notes that required courses can be "a hodgepodge of arbitrary, esoteric classes that cohere into nothing at all." Still, to keep the students happy, the universities hand out inflated grades: for example, an absurd ninety-one percent of Harvard graduates gain honors. The result is that, trained to be workaholics, functionaries, and careerists "cohering to nothing at all," students have no intellectual or spiritual tools to explore the meaning of life or moral imperatives. A spate of recent books with such titles as *Our Underachieving Colleges* (Derek Bok), *Excellence Without a Soul* (Harry R. Lewis), and *A Larger Sense of Purpose* (Princeton's former president, Harold Shapiro)—implying that universities don't have one—spell it all out.

Eventually with no moral, philosophical, or aesthetic underpinnings, we get our inevitable parade of degreed felons in corporate and political life. As for our children, we frequently get those who know nothing of Atticus Finch and everything of Charles Manson. They know a little about Rosa Parks but much more about Britney Spears. This not true of all students, of course, but enough to make us wonder. Or, if it's always a Bruce Willis and never a Saint Francis, always a Pamela Anderson and never a Dorothy Day, always a Howard Stern and never Bono, then the resulting imagery, symbols, sights, sounds, and story values will produce a confused, amoral, reed-in-the-wind populace.

None of this is to imply that we all have to always read "serious" books or that nonsensical entertainment, stupid tricks, utterly mindless diversions, or outrageous stories are useless or always harmful. Not at all. They have their place. Thank God. Where would we be without the satire and one-liners:

A man walks into a restaurant and says, "How do you prepare your chickens?" The cook says, "Nothing special. We just tell them they're gonna die."

Did you hear about Zeke's nephew, Clem, who won the gold medal at the Olympics? He had it bronzed.

"Grandpa, can you make a noise like a frog?" "Why would I want to do a thing like that?" "Well, Grandma says when you croak, we're going to Hawaii."

A little old Jewish woman is walking down the street in the garment district. A flasher comes toward her and whips open his raincoat. She looks and says, "You call that a lining?"

Where would we be without Chaucer's bawdy *Canterbury Tales*, the Marx Brothers's *Duck Soup*, or John Cleese's *Fawlty Towers*? The alarm comes when these things are not diversions but become mainstream, the template against which we live, the common coin of conduct, reference, and communication. Then we lose the ability to tell the difference between a movie like *Hostel* where dismemberment and torture are splayed for the sheer joy of it, and the brutality of *All Quiet on the Western Front* that provokes one's conscience.

Once again, it is the remembered experiences, images, symbols, and stories that shape the moral person, which is why the right balance is necessary. Dostoevsky had it right in *The Brothers Karamazov*, when in the closing scene Alyosha Karamazov, the youngest brother, addresses a group of boys for whom he has become a mentor and role model. This takes place following the funeral of one of their young comrades whom the boys had once taunted and persecuted but later were reconciled with and came to love. He says:

> You must know that there is nothing higher, or stronger, or sounder, or more useful afterwards in life, than some good memory, especially a memory from childhood, from the parental home. You hear a lot said about your education, yet some such beautiful, sacred memory, preserved from childhood, is perhaps the best education. If a man stores up such memories to take into life, then he is saved for his whole life.

> And even if only one good memory remains with us in our
> hearts, that alone may serve one day for our salvation…and
> keep us from great evil.

That Russian wisdom concerning image, symbol, ritual, and story forms the bridge to our next thought, and (according to some devotees) an introduction to the greatest Catholic poet of our time.

The Catholic Imagination

Before we introduce him, we must first review and expand what we saw in Chapter 4, namely, the loss of the Catholic sacramental imagination. The Catholic sacramental imagination refers to the fundamental instinct that there is more to reality than meets the eye. You find this in Joseph Mary Plunkett's poem.

> I see his blood upon the rose
> And in the stars the glory of his eyes.
> His body gleams amid the eternal snows,
> His tears fall from the skies.
>
> I see his face in every flower;
> The thunder and the singing of the birds
> Are but his voice—and carven by his power
> Rocks are his written words.
>
> All pathways by his feet are worn,
> His strong heart stirs the ever-beating sea,
> His crown of thorns is twined with every thorn,
> His cross is every tree.

It is part of the Catholic genius to intuit that there are hidden presences hinted at by the sensuousness of the material world of roses, stars, flowers, birds, and rocks. We do not destroy images, as did the Greeks in the great Iconoclast heresy of the eighth and ninth centuries, burn books, paintings, and works of art in the "bonfire of the vanities," as the Dominican monk Savonarola did in fifteenth-century Florence, or as did the Protestant fundamentalist Oliver Cromwell in seventeenth-century England. Catholics have always believed that what you see is not what at first you get. For the Catholic, beyond sight there is insight. Nature, music, art, and story are a summons to deeper realities. The narrative, icon, sculpture, oratorio, painting, cathedral, and stained glass are windows to another world. Charles Scribner III, a Catholic convert and the great-great-grandson of the founder of the Charles Scribner Publishing House, writes in his book *The Shadow of God*, "I had long taken it for granted that spirituality could generate great works of art from the Gothic cathedrals to Handel's *Messiah* but it struck me that the opposite is equally true: works of art nourish religious faith and spiritual growth."

Especially story. It is no accident that our faith in fact comes from stories with all of their powerful metaphors, and is grounded in them, stories bound in a book we call the Bible, interpreted and retold in what we call Tradition and expressed through the arts. Which is why Catholicism is—has been—famously material, visual, sensual, and sacramental; it is, in fact, loaded with symbols: water and wine, oil and beeswax, incense and vestments, palms and ashes, songs and processions, stained glass and arches, chants and fonts, statues and icons, rituals and rites, novenas and litanies, rosaries and scapulars, religious garb and lives of the saints. Catholicism virtually assaults the five senses.

(This is why, when mocking a religion, the movie or television producers always pick on Catholicism: the three-piece-suited minister with his fabulous hairstyle standing in front of a plain pulpit and plain walls is no match for the mitered, incense-swinging, hand-kissed, gold-vested cleric surrounded by minions, gargoyles, stone saints, clerestory windows, and all that "medieval" furniture—the very word "medieval" connoting something regressive, sinister, and conspiratorial and therefore marketable.)

This "thick Catholicism," as it is called, points to the Glorious Unseen, the immanent and transcendent God. You walk into a great cathedral, for example, and are faced with a coherent and compelling vision that evokes the presence of God and the possibilities of transcending ordinary consciousness. This is the Catholic imagination at work; it pulls you into something else, something more, Someone more.

Today, the plain, computer-room type of some Catholic churches, devoid of statue and symbol, ritual, folkloric devotions, the old richness of the sacraments and the other-worldly chants, are more like the Protestant version, focusing on the individual, the word, and the congregation. There is no upward lift. What you see is what you get. There are few things to coax one higher. There are few stories to inspire, few images to fire the imagination, few symbols to point to Another.

Yet symbol and ritual are so essential to human nature that, as we drop them, others, especially our youth, pick them up and compulsively substitute stereotyped jeans, tattoos, rock music, dangling crucifixes, strobe lights, posters, and special language. They idolize their high priests and priestesses—called celebrities—who are decked in the required vestments of hats peaked to the side, earrings, midriffs, pierced bodies, and, of course, lots of hair. Gangs are fiercely rigid in their imagery and ritual: you must wear certain identifying colors, certain prescribed tattoos, protect well-defined territory, have exclusive rights to mottos, girls, and hand signals. No one else, on pain of reprisal, may infringe on such moral copyrights. The point is we are a symbol-making and symbol-bearing people; think of your devoted allegiance to brand names and status symbols.

The Catholic imagination was there first, but in many ways it has relinquished its heritage, even though, on Ash Wednesday and Palm Sunday we still see its drawing power. We don't even have the Catholic novel any more, which thrived in the 1940s and 1950s. Robert Hugh Benson, Georges Bernanos, Sigrid Undset, Hilaire Belloc, G.K. Chesterton, Francois Mauriac, Evelyn Waugh, Graham Green, Flannery O'Connor, Walker Percy, J.R.R. Tolkien have not, for the most part, been replaced.

Even Catholic pop culture (except in a sinister way as in modern movies like *Stigmata* or *The Da Vinci Code*), which played such a supportive role in the Catholic imagination, has faded. Here's an excerpt from Jim Martin's fine book, *My Life with the Saints*:

> One Friday evening during my second year as a novice, I wandered into the TV room to see what video was being served up.

Television watching was a popular pastime for novices on a thirty-five dollar monthly stipend....

"What's on?" I asked the other novices as I walked into the TV room.

"*The Song of Bernadette*," said one barely glancing up from the TV.

"What's it about?" I asked. Everyone looked up from his chair aghast.

"You're kidding, right?" said another novice. "Please tell me you're kidding."

I shook my head dumbly.

One thing I realize after joining the Jesuits was how little Catholic culture I had grown up with, or at least absorbed. While the other novices had grown up in families that went to daily Mass, attended novenas, said grace at meals, and knew the difference between the Immaculate Heart and the Sacred Heart, I was still trying to remember how many sacraments there were.

My ignorance extended not just to weightier theological matters but also to Catholic pop culture. In the space of just a few months I had already been teased for not having seen *Going My Way*, *The Nun's Story*, and *The Trouble with Angels*. I feared that this was another instance of my not knowing a movie that everyone else had seen by age ten.

"Sit down," the novice said. "You can't say that you're Catholic and not have seen this movie."

Bruce Springsteen

Could it be, then, that the reason our greatest Catholic poet today is acknowledged and honored everywhere is precisely because he has tapped deeply into the Catholic images of his youth? I refer, of course, to Bruce Springsteen. It is interesting that Bruce Springsteen, a Catholic in name only and who does not go to church, sings about redemption, moral decisions, and invocations of God.

Think of his *Thunder Road*, rife with Catholic imagery, and *Darkness on the Edge of Town* and *The River*. As Father Andrew Greeley wrote in 1988:

Tunnel of Love [the Springsteen album] many be a more important Catholic event in this country than the visit of Pope John
Paul II. The Pope spoke of moral debates using the language
of doctrinal propositions that appeal to (or repel) the mind.
Springsteen sings of religious realities—sin, temptation, forgiveness, life, death, hope—in images that come (implicitly
perhaps) from his Catholic childhood, images that appeal to
the whole person, not just the head, and that will be absorbed
by far more Americans than those who listened to the
Pope....The piety of these songs—and I challenge you to find
a better word—is sentient without being sentimental."

When asked how such colorful imagery got into his songs,
Springsteen replied, "Catholic school, Catholic school, Catholic
school." (He was, in fact, very unhappy there; a "disaster" he called it.)
He said, "You're indoctrinated." He grew up a block away from St. Rose
in Freehold, New Jersey. "I'm not a churchgoer, but I realized, as time
passed, that my music is filled with Catholic imagery. It's not a negative
thing. There was a powerful world of potent imagery that became alive
and vital and was both very frightening and held out the promise of
ecstasies and paradise. There was this incredible internal landscape that
they created in you" (*New York Times*, April 2, 2005).

Lost Heritage

Springsteen is a product of that Catholic imagination. His childhood
landscape has for the most part disappeared, and so I must remind you
that today's youth are the first full generation to grow up bereft of the
old Judeo-Christian symbols, visuals, and stories. Absent from church
(only fifteen percent attend), they get their knowledge and images of the
church and Jesus, such as they are, from *Godspell*, *Saturday Nite Live*, the
media, and *South Park*. As a result, for them, God is not Michelangelo's
awesome figure on the ceiling of the Sistine chapel, but Walter Cronkite;
Jesus is not El Greco's raging figure casting out the moneychangers from
the Temple. He is Paul Lynde, a toothy buddy, and everyone's going to
heaven. He is not the fearsome Byzantine Lord set in mosaic over the
sanctuary in the National Shrine in Washington, DC, warning of hellfire

if we do not feed the hungry or give drink to the thirsty. He is wise, live-and-let-live Sheriff Andy Taylor. He is not the luminous figure wrapped in Raphael's clouds and ascending into heaven. He is Brad Pitt in jeans. He is not the troubled Jesus ritually breaking bread in Da Vinci's Last Supper or Carravaggio's dead corpse being taken down from the cross. He is savvy Captain Kirk of the earthship Enterprise.

Devoid of authentic religious imagery, it is no surprise that surveys show that only thirty-eight percent of Catholics born after 1978 feel that "the sacraments are very important" and only fifteen percent, as I mentioned, attend Mass weekly. As I also mentioned in another chapter, Catholic kids score lowest of all denominations in religious literacy, knowledge, and practice. These statistics, of course, grow stronger where there are non-practicing parents.

There is no sensuousness to lure them back. Thus the link to Catholicism in general and imaginative Catholicism in particular has been broken. This is not to disparage children whose hearts and minds are readily open to the good and the beautiful and who can be generous and caring to a fault. Not at all! Rather, it is an invitation to parents and teachers to feed their souls, the earlier, the better.

I stress how critically important it is to reclaim our stories, our visuals, our art, our rituals, and our religious folklore to catch the imaginations of adults and children, especially since Catholicism's future lies with southern hemisphere Catholics, such as the conservative and image-loving Hispanics. Storytelling and its attendant ritual and artistic expressions and the images, metaphors, and symbols it offers are vitally important.

Eight Goals of the Spiritual Journey

Let us now examine the eight goals of the spiritual journey: spirituality, cooperation, priorities, humility, detachment, legacy, wisdom, and memories. To do this we have stories for the spiritual journey to illustrate each. They are rich and deserve much reflection. First, spirituality and the story of Christopher.

> Christopher was a mild and gentle giant of a man who served
> the king of Canaan faithfully. Though he cared deeply for his

lord, the king, he dreamed of serving the strongest master in the world. Taking leave of Canaan, he traveled until he came to the castle of the one said to be the greatest ruler in the world. When the king saw the size and strength of Christopher, he made him second in command and invited him to dwell in his court.

One day when a minstrel was entertaining the king, he sang a song about the devil. Whenever the name of the devil was mentioned, the king made the sign of the cross. Christopher asked the king about his actions.

"It is to ward off the devil," the king answered.

"Do you fear his power?" asked Christopher.

"Ah, yes," said the king, "he has great might."

Christopher shook his head sadly. "I must leave you, my Lord, for I have a great desire to serve the most powerful one in this world. It seems the devil is that one."

Christopher began his search for the devil, wandering until he met a great company of knights. The leader of the knights, a man who appeared cruel and horrible, approached him and asked him what he wanted.

"I am in search of the devil to be my master," said Christopher.

"I am the one you seek," said the terrible knight.

Christopher immediately bowed before the devil and promised his allegiance.

A bit later, as the company of knights walked together, they came upon a cross standing at an intersection. Immediately the devil turned to the side, taking his followers in a circuitous route until he finally came back to the highway.

"Why did we take this route?" asked Christopher. At first the devil was reluctant to answer, but Christopher persisted. "There was once a man called Christ who was killed on a cross," the devil explained. "When I see his sign, I am afraid and attempt to avoid it."

"Then he is greater and more powerful than you," said Christopher. "I see that I have yet to find the one who is the greatest lord on the earth. I will leave you to find Christ, whoever he is."

Christopher began a long search for the one people called Jesus, the Christ. At last he came upon a pious hermit who welcomed him and began to teach him about Jesus.

One day the hermit spoke to Christopher. "You are not ready to serve Christ. In order to do this you must fast."

Christopher said, "It is most difficult for me to fast. Ask me to do something else."

"You must wake early in the morning and pray long hours each day," the hermit said.

"Please," said Christopher, "find me a task more to my ability. I am not a man who can pray for long periods of time."

The hermit thought for a moment before he spoke again. "You are indeed tall and strong. You shall live by the river and carry across anyone who comes in need. In that way you will serve Jesus. I hope that our Lord Christ will one day show himself to you."

So Christopher began his life of service at the river, where the current was strong. There, with the help of a huge pole, he carried rich and poor alike over the treacherous river.

One day as he slept in his lodge by the river, Christopher heard the voice of child calling, "Christopher, come carry me over." When he looked outside, he saw no one. Back in his lodge, he again heard the voice call. Again his search was unsuccessful. The third time he went outside, he found a child who begged Christopher to carry him over the river. The giant took the child on his shoulders and began his walk across the river. As the water rushed against his body, the weight of the child was almost too much to bear. The farther he walked, the more the water swelled and the heavier the child rested on his shoulders. For the first time in his life, the giant Christopher was gripped with a fear of death. At last, using all his might, Christopher reached land and put the child down.

Lying nearly exhausted, Christopher spoke to the child. "I was in great trouble in the water. I felt as if I had the weight of the whole world on my shoulders."

Then the child spoke. "Indeed you have borne a great burden, Christopher. I am Jesus Christ, the king you serve in your work. This day you have carried not only the whole world, but the one who created the world. In order that you might know what I say is true, place your staff in the earth by the house, and tomorrow it will bear flowers and fruit." Then the child disappeared.

The next morning Christopher walked outside, and there he found his staff bearing flowers, leaves, and dates. Christopher now knew that he served the greatest and most powerful master in the world.

REFLECTION Among the principles of spirituality embedded in this story is the one of finding God where you are. Here is a man who could not fast and could not pray for long—these were not for him—but in his own gifts he found the Christ. He found his sanctity, as we would say, where he was planted. He uncovered his story where he was. In turn, his became a story for us to live by. Each person's spiritual path may be different. The late Blessed Pope John XXIII put it well: "From the saints I must take the substance, not the accidents, of their virtues. I am not Saint Aloysius, nor must I seek holiness in this particular way, but according to the requirements of my own nature, my own character, and the different conditions of my life" (*Journal of a Soul*).

Our second story illustrates cooperation or, if you will, the dangers of division and pride. It is called "The Quail and the Hunter."

Once upon a time, a flock of quail lived near a marsh and they would fly to the nearby fields every day to feed. The only problem was that there was a Bird Hunter who lived nearby, and of late he had gotten to snare many quail in his net to take them to a nearby market to be sold. The reason he had grown so successful in catching them was that he had learned to imitate perfectly the call of the Leader. The Bird Hunter gave the call, and the quail, thinking it was the Leader, flew to his area where he tossed his net over them and captured them.

One day the Leader called all the quail together for a conference. He said, "We are becoming decimated! Soon there will be none of us left. The Bird Hunter is catching us all. But I have found out how he does it. He learned my call and deceives you. But I have a plan. The next time you hear what you think is my call and fly to the area and the Bird Hunter throws his net on top of you, here is what you are to do: all together you stick your heads through the openings in the net, and in one motion fly up with the net and land on the thorn bush. The net will stick there, you extricate yourselves, and the Bird Hunter will have to spend all day freeing his net."

And this is what they did. The Bird Hunter came, gave the imitation call, and the quail came. When the net was thrown over them, as one body they stuck their heads through the openings, and flew away to the thorn bush. They left a frustrated Hunter trying all day to get his net loose. This went on for some time until the Hunter's wife bitterly complained that her husband was bringing home no quail to bring to market. They were becoming poor. The Bird Hunter listened to his wife, told her of the actions of the quail, and with his hand on his chin, added, "But be patient, dear wife. Just wait till they quarrel. Then we shall catch them again."

Well, it so happened that one day when the Bird Hunter made his call, all the quail rose up and flew to the area where he was. But as they were landing, one quail accidentally brushed against another. "Will you watch where you're going, you clumsy ox!" cried the one quail.

The other said hastily, "Oh, I'm sorry. I really am. I didn't mean to do it. It was an accident."

"An accident, was it?" cried the first quail. "If you'd watch where you're going instead of peering all about, you wouldn't be so clumsy."

"Well," said the second quail, "I don't know why you take that attitude. I said I was sorry, and if you can't accept that..."

And they got to quarreling. Soon the others, perceiving the argument, gathered around and took sides, one for the first quail and the others for the second quail.

Meanwhile, the Bird Hunter had his net ready and threw it over the birds. They began to cry to one another, "Come, let us stop arguing and hurry or else we'll be caught. Let's fly over that way!"

But the other quail responded, "No, we're always flying over that way. We're always doing what you want. Come, let us fly this way!"

And while they were arguing which way to go, the Bird Hunter, with a smile on his face, gathered them up in the net, brought them to market, and that day made a fine penny.

REFLECTION A wonderful story and a wonderfully obvious one. We should not let our petty feelings and foolish pride hinder good and sensible actions. It is obvious that we have deep and terrible divisions in the church today, with far right and far left Catholics railing at each other. Meanwhile the secular folk, unencumbered by a disunited front, hawk values hostile to the gospel.

Our next story is neat and is about spiritual priority. It's called "The Very Pretty Lady."

There once was a very pretty lady who lived all alone. She didn't have to live all alone; she was so pretty that there were many young men anxious to marry her. They hung about in her dooryard and played guitars and sang sweet songs and tried to look in through the windows. They were there from dawn to dusk, always sad, always hopeful, but the very pretty lady didn't want to marry any of them. "It's no use being loved for the way one looks," she said to herself. "If I can't find someone who will love me in spite of my face, then I will never marry anyone at all."

This was wise, no doubt, but no one is wise all the time. For the truth is that the very pretty lady rather liked the fact that she was pretty and sometimes she would stand in front of the mirror and look and look at herself. At times like that she would be pleased with herself and would go out to the dooryard and talk to all the young men and let them go with her to market and carry home her bags and packages for her. And for a long time afterward they would all look a good deal more hopeful than sad. But most of the time the very pretty lady stayed inside her cottage, feeling lonely regardless of all the young men in the dooryard, longing for someone who would love her as she wanted to be loved.

Now, after a while, one way or another, the Devil heard about the very pretty lady and he decided that she was the very thing he needed to brighten up his days in Hell. So he packed a satchel of disguises and went up to have a look at her. He had heard how very pretty she was, but no one had told him that she never let anyone inside the cottage. He went disguised as a beggar, but she wouldn't open the door. He tried appearing as a preacher and then as a king, but that didn't work either. So at last he simply disguised himself as one of her suitors and hung about with the others waiting for market day. When the pretty lady came out at last, the Devil walked beside her all the way to town, looking at her every movement, and he carried back the heaviest package. By the time she had gone inside her cottage again, his mind was made up: she was indeed exactly what he needed in Hell, and he had waited long enough to have her.

When night came and the sad and hopeful young men had gone home, the Devil threw off his disguise and wished himself into the pretty lady's bedroom with a puff of red smoke and a noise like thunder. The pretty lady woke up at once, and when she saw him she shrieked.

"Don't be alarmed," said the Devil calmly. "It's only me. I've come to take you away to Hell."

"Never!" cried the pretty lady. "I shan't go and there's no way you can make me."

"That's true," said the Devil, "there isn't. You have to come of your own free will when you come before your time. But you'll like it so much down there—you'll be the prettiest thing in the place."

"I'm that already, right here," said the pretty lady, "for all the good it does me. Why should I go away to have the same thing somewhere else?"

"Ah, but in Hell," said the Devil, "your beauty will last forever and ever, whereas here it can only fade."

For the first time the pretty lady was tempted, and the Devil knew it. He fetched a mirror from her bureau and held it up in front of her so she could look at herself. "Wouldn't it be a shame," he coaxed, "to let such a pretty face go to waste? If you stay here, it can only last fifteen or twenty more years, but in Hell there is no time. You will look just as you do now till the stars fall and a new plan is made, and we all know that will never happen."

The pretty lady looked at herself in the mirror and felt, as she sometimes did, that it was rather nice to be pretty but in the nick of time she remembered what it was she really wanted. "Tell me, she said. "Is there any love in Hell?"

"Love?" said the Devil with a shudder. "What would we want with a thing like that?"

"Well then," said the pretty lady, pushing away the mirror, "I'll never agree to go. You can beg all you want from now till Sunday, but it won't be any use."

At this the Devil grew very angry and his eyes glowed like embers. "Is that your final word?" he demanded.

"That is my final word," she answered.

"Very well!" he said, "I can't take you against your will, that's true. But I can take your beauty. I can and I will."

There was another clap of thunder and the Devil disappeared in a cloud of smoke. He went straight back to Hell and took all the pretty lady's beauty with him, and he tacked it up in little fragments all over his throne room, where it sparkled and twinkled and brightened up the place very nicely.

After a couple of years, however, the Devil grew curious about the lady and went to see how she was getting along. He arrived at her cottage at twilight and went to peer in through the window. And there she was, ugly as a boot, sitting down to supper. But candles lit the table and she was no longer alone. Sitting with her was a young man just as ugly as she, and in a cradle near her chair lay a very ugly baby. And the strange thing was that there was such love around the table that the Devil reeled back as if someone had struck him.

"Humph!" said the Devil to himself. "I'll never understand this if I live to be a trillion!" So he went back to Hell in a temper and tore down all the lady's beauty from the walls of his throne room and threw it away, and it floated up out of Hell into a dark corner of the sky and made itself, more usefully, into a star.

REFLECTION We are constantly and cleverly being seduced by a thousand advertisements and messages to purchase items that will make us "successful" on the outside: clothes, body image, makeup, money, high consumption, endless sex. Yet the success of the interior life and moral values are what count.

The fourth story illustrates humility. It is called "The Fake Rabbi."

Once upon a time, three pious Jews decided to travel to a distant city to spend the high holy days with a famous rabbi. They set out on their journey, without food or money, intending to walk the entire way. Several days into the journey, weak from hunger and still a long way from their destination, they knew they had made a mistake and they must do something. They came up with a plan. They decided that one of them would disguise himself as a rabbi. That way, when they came to the next village, the people would offer them food, honored to have a rabbi visit their town. None of the three, being pious, wished to be the deceitful one, so they drew straws, and the unlucky one who drew the short straw had to don the clothing of a rabbi. Another dressed as his assistant.

When they drew near to the next village, they were greeted with excited cries of joy, "A rebbe is coming! A rebbe is coming!" Escorted with great ceremony to the local inn, the hungry threesome were treated to a sumptuous meal.

When the meal was done, however, the innkeeper approached the "rabbi" and spoke with great sorrow. "Rebbe, you must pray for my son," he said. "He is dying, and the doctors have given up hope. But the Holy One, blessed be his name, may respond to your prayers." The counterfeit rabbi looked desperately to his friends for help. They motioned for him to go with the innkeeper to his son's bedside. They had begun this hypocritical ruse, and now there was no choice but to keep on playing the game. The mock rabbi accompanied the distraught father to his son's sick bed.

That night, the three travelers slept fitfully. They were eager to leave town before their deception was discovered. In the morning, the innkeeper, still hoping for a miracle and grateful for the prayer of this visiting rabbi, sent the party off with the loan of a carriage and a team of horses. They left the village and traveled to the great city where they spent magnificent holy days under the spell of the famous rabbi. His teaching of the Torah carried their spirits to the very vault of heaven. But too soon, the holy days were at an end, and the three companions had to go back home through the same village to return the borrowed carriage and horses.

Terrified, the mock rabbi resumed his disguise; his heart was in his throat as they approached the village, especially when he saw the innkeeper running toward them, waving his arms furiously. But to the pretender's delight and surprise, the innkeeper embraced him with joy, exclaiming, "Thank you, rebbe. Only one hour after you left our village, my son arose from his bed well and strong. The doctors are amazed, but my son lives, and I am grateful for your faithful prayer." The two companions looked with astonishment at their phony rabbi companion. What had happened? Had his prayer healed the boy? Was he truly a rabbi all along, without telling them? When they were alone, they turned on him with their questions. "What had he done at that boy's deathbed?" they demanded to know.

He replied that he had stood at the boy's side in silence and, then, began to lift his thoughts to heaven: "Master of the universe, please; this father and son should not be punished just because they think I'm a rabbi. What am I? I am nothing! A pretender! If this child dies, his father will think a rabbi can do nothing. So, Master of the universe, not because of me, but because of this father and his faith, can it hurt that his son would be healed?"

REFLECTION The Hasadim tell this story because of its profound insight into all of us. We are all pretenders, hypocrites. None of us is so worthy as to merit God's favor; our religion is a mask we hide behind. But God is gracious and redemptive in spite of our pretense. Perhaps, then, Jesus reprimands the hypocrites because only a sharply pointed rebuke can poke a hole in the hypocrite's facade, allowing just enough light of the gospel to stream through with the news that every human being longs to hear: that when the applause of the admiring crowd dies out and the theater stands dark and empty and the pretender in all of us removes the mask and stands there, like the false rabbi in the old tale, all alone, there is still God, the God who looks behind the mask to find the child yearning to come home, and the God who beckons us to come just as we are.

Our next story speaks delightfully of detachment. It's an old English story, "The Hedley Kow."

> Now, it happened that an old woman, Mrs. Miller, was on her way back home from market one day, trudging peacefully through the twilight, thinking of her nice, warm fireside, when she saw something lying in the road ahead. "Why, it's a pot, a big iron pot. It must have fallen off someone's wagon. Or else there's a hole in it somewhere, and so it's been just thrown away. A good, useful thing like that…why, I can use it, hole or no hole, to plant some flowers in."
>
> But when she looked in the pot, the old woman gasped. "Gold pieces! The pot is full of gold pieces! Why, what a lucky woman I am!" Tying her sturdy woolen shawl around the pot, she began to drag the heavy thing home. But something felt very strange about her burden. And when she turned around to see what was wrong, the old woman gasped again. "My eyes must have played a trick on me. How could I ever have mistaken that for a mass of gold coins? It's a lump of silver. Better and better! If I tried to spend all of those coins, folks would wonder where I got them. They might even think I was a thief! No, no, a lump of silver will be much simpler to sell. Why, what a lucky woman I am!"
>
> Off she went again, dragging the lump of silver behind her. But once more, something felt very strange about it, and she turned around to see what was wrong. "Now, isn't this the silliest thing? My eyes really are playing tricks on me. How could I have thought this was a lump of silver when it's a nice mass

of iron, good, solid iron. Better and better yet! Silver would be odd to sell, and folks would still be wondering if I was a thief, but iron, well, any ironsmith will gladly buy it from me. What a lucky woman I am!"

Off she went again, dragging the mass of iron after her. But once more, something felt very strange about her burden, and she turned to see what was wrong. "Oh, my. Oh, dear. Oh, my dear. It must be the dim twilight fooling me, that's what it is. That's no mass of iron I'm pulling along, it's a good, heavy stone. A nice, smooth, round one, too—exactly what I've been needing to prop open my door. What a lucky woman I am!"

She hurried home with her prize and set it beside the door. But no sooner had she untied the shawl from the rock than Whoosh! The rock was suddenly growing, sprouting ears and legs and a long donkey tail. Before the old woman could so much as gasp, the creature was gone into the night, braying and laughing. "Oh, my dear, dear me, that was no stone; that was the Hedley Kow! And to think I had a chance to see him. What a lucky, lucky woman I am!"

REFLECTION An enjoyable story! Talk about simplicity and detachment! The woman was ready to let go as soon as something did not seem right.

Our next story talks about legacy, what we should want to leave behind; it reflects the themes of the *Epic of Gilgamesh* and Homer's work. It's a Japanese tale called "Santoro."

There once was a man named Santoro who was a very good businessman and very rich. He had a magnificent house, the best of food, beautiful clothes, and an exquisite garden full of exotic trees and plants. One day Santoro got sick and he called the doctor. The doctor came, treated him, and said casually as he was leaving, "Take care of yourself, Santoro. You know you're going to die someday. Don't let Death come sooner than he should." When he left, Santoro began to think. He found himself saying in amazement, "Die! Die? But I don't want to die. I don't want to die!" Dejected and perplexed, he sat down on his velvet chair, put his head in his hands, and said to himself, "What shall I do?" Then it hit him. He stood up saying, exclaiming, "I know. I have learned that somewhere there is the Fountain of Youth. I shall find it, drink from it, and live forever. I shall not have to die!"

So Santoro sold all his possessions, took his riches and went in search of the Fountain of Youth. He traveled over hill and dale, asking everyone. Everyone had heard of it, but no one could tell him where it was. Days passed into weeks and the weeks into months and the months into years. One day, tired and discouraged, Santoro climbed a mountain and came upon the ruin of an old temple. He laid his head on his knees and closed his eyes.

When he opened them again, there was a venerable Monk, arms in long sleeves, standing before him. "Santoro," he said, "you are looking for the Fountain of Youth. I can't tell you where it is, but would you like to go to the Land Where People Never Die?"

"Oh, yes!" exclaimed Santoro, "That's what I want. Take me to the Land Where People Never Die."

The old monk withdrew his hand from his sleeve and pulled out a small paper bird and laid it on the ground. The paper bird grew bigger and bigger until it was large enough for Santoro to climb aboard his back. The bird took off over the sea and dale, over mountain and rock, traveling for days until at last there was an opening in the sky and Santoro saw a lovely green island below. The bird landed. Never had Santoro seen such beauty. And there were people there. They were more or less sitting on the shoreline staring into space, but he didn't notice that. Here he was in the Land Where People Never Die.

Soon, because he was such a good businessman, Santoro once more had the magnificent house, the best of food, beautiful clothes, and an exquisite garden full of exotic trees and plants. He was very happy. And time just went on, and on, and on…and on…and on. One day Santoro said to himself, "You know, you keep thinking that something is going to happen, but it never does." It was getting to him so much that one day he again said to himself, "I know what I shall do. I shall go out into the woods and pick all those berries that my father taught me are poisonous. And I will eat them and I shall die."

So he did. He picked all the poison berries and gobbled them down. But, of course, he didn't die since he was in the Land Where People Never Die. Then he decided that when the next ship came in bringing supplies he would bribe the sailors to get all the terrible and poisonous medicine out of the medicine chest and he would swallow the iodine and mercurochrome and all the rest, and so would die. He bribed the sailors, downed the poison, but he did not die because he was in the Land Where People Never Die.

Soon he too had joined all the others sitting on the shoreline staring into space. One day, dejected, bored and sad, he happened to put his arm up his sleeve. "What's this?" he said. He pulled it out and it was the paper bird! He quickly put it on the ground. It grew bigger and bigger, and he climbed on its back and off he went. He was ecstatic! At last he was free.

But while soaring over the ocean, a swift and terrible storm came up. Thunder and lightning sounded and flashed. Hard rain pelted him. The bird, being only paper, soon got drenched, crumpled, and fell toward the water with Santoro. He dropped into the pit full of water and when underneath he opened his eyes, he saw the largest White Shark he had ever seen coming straight toward him with open jaws. It opened them wider around the head of Santoro. He screamed an awful scream—and woke up.

There before him was the old monk asking, "Santoro, do you want to go to the Land Where People Never Die?"

"Oh, no, no, no," responded Santoro. "I've quite changed my mind about that."

"Santoro," said the Monk, "listen to me. You go home and rebuild your magnificent house and have the best of food and beautiful clothes and an exquisite garden full of exotic trees and plants, but instead of building these things for yourself, do them for others. Then when it comes your turn to die, they will miss you and sing your praises."

And that's what he did. And that's what happened.

REFLECTION It's the gospel, Japanese style. The one who would save his life will lose it; the one who will lose his life will save it.

Our next story gives us a wisdom figure. It's a moving one about a woman called Maum Jean.

> I was a timid six year old with braces on my legs, a frail, lost, lonely little boy when I first arrived at the farm in Georgia. Had it not been for an extraordinary woman, I might have remained that way. She lived on the farm in a two-room cabin where her parents had been slaves. To an outsider she looked like any of the black people on the farm, in her shapeless gray dress. But to those who knew her she was a spiritual force whose influence was felt everywhere. She was the first person called when there was sickness; she made medicines from roots and herbs that seemed to cure just about anything. She had a family of her own, but all the children in the area felt that they belonged to her. Her name reflected this. In the soft speech of the Georgia lowlands, the word "maum" is a slurred version of "Mama." We called her "Maum Jean." Maum Jean talked to the Lord often and we all suspected that when she did he stopped whatever he was doing and listened and took appropriate action.
>
> Her heart reached out to small, helpless things, so she took particular interest in me from the start. When I was stricken with polio at the age of three, I'm sure my parents didn't know what was the matter with me. All they knew was that times were hard and suddenly they had a crippled child on their hands. They took me to a New York City hospital, left me, and never came back. The people who took me into their foster home had relatives on the Georgia estate where I was sent in the hope that the warmer climate might help. Maum Jean's sensitive emotional antenna instantly picked up the loneliness and withdrawal inside me. Moreover, her marvelous diagnostic sense surveyed the polio damage and decided that, regardless of what the doctors might have said, something more ought to be done.
>
> Maum Jean had never heard the word "atrophy," but she knew that muscles could waste away unless used. And so every

night when her tasks were done she would come to my room and kneel beside my bed to massage my legs. Sometimes when I would cry out with pain, she would sing old songs or tell me stories. When her treatments were over, she would always talk earnestly to the Lord, explaining that she was doing what she could but that she would need help, and she asked him to give her a sign when he was ready.

A creek wound through the farm and Maum Jean, who had never heard of hydrotherapy, said there was strength in running water. She made her grandsons carry me down to a sandy bank where I could splash around pretty well. Slowly I grew taller, but there was little change in my legs. I still used crutches. I still buckled on the clumsy braces. Night after night, Maum Jean continued the massaging and praying. Then one morning, when I was about twelve, she told me she had a surprise for me.

She led me out into the yard and placed me with my back against an oak tree. She took away my crutches and braces. She moved back a dozen paces and told me that the Lord had spoken to her in a dream. He had said that the time had come for me to walk.

"So now," said Maum Jean, "I want you to walk over here to me."

My instant reaction was fear. I knew I couldn't walk unaided. I had tried. I shrank back against the solid support of the tree. Maum Jean continued to urge me. I burst into tears. I begged. I pleaded.

Her voice rose suddenly, no longer gentle and coaxing, but full of power and command. "You can walk, boy! The Lord has spoken! Now walk over here!"

She knelt down and held out her arms. And somehow, impelled by something stronger than fear, I took a faltering step, and another, and another until I reached Maum Jean and fell into her arms, both of us weeping. It was two more years before I could walk normally, but I never used the crutches again. For a while longer I lived in my twilight world. Then a circus came through town and when it left, I left with it.

For the next few years, I worked with one circus or another. Then the night came when one of Maum Jean's tall grandsons knocked on my door. Maum Jean was dying. She wanted to see me. The old cabin was unchanged. Maum Jean lay in bed surrounded by silent watchers. Her frail body was covered by a patchwork quilt. Her face was in shadow, but I heard her whisper my name. I sat down and touched her hand. For a long time I sat there. Now and then Maum Jean spoke softly, her mind was clear. She hoped I remembered the things she had taught me.

Then the old voice spoke, stronger suddenly, "Oh," said Maum Jean with surprise and gladness, "it's so beautiful!" She gave a little contented sigh and died. And then something quite unbelievable happened. In the semidarkness her face seemed to glow. No one had touched the lamp. There was no other source of light. But her features, which had been almost invisible, could be seen plainly and she was smiling. It lasted for perhaps ten seconds.

It was most strange, but not at all frightening. I couldn't account for it then and I can't account for it now. But I saw it. We all saw it. Then it faded and was gone. That happened a long time ago. But I still think of Maum Jean often. And I will always remember the main thing she taught me: that nothing is a barrier when love is strong enough. Not age. Not race. Not death. Not anything!

REFLECTION We can hear this several ways: we are the child crippled with need, sin, longing, illness, and there is One who will heal us. Or we can see the story as one of imitation: we are called to be Maum Jean in this world using our prayer, charity, and gifts to heal others.

Finally, we come to our last story, a favorite of mine, "The Tin Box" by Ed Hayes. It's about memories and is a good summary of this book's message.

The long gravel driveway that led up from the highway was filled with cars and pickup trucks. The two-story, white farmhouse and large barn were surrounded by tractors and other farm machinery, together with furniture and a variety of household articles. The farm had been in their family now for two generations and like so many other Midwestern farms, it had been sold recently to some European businessmen. Today, Tom and Mary would sell their furniture and all of their farm machinery. After trying different solutions, even a part-time job in town, Tom was giving up at attempting to make a living from farming.

The farm auction had attracted neighbors and strangers alike. The farmers gathered in small clusters, chatting about the price of cattle or recent futile efforts of the government to help farm prices. Their wives exchanged local news and gossip. But the general mood was sad. The auctioneer, a fat man wearing a white cowboy hat, stood on the hay wagon and began the auction with gusto. The furniture went first. The antique oak dining room table and Victorian picture frames were purchased by strangers.

After the furniture and antiques came the machinery. The large, orange Allis-Chalmers tractor, the combine, and cultivator changed hands to the Morse code of the auctioneer's chant. Most of the sale items had been sold when the auctioneer held up a small tin box and began his usual spiel: "How much do I hear for this small tin box?" Before a single bid could be placed, Tom shouted, "Sorry, friends, the tin box is not for sale…everything else is, but not that!" He came forward and took the tin box from the auctioneer's hand saying, "Sorry, it must have gotten mixed up with the sale things by mistake." Tom walked away through the crowd smiling, with the battered tin box under his arm. The remaining items went quickly; the auction was over.

The day also began to quickly disappear as the long shadows of afternoon crisscrossed the old white farmhouse and the barnyard. The pickup trucks slowly rolled down the gravel driveway, the life possessions of Tom and Mary stacked on them or being towed behind. The ladies of the VFW auxiliary, who had served the sale with a lunch of sandwiches, donuts, and coffee, gave Mary some of the leftover food and drink. She carried them into the kitchen as Tom settled with the auctioneer, who echoed the sympathies of their neighbors about having to sell. He placed his fee into a worn-out, brown billfold and drove down the drive…the last car.

Mary was alone at the kitchen table as Tom entered the back door. The glare from the single bare light bulb (the antique glass shade had brought a good price) made that once cozy room now seem as stark as a morgue. The house was empty except for the kitchen table and three chairs, and the large, old bed upstairs. The antique bed had belonged to Tom's parents and was solid walnut. It and the table were not included in the sale but had been given to one of their sons. Tomorrow he and his wife would pick them up.

Tom and Mary had planned on leaving the farm that night. Their suitcases and a pile of cardboard boxes stood ready by the door. The couple sat in silence at the kitchen table sharing the unsold ham sandwiches and coffee. The tin box had a place of honor in the center of the kitchen table. Mary was the first to speak: "They almost sold your little tin box."

"Yeah, that was close, wasn't it?" said Tom, as he slowly opened the lid of the box.

To the average eye the box appeared to be empty, but in reality it was filled almost to the top. The old battered tin box was filled with memories. Mary opened a suitcase and removed a small tin box that could have been a twin to Tom's. Slowly, one after another, they took out memories from their tin boxes and passed them to each other. One memory would awaken another one or be the leader of an entire parade of memories: "Remember the first night we stayed here after we were married…or when Dick came home from the Army…or that Christmas day in the '50s when we and the kids were snowbound?" Their little tin boxes held memories that went back to their early childhoods. In one corner of Tom's box was a memory of him and his friends, when they were young men, swimming in that deep pool down the creek, the one that's surrounded by the giant cottonwoods.

These small tin boxes were what made Tom and Mary the richest people in the county. Early in life they had learned a great secret from Tom's grandfather. "The purpose of any possession," the old man had said, "is to make memories! The only purpose of money—only purpose—is to make memories. Things and possessions only rust and age, but memories, Tommy, memories are like fine wine…they grow in value with time." Now that the farm sale and auction had completely dispossessed them of their belongings, they knew the wisdom of what Grandfather had said to them in his funny, broken German accent.

Tom returned the last memory to his tin box. He had to rearrange some memories for it to fit. He closed the lid and looked at his watch. They had visited over their memories so long that it seemed too late now and too much trouble to drive into town to their new apartment. Instead, they decided to spend just one more night at the farm. Mary unpacked some sheets from one of the cardboard boxes by the door and made the bed.

By now the moon had risen and the wind blew waves of moonlight through the open windows. With no curtains or pictures, the bedroom was empty of things but full of pale, white moonlight. Tom placed his little tin box on the windowsill as he climbed into the ancient great bed. Their last night on the farm was one of the most beautiful of their lives.

Mary was asleep as Tom arose and stood by the open window. The fields, the barn, the windmill, and, off in the distance, the cottonwoods along the creek were all silent but beautiful, bathed in the light of the giant moon. Tom smiled as he opened, once again, his little tin box and gently placed inside it the memory of this beautiful night. He attempted to close the lid, but it wouldn't close; the box was so full. Gently he rearranged the memories so they would all fit. Then he closed the lid. As he did, it made a strange click that he had never heard before. Tom placed the old tin box on the windowsill and slowly laid back on the bed. He closed his eyes and was asleep almost at once. The next morning when she awoke, Mary found him sleeping peacefully in the gentle arms of death.

The following days were hectic. The arrangements for the funeral, the arrival of their children and relatives, and the visits of friends and neighbors took Mary's time. Three nights later, accompanied by the family, she went to the funeral home. As they entered, the lobby was filled with many of the same farmers who, only a few days before, had stood in their yard on that auction day. They stood in small groups, discussing how selling the farm had been just too much for Tom. As she passed, Mary overheard their comments.

She smiled to herself as she walked down the aisle toward the casket in the center of a sea of flowers, for she knew that selling the farm had nothing to do with Tom's death. Dressed all in black, she was regal in her serenity as she stood by the casket, looking down at her husband. Tom looked peaceful, his worn face relaxed, his hands folded across his chest. His fingers still had tiny grease-darkened lines from all the years of hard work. Intertwined among his fingers was a black rosary. Mary opened her handbag and then, reaching down, she removed the rosary from Tom's hands and placed it in her bag. She then took from the handbag the little tin box and placed it in Tom's hands.

The parish priest, who had been standing by the foot of the casket, stepped forward and, with his authoritarian but hushed voice (the one that came from years of speaking in the confessional), said to her, "Mary, Mary...you can't do that!" He started to reach down to remove the tin box from Tom's hands.

"Leave it there, Father Cryziski," Mary said, in an equally authoritarian voice, "that's Tom's rosary. Hardly a day would pass that he wouldn't take some memory out of that box and be filled with gratitude. He was a holy man and he understood what poverty and prayer were all about. No, Father, the box remains because it's the only thing he's taking with him to heaven."

The priest began to object, but Mary outwitted him. She turned to the crowded funeral home, filled with people wall-to-wall, and said in a loud, clear voice, "Father Cryziski is now going to lead all of us in the rosary"; and with that she knelt beside the casket. The priest was trapped...and so, forced to kneel beside her, began, "In the name of the Father, and of the Son..."

When the wake was over, and family and friends had all departed—even the Polish pastor who, while unhappy about the seeming sacrilege, had decided to let it go without further discussion—Mary returned to her apartment. Her black dress hung on the back of the bedroom door as she sat on the bed and smiled, thinking of how much Tom would have approved of what she had done that night. Then she carefully took out her own little tin box and opened it. She placed the memory of the wake—the many, many kind words about Tom, even the expression on Father Cryziski's face—all of it, into her little tin box. That memory fit perfectly on the very top of the full box. As she closed the lid, it made a strange little click. Mary smiled and lay back on the pillow. She was asleep, peacefully, almost at once.

REFLECTION Those memorable words of Tom's grandfather—"The purpose of any possession is to make memories"—are at the heart of this book. Early stories, rituals, and celebrations provide the first associative symbols and images that nourish our moral lives. I remember hearing psychiatrist and prize-winner (for his *Moral Lives of Children*) Robert Coles speak about the little girl, Ruby, who featured so famously in the early civil rights movement in the South. She appears in the Norman Rockwell painting of a little black girl marching to a newly integrated school surrounded by protective marshals while the angry crowd is harassing her. When he got to know the family, he asked Ruby how she withstood the terrible threats and name-calling as she went to school. Ruby replied that as she walked she thought of Jesus carrying his cross and praying for his enemies. That sustained her. The point is that, at an early age, she had absorbed the images of Christianity as a template against which to interpret her life and guide her conduct. This is a powerful and significant example and the thesis of this book. It is no exaggeration to say that in another context she may well have plotted revenge or urged her siblings or relatives, Columbine-like, to machine gun the crowd. That may sound extreme, but for those raised on violent images or absent parents or poor role models, whose storyline, as we might say, is empty of redeeming metaphors, they may well have reacted that way.

Make memories. Grandpa is right, "Things and possessions only rust and age, but memories, Tommy, are like fine wine…they grow in value with time."

CHAPTER SEVEN

Nursery Rhymes

*When the will comes in conflict with the imagination,
the imagination invariably carries the day.*

EMILE COUE

One would not normally think of nursery rhymes as part of the human journey, but in fact they have played a crucial part. They, so to speak, got there first. That is to say, nursery rhymes stand at the very beginning of feeding the imagination. They are precious, generation-tested stories and poems polished by long years of telling and retelling, and babies need them as much as they need food. Moreover, as we might suspect by now, these rhymes often have a history and in fact many are disguised stories (some rather dark and salacious), originally and primarily intended for adults.

I can only give you a teaser, but let me share some of the best-known ones. You will notice that many of them are transported English rhymes for the simple reason that the British formerly occupied the country. So, Mary, Queen of Scots, much into high fashion, like some folk of today, got her clothes from France, some of which were decorated with gold-plated seashells and tiny bells. So people could comment on this frivolity without losing their heads by reciting:

> Mary, Mary, quite contrary
> How does your garden grow?
> With silver bells and cockle shells
> And pretty maids all in a row.

The Bishop of Glastonbury, responsible for title deeds to estates, sent twelve deeds to Henry VIII via his faithful steward, Jack Horner, who, for safety's sake, carried them in an empty pie shell. Apparently Jack wasn't *that* faithful, for only eleven arrived since Jack snatched or "pulled" one (a good one, a "plum") and kept it. (Believe it or not, the Horner family still owns that estate today.) So no wonder we got:

> Little Jack Horner
> Sat in a corner
> Eating his Christmas pie.
> He put in his thumb
> And pulled out a plum
> And said, "What a good boy am I."

Elizabeth, Queen of Bohemia and daughter of King James of England, was known as the "Queen of Hearts" for her beauty and charm. She is remembered in this rhyme:

> The Queen of Hearts,
> She made some tarts,
> All on a summer day;
> The Knave of Hearts,
> He stole those tarts,
> And took them clean away.

> The King of Hearts
> Called for those tarts,
> And beat the Knave full sore;
> The Knave of Hearts
> Brought back the tarts,
> And vowed he'd steal no more.

As usual, there's more to this rhyme than meets the eye. The Knave of Hearts was Ferdinand II, the adopted son of the deceased Emperor Matthias. The "tart" was the possibility of having the throne through marriage, thereby legitimizing his right to kingship. However, Ferdinand II proved unpopular, and the kingship went instead to Frederick the Palatinate, who became the King of Hearts.

Then we have this rhyme:

> Rain, rain, go away,
> Come again another day.
> Little Johnny wants to play;
> Rain, rain, go to Spain,
> Never show your face again!

This ditty, fervently sung by the Spanish we presume, goes back to Queen Elizabeth I's time, when there was bitter rivalry between England and Spain, culminating in the attempted invasion by the Spanish Armada in 1588. It had over 130 large galleons while the British had only 34 small naval vessels and 163 merchant ships. But the British won the battle both because of the swift hit-and-run ability of the smaller boats and also because of the very stormy weather that scattered the clumsy Spanish fleet.

Speaking of Queen Bess, one of her ladies in waiting had an old cat that roamed around Windsor castle. One day it ran beneath the throne where its tail brushed against the Queen's foot, startling her. Fortunately, this queen *was* amused and decreed that the cat could wander around the throne room as much as it wanted, as long as it made a dent in the mice population. In any case, from this we got:

> "Pussycat, pussycat, where have you been?"
> "I've been up to London to see the Queen."
> "Pussycat, pussycat, what did you there?"
> "I frightened a little mouse under the chair."

Most people do not know that Humpty Dumpty was not a person at all. He, or rather it, was an object, a cannon, a very large cannon. It was used during the English Civil War in the besieged city of Colchester and was prominently displayed on a wall next to the local church. When the wall was blasted, the cannon fell and was destroyed. The Royalists tried to raise it up but it was too heavy. Literally, all the king's horses and all the king's men couldn't fix it.

> Humpty Dumpty sat on a wall,
> Humpty Dumpty had a great fall.
> All the King's horses,
> And all the King's men
> Couldn't put Humpty together again!

In the scandal department, a handsome courtier named George Villiers caught the eye of King James I, who took him as his gay lover. But George was versatile. He also had an affair with the French king's wife and caused quite a scandal. (He had other liaisons.) Nevertheless, he continued to exercise great influence over the king, although hated by both commoners and courtiers. Finally Parliament had enough of "Georgie Porgie," as they called him, and got the king to stop protecting him. So, he lives on in a very sanitized version—unless you read between the lines:

> Georgie Porgie, pudding and pie,
> Kissed the girls and made them cry.
> When the boys came out to play
> Georgie Porgie ran away.

Cardinal Wolsey, who gives a notable speech in Shakespeare's play *Henry VIII*, was in fact that king's servant and, although very powerful, was unable to push through Henry's divorce from Katherine of Aragon (so Henry could marry Anne Boleyn). In the rhyme we know as "Old Mother Hubbard," King Henry is the "doggie" and the "bone" refers to the divorce not obtained from the cupboard (the Catholic Church).

> Old Mother Hubbard
> Went to the cupboard
> To get her poor doggie a bone,
> When she got there
> The cupboard was bare
> So the poor little doggie had none.

Beyond the political, some rhymes dealt with tragedy. We hardly sense the terror of the Bubonic Plague in the fourteenth century in such a pastoral rhyme as

> Ring around the rosy
> A pocketful of posies
> "Ashes, Ashes"
> We all fall down!

But the plague caused a rosy red rash in the shape of a ring. Posies were carried to sweeten the air as bad odors were thought to transmit the disease. "Ashes, ashes" refers to the cremation of the dead bodies.

And what about this popular rhyme?

> Baa, Baa Black Sheep, have you any wool?
> Yes sir, yes sir, three bags full!
> One for my master, one for my dame,
> And one for the little boy that cried in the lane.

This rhyme actually reflects the dissatisfaction of the working people of England where there was a tremendous demand for wool, resulting in an enormous wool industry and leaving few people, as a result, working in the fields. So food prices rose and wages declined. The rhyme reflects the idea that the king or master received ample wool as did the dame or wealthy folk, but the vast populace, represented by the little boy who cried in the lane, received a meager share. Times haven't changed.

Of course, not all nursery rhymes have political history behind them, but most have some social history. For example, owls appear to be very patient in watching out for prey and they figure in many mythologies. In Greece, the owl is Athena's bird, she the goddess of wisdom; hence the association of the "wise owl." Since the owl hunts only at night, it also became associated with evil spirits who also prowl around at that time. Anyway, the owl has been conscripted to get children to keep quiet.

> A wise old owl lived in an oak
> The more he saw the less he spoke
> The less he spoke the more he heard
> Why can't we all be like that wise old bird?

The Importance and Power of Rhymes

Little would one think that our precious nursery rhymes had such a loaded history! But, for our purposes, it is enough once more to realize the theme of these pages, namely, that language is rich and deep; stories are multi-layered and subversive. Things are not always what they seem. There is always in the best of stories the question behind the question, and we must learn how to sensitize ourselves to deeper meanings. But beyond all that, on the very formative human level, the invaluable power of nursery rhymes is in their interaction. Many rhymes are sing-song and the child gets to delight in the sounds and tossing and poking and hugging that go with the telling. Imagine, for example, a child gazing at the moon looking for cobwebs after hearing this (and being tossed upward):

> There was an old woman tossed up in a basket
> Seventy times as high as the moon;
> And where she was going I couldn't but ask it,
> For in her hand she carried a broom.
> Old woman, old woman, old woman, quoth I,
> O wither, O wither, O wither so high?
> To brush the cobwebs off the sky!
> Shall I go with thee? Aye, by and by.

In the telling or singing of these rhymes, what is happening, of course, is the patterned sound of a familiar voice. Very quickly babies can identify their mother's voice above all others. This interactive language experience is vital to the development of the brain. Small children soon learn by repetition to become accustomed to the sounds and take ownership of the rhymes. Moreover, since so many of the rhymes plumb symbol, myth, and metaphor, children soon learn to suspect the question behind the question and their imaginations grow wonderfully. Until we send them to school.

CHAPTER EIGHT

Stories That Challenge

"Storytelling is so natural to human beings it suggests a definition: we are creatures who think in stories."

—JOHN AND MARY HARRELL, *To Tell of Gideon*

Good stories won't let go. They nitpick at our hearts. We go back and re-read them or review them. How many times I have replayed movies such as *Pride and Prejudice*, the Greer Garson-Lawrence Olivier gem, or *Now, Voyager* with Bette Davis. Some, younger than I, can't count the times they've seen *Star Wars*, the Harry Potter series, or read old favorites. In this chapter I have collected some favorite "nitpicking" stories that range from the soulful "The Stolen Child" to Joan Windham's charming saint stories for children. Each, in its own way, advances the human journey. Let me begin with *The Wizard of Oz*.

I devoted an entire book, *The Yellow Brick Road* (Twenty-Third Publications), to opening up the themes and symbols of this beloved tale, now shown yearly on television. Here is a summary of one chapter that unfolds the now familiar question behind the question. There are wonderful metaphors found in *The Wizard of Oz*, basically a quest and voyage-and-return type plot. The story follows predictable steps, so let's review them.

First of all, these hero-story sagas start off with the heroine in a state of mild discontent. Dorothy Gale was happy on her Kansas farm with Uncle Henry and Auntie Em and the three farm hands. Still, she was uneasy and wondered what was over the rainbow. Were there, perhaps, bluebirds? Is there something more? Can I be something more? These questions, these enticements, set up the journey. This is what the spiritual writers call "holy discontent," and Dorothy was feeling it.

With that holy unease inspired by the Spirit, one is set up for the second step: a call to find out, a call to adventure, a call to start the journey, that call being a fearsome and hard-to-ignore tornado in Dorothy's case. For some, such a call may indeed be as dramatic as a tornado, like God's call to Moses in the Burning Bush; Jesus knocking Saul off his horse on the way to Damascus; Yahweh's threefold call to the yet-to-be prophet, the boy Samuel; the beckoning of Virgil out of the mist to Dante. But for many, the call is not so dramatic or sudden; it may be far more subtle. So, for example, on this particular day a person suddenly experiences a lovely moment of intense friendship, a stunning sunset, the Grand Canyon, or the total trust of a small child who falls asleep in one's lap.

In such experiences a person is pulled out of self and feels a sense of wholeness and harmony. Everything for the moment has fallen into place. Life is not absurd at all. There really is meaning to it. It all makes sense, marvelous sense, grand sense. There is a harmony, without and within, that is quite compelling. Some may pause in a momentary trance or a longer ecstasy (literally: to stand outside of oneself). A new reality looms and beckons.

THE NEXT STEP The heroine starts out and begins the third step in this voyage and return saga: a time of testing. The journey starts out quite excitingly at first but then Dorothy soon finds out this whole venture is not as easy as she thought, not as romantic. And just as in *The Inferno*, as Dante began his journey, he immediately ran into the three beasts, a leopard, a lion, and a wolf (the love of pleasure, fierce pride, and ravenous greed), so Dorothy would meet her own inner demons ("lions and tigers and bears, oh my") and flying monkeys, not to mention the wicked witch! These are the sins that block the journey, the evils to be confronted in order to come to insight, to self-transformation. Those lions and tigers and bears represent her own inner demons, such as discouragement, depression, addiction, pride, as well as the many external forces of evil and temptation that are ready to thwart her journey.

Sooner or later—and here comes the next step—she comes to the realization that she can't go it alone. She will need allies, friends on this freely-chosen adventure. She needs resources. Suddenly in such hero-myth stories, they appear—which is in line with the old Eastern adage, "When the student is ready, the teacher appears." Such a friend is usually a wise animal, usually a turtle in the African myth stories or a fox, such as the fox in *The Little Prince*, or an angel like Raphael who watched over little Tobias on his journey, a fairy godmother who comes to the aid of Cinderella, a cricket for Pinocchio.

In our story, the friends turn out to be a scarecrow, a tin man, and a cowardly lion, not the most stable group, but friends nevertheless and friends who come through in a pinch.

Note that this whole first scene, as it were, is deep storytelling. Its subject is the human condition, the unease of existence, the yearning for something more, the restless hearts that are restless till they rest in God. Responding to the spiritual journey is easy at first, until sin reminds us of the obstacles, till the wild beasts distract us, block us. Dorothy is us. So are the lions, tigers, and bears.

TREES AND APPLES With her newfound companion Scarecrow at her side, Dorothy starts off again on the yellow brick road. She has another discovery to make. There is, you see, a scary forest to go through, complete with grotesque apple trees that frighteningly try to reach out and grab her. When Dorothy barely escapes their clutching branches, the Scarecrow taunts them into throwing their apples at them. Surprisingly, the apples turn out to be not as nasty as the trees but quite tasty indeed. And here, behind the figure of these distorted trees and their sweet apples, is a powerful metaphor. The lesson of sweet apples from the grotesque trees is telling us of the discovery of grace in unlikely places, even in the deformities of our own lives; that grace is not always gentle but harsh, like Francis embracing the leper and Mother Teresa cradling bodies on the streets of Calcutta. We must beware of the temptation to flee our limitations and ugliness instead of confronting them in order to discover the grace of broken places. That's a lesson that must be learned on all spiritual journeys.

FORGETFULNESS Even with friends, there awaits that most potent and most dangerous of all roadblocks on the spiritual journey that very few heroes avoid, the temptation, I must say, that almost always works. It is called the seduction of forgetfulness. Even Jesus was not exempt from this temptation. In the desert Satan told him to change the stones to bread, to jump from the temple's pinnacle, to own the whole world, in a word, to forget who he is in exchange for the role of a magician and self-serving tyrant. It happens in *The Wizard of Oz*. In the movie, the Wicked Witch looks into her crystal ball, watching the foursome on their journey and knows she has to stop them. So what does she think of? Poppies! Yes, poppies. They will make them…what? Forget! Dorothy and her allies are overcome by the field of poppies, narcotized into unconsciousness, forgetfulness. They stop their journey.

This is a very common metaphorical theme. Remember the fox and his silly sidekick in Disney's *Pinocchio*? Pinocchio is the typical hero-myth figure; he is someone on a journey to become real, but he gets distracted into Pleasure Island where he forgets who he is becoming and begins instead to become something quite different: a jackass! Remember the modern version of *The Lion King*, another hero-myth figure? He is seduced and forgets his regal responsibilities and adopts the carefree lifestyle of "Hakuna Matata."

In much of the early spiritual writings, the primary sin was forgetfulness. You forget who you are. You forget your mission. You forget where you came from. The very atmosphere makes you forget: the crowd, the language, the dress, the attitudes, the values. On the everyday home level, parents say to a son or daughter caught in some disappointment, "I don't care what everyone else does. You are who you are!" Or, if we commit some blunder, we apologize, "I don't know what came over me. I'm sorry. I forgot myself for the moment."

TRANSFORMATION Dorothy and friends recover and indeed make their way to Oz. But something's missing. The fact is, although they have completed their physical journey, they haven't completed their spiritual journey. Inner transformation, we might say, hasn't taken place yet. The Scarecrow is still brainless, the Tin Man heartless, the Lion courageless, and Dorothy clueless. Further scary adventures help the quartet find their true selves.

When this happens, it is the Wizard who points out the transformation of the three companions and it is Glinda, the Good Witch, who points out Dorothy's transformation, Dorothy who is still wondering how she'll get back to Kansas. Glinda says that even though the Wizard has accidentally taken off in the balloon, "You've always had the power to go back to Kansas."

Dorothy responds, "I have?"

The Scarecrow asks, "Why didn't you tell her before?"

"Because she wouldn't believe me. She had to learn it for herself."

The Scarecrow asks, "What did you learn, Dorothy?"

Dorothy thinks a minute and replies, "I think it wasn't enough just to want to see Uncle Henry and Auntie Em, and if I ever go looking for my heart's desire again, I won't look any farther than my own backyard because if it isn't there, I never lost it to begin with. Is that right?"

Dorothy has learned something. A new inner awareness has taken hold of her, a spiritual transformation. Time to go home. There's no place like it. End of story, end of journey.

And you thought *The Wizard of Oz* was just a fairy tale! Once more, being sensitive to language and metaphors will lead you beneath the surface to deeper meanings and deeper truths for, as it has been said, a truth wrapped in story is more memorable than truth merely exposed.

This story, "The Stolen Ax," offers a nice bit of psychological wisdom.

> A woodcutter went out one morning to cut some firewood. He looked around for his favorite ax and discovered to his alarm that it was missing. He anxiously searched around the woodpile, behind his house, and in his shed, but could not find it anywhere.
>
> The woodcutter became more agitated the longer he spent trying to find his tool. Then, out of the corner of his eye, he noticed his neighbor's son standing near the woodshed. The

woodcutter stared at the boy and thought, "Look at him lurk-ing about the shed, shifting uneasily from foot to foot, greedy hands stuffed into his pockets. What a guilty look on his face! I cannot prove it, but he must have stolen my ax!" The wood-cutter fumed and promised himself he would get even for this crime.

The next day, the woodcutter stumbled on his ax laying beside a pile of firewood. "I remember now!" he exclaimed. "It is just where I left it when I was splitting wood!"

The next time he saw his neighbor's son, the woodcutter looked intently at the boy. He scrutinized him from head to toe. "How odd," he thought. "Somehow, between yesterday and today, that boy has lost his guilty look."

This strong story, "The Stolen Child," is related to Chapter Three: The Healing Power of Stories.

Once upon a time, there was a path that stretched from here to there. On one side of the path, tall mountains loomed. Along the other, the cold sea moaned. Along this path came two fairy women, wrapped tightly in dark cloaks. As they walked along, they saw a bundle in the path. It mewed faint-ly, like a tired cat. Snatching it up, they tore off the cloths. "It's a baby," said one. "A mortal baby," crowed the other.

After looking around to make sure no one was watching, one fairy hid the baby under her cloak, and the two fairy women scurried away, more quickly than they had come before. After the fairy women disappeared, a fishing boat came sailing along the coast. The man at the tiller happened to glance at the cliffs. "What's that!"

"Nothing," said the other.

"There's something on those cliffs."

"You're daft."

But the man at the tiller turned about and headed for shore. He steered through the rocky shoals and landed at the foot of the cliffs. The men climbed steadily until they came to a rocky ledge. A young woman lay there, still as death. The tillerman knelt down and put his ear to her mouth. When he felt a faint puff of breath, he knew she was still alive. The men carried her down to the boat and sailed off as fast as they could. When they reached the harbor, they called for the women folk to come and take care of her. For several days she lay still, more dead than alive. The women took turns staying by her side, moistening her lips with damp cloths, tucking the blankets around her chilled body.

At last, she opened her eyes. "Where is my baby?" she cried. "Bring me my baby."

At that the women looked at one another. For they had no baby to give her. An old woman took her hand. "Be brave, daughter. For your baby must have fallen from your arms and landed in the sea."

"He did not!" the mother cried. "I wrapped him in his blanket and laid him in the path when I went to find water. I know he is safe."

At that the women shook their heads, but they summoned the menfolk and sent them up and down the path, seeking any news of the baby. The men searched the livelong day, but came back shaking their heads. No one had seen or heard of a baby left on the path.

When they brought the young mother the sad news, she tossed her blanket aside. "My baby is alive. I will find him."

"Shhh," the women soothed her. "You are still weak. Wait till you are stronger. Then you can go on your way."

At that the young mother fell back into bed. She bided her time, eating the food they brought her and resting until her strength returned. Then she rose from the bed. "Farewell," she said. "If I live, I will return with my son. If I die, so it must be." The villagers were sad to see her go, for they had grown to love the brave young mother and they were sure her baby was dead.

The young mother journeyed for many weeks, stopping at every croft and village. But no one had heard of a baby left on a path by the sea. She journeyed until her feet were bleeding and her clothes were torn. At last she came upon a camp of gypsies and her heart beat faster in her chest, for the gypsies traveled far and wide, and if any had news of her baby, it would be them. When she appeared at the edge of their circle, they fell silent, staring at the gaunt young woman with tangled gold hair and wild eyes. They made room for her beside their fire and brought warm water to bathe her feet. They gave her food from their pot. But when she asked if they had news of her baby, they shook their heads and said no, all the babies in the camp were their own. At that the young mother broke into sobs and said she could not go on, for her baby was all she had in this world.

The gypsies huddled together, dark heads bent close in a circle. When they broke apart, their leader came to the young mother. "Do not despair," he said. "We will bring you to our ancient grandmother, the Wise One, who knows all there is to know on earth." And they did. They brought the young mother with them in their own caravan, feeding her and caring for her as if she were one of their own. And at last they came to a great gypsy encampment, and they brought the young mother to an old crone sitting beside a fire. The two women sat side by side, holding hands in silence. At last the grandmother rose and threw some herbs into the fire. When she returned to her seat, she held the young mother's hand tightly. "The news I have is not good. Your baby has been taken by the fairy women of the Sidh. He is being held in their dark underground kingdom. Nothing that has entered that kingdom has ever returned to the light of day."

"What must I do?"

The grandmother sat silent for a long while. At last she spoke. "The Sidh are a greedy folk, always lusting after precious things. But they have no art or skill of their own. Whatever they get, they get by thievery or bargaining. You could buy your way into their dark realm with something rare and beautiful."

"I have nothing. No family. No money. How can I get something so rare?"

"There I cannot help you. And you will need something else, even more precious, to buy your baby back once you are in the dark realm." At that the mother hung her head, so confused and despairing was she. The ancient grandmother put her hands on the mother's head and blessed her, protecting her against all things made of earth, air, fire, and water. Then she sent the young mother on her way.

For a while the young mother was numb and dazed, so impossible did the task seem. But gradually the haze cleared. She set herself to remembering all the wondrous things she had heard of, and at last two came into her mind: the white cloak of Nechtan and the golden harp of Wrad. And she knew what she must do.

She set off for the sea and ended up not far from the place where she had fallen. On hands and knees she crawled over the rocks, gathering the downy white feathers that had fallen from the breasts of the eider ducks. And the ancient grandmother's blessing held true, for she was not bruised by the rocks, nor torn by the wind, nor burnt by the sun, nor drenched by the sea. And when she had gathered armfuls of the white feathers she sat on the shore and wove them into a cloak. And when she was finished, the cloak looked like a cloud that had drifted down from the sky. And then she took her hair, her golden hair that fell to her waist, and chopped it all off. She took the golden strands and wove them into a border, a shining border of suns and moons and stars. Then she folded the cloak and lay it safe under a rock and went down to the beach again, gathering the skeletons of long-dead sea creatures, creatures that had lain so long on the bottom of the sea that their bones were polished smooth as ivory. She took those bones and bent them into a harp frame and then strung the harp with her own golden hair. When she was finished, she plucked the harp. The note rang out so full of grief and love and longing that the wild birds themselves paused in the air at the sound of it. Then she took her harp under her arm and placed the cloak on her shoulders and headed for the dark kingdom.

She traveled by night and by day, by highway and byway, over mountains and across rivers, and at last she came to Sidhean, the dark kingdom of the fairy folk of the Sidh. She hid behind a tree, watching the fairy folk enter. Now the Sidh do not look so different from you and from me. Their ears are a bit pointed, and their hands—those hands that have no skill to make or mend—are a bit like claws, but except for that the Sidh look like ordinary mortals. As the moon rose full, a late-arriving fairy hurried toward the gate. The young mother stepped from behind the tree, swirling the cloak as she faced the fairy. "What!" began the fairy, whose eyes narrowed at the sight of the shining cloak. "How much do you want for it," she said, hands darting to pluck at the shimmering border.

"It is not for sale."

"Place it on the ground, and I will cover it with gold."

"I made this cloak with my own hands and embroidered it with my own hair, and I will not sell it—but I will give it to you if you bring me into your kingdom."

"Yes," said the fairy, greedily snatching at the cloak, "Give it to me."

"I will give it to you once we are inside," said the young mother, who knew the Sidh were a thieving folk who would steal whatever they could.

The fairy grabbed the young mother's hand and drew her through the dark gates. They hurried through long winding passageways and at last entered the great hall. Fairies came up hissing at the young mother, but she swirled the cloak cunningly, and thrust it at the fairy who had brought her through the gates. Seeing the cloak, the fairies lost all interest in the mother. They swarmed the fairy, snatching at the cloak as the young mother strode toward the throne at the end of the hall.

The king sat on the throne, his head wreathed in gold, his clawed hands toying with a jeweled necklace. "A mortal," he hissed and sat upright as the young mother approached.

"I have brought you this," she said, holding aloft the harp.

"I have harps aplenty."

"But have you one like this?" And she plucked a golden note strung from her own hair, and the sound was so full of grief and love and longing that the hall fell silent, and all turned to look at her.

"What do you want for it," the king asked casually, trying to hide his desire.

"It is not for sale."

"Everything has its price," he said and ordered his servants to bring gold.

"I don't want gold," she said as they heaped it around her feet.

"Jewels?" he said and his servants ran to bring armfuls of emeralds and rubies.

"Neither gold nor jewels," she said, and plucked the harp again.

"Anything," he said, "I will give you anything."

"Then give me back my baby, the one your women stole from the path by the sea."

And the king was displeased for he'd had a mind to keep that mortal baby to serve him in his dark realm. But he wanted that harp. He motioned his servants to fetch the child and then reached out his hand for the harp.

"Not till my baby is in my arms," she said.

And when the servants brought the baby, he saw his mother and held out his arms to her. When she pressed him safe against her breast, she handed over the harp, and the king began to play. The notes were so full of grief and love and longing that the fairies froze in place, listening, and for all we know they are still there today. But the young mother made her way out of that dark kingdom and back up into the light of day. She journeyed back to the village of fisherfolk who had loved her well, and she and her son lived there many a day.

One person commented on this story:

This story has deep power and significance for me. The first time I told it was at a Family Camp in northern California. I had just heard that a teen girl, Carrie, a close friend of our family, had been killed in a bike accident that day. As I told the story, I felt that Carrie was quite close, listening from another realm, and I continue to feel her presence when I tell this story. I have told it maybe two dozen times, mostly in shelters for

homeless and abused women. It is a powerful tale for those
women, many of whom have had custody issues, and many of
whom feel deeply conflicted and ashamed about their ability
to protect and care for their children. Since the subject matter
of the story is so likely to be loaded, when I tell it in a shelter,
I always warn the women that I am going to tell a story about
a woman's journey to recover her stolen child, but I add that
it could be heard as a journey to recover anything of deep personal importance.

"The Sacrifice Flower" by Sr. Jose Hobday, a wonderful storyteller and
part Seneca Indian, could also be included in the healing category.

My mother, who was a Native American, taught me all kinds
of wonderful ways to pray when I was a child. A very special
one was the Sacrifice Flower prayer, which she adapted from
the heritage of her people, the Seneca Iroquois. She taught me
to say this prayer when I was feeling low or had a burden I
wanted lifted. Later, I learned to use it for happy occasions and
when I had a special request I wanted to make of God. Like all
mothers, she could always tell when something was bothering
me. She'd say to me, "All right, Jo, I think it's time you went
outside and found yourself a Sacrifice Flower. It's time you get
your burden lifted from your heart and give it to God."

So I would go looking for a flower. Sometimes Mother
would go out with me to help me with my flower or talk about
what was bothering me. Sometimes, too, she had something
weighing on her heart and she would find a Sacrifice Flower of
her own. That flower was supposed to be special, one that
meant a lot to me. As a girl, I picked a dandelion, hollyhock,
and daisy. Mother said I was to be very careful with the flower
because it had been selected for a holy purpose. I lovingly
cupped it in my hands so nothing would happen to it.

When I got home, I did as my mother instructed and told
the flower what burden I wanted lifted and taken to God. How
was the flower to do this? Remember, this was a Sacrifice
Flower, one that was going to die. The idea was that as life
went out of the flower, it would carry my prayer to God. That

meant, of course, the flower was not to be placed in water. I had a shelf in my room that I liked to use for my Sacrifice Flower because it was sort of private and yet I could see it as I went in and out.

Every time I saw the flower, I could see it giving its life for me and I could imagine my prayer being carried to God. That was true even when I was elsewhere and was just thinking about the flower. Either way, I had a strong sense my prayer was being heard. My flower and I were in union. Sometimes it took a few days, sometimes a couple of weeks.

When the flower finally died, I would take it outside, say good-bye to it, and thank it for giving its life for me and for delivering my prayer. Then I would bury it so it would have a chance at a new life, and I always hoped it would come back as an even nicer flower. In this simple, graphic way my mother taught me how uplifting prayer can be. And, in the process, she taught me about life, too, how basic both dying and rising are to living and how important it is that we become Sacrifice Flowers for each other.

The following stories relate to Chapter Four: The Moral Lives of Children. The first one is called "Hans the Shepherd Boy."

Hans was a little shepherd boy who lived in Germany. One day he was keeping his sheep near a great wood when a hunter rode up to him.

"How far is it to the nearest village, my boy?" asked the hunter.

"It is six miles, sir," said Hans. "But the road is only a sheep track. You might easily miss your way."

"My boy," said the hunter, "if you will show me the way, I will pay you well."

Hans shook his head. "I cannot leave the sheep, sir," he said. "They would stray into the wood and the wolves might kill them."

"But if one or two sheep are eaten by the wolves, I will pay you for them. I will give you more than you can earn in a year."

"Sir, I cannot go," said Hans. "These sheep are my master's. If they are lost, I should be to blame."

"If you cannot show me the way, will you get me a guide? I will take care of your sheep while you are gone."

"No," said Hans, "I cannot do that. The sheep do not know your voice, and—" Then he stopped.

"Can't you trust me?" asked the hunter.

"No," said Hans. "You have tried to make me break my word to my master. How do I know that you would keep your word?"

The hunter laughed. "You are right," said he. "I wish I could trust my servants as your master can trust you. Show me the path. I will try to get to the village alone."

Just then several men rode out of the wood. They shouted for joy. "Oh, sir!" cried one. "We thought you were lost." Then Hans learned to his great surprise that the hunter was a prince. He was afraid that the great man would be angry with him. But the prince smiled and spoke in praise of him.

A few days later a servant came from the prince and took Hans to the palace. "Hans," said the prince, "I want you to leave your sheep to come and serve me. I know you are a boy whom I can trust."

Hans was very happy over his good fortune. "If my master can find another shepherd to take my place, then I will come and serve you." Hans went back and tended the sheep until his master found another shepherd. After that he served the prince many years.

The next two stories of the lives and legends of the saints are from the wonderful works of British author Joan Windham. No one does it better. Here, for example, is a story for kids and others who get teased. It's called "St. Mungo."

Once upon a time there was a monastery at Culross, in Fifeshire, Scotland, and it was a Boy's School, and it was near the sea.

Very early one morning one of the monks (whose name was Servan) was saying his Office when God said to him, "Servan, go down to the sea and you will find something."

So Servan got up and put his Breviary away, and then he went outside. It was so very early in the morning that it was still nearly dark, but he found the path that led to the sea, and very soon was on the beach. There he saw a Dark Bundle. He peered at it and found that it was a Girl wrapped up in a dark cloak with a tiny, brand-new baby! They were sopping wet, and the girl was Very Ill with Temperature.

"Poor things!" thought kind old Brother Servan. "They must have been wrecked or something!" And he lifted up the girl and her baby and carried them back to the Monastery. He called the other Monks, and they gave the girl a Hot Tot to try and warm her up, but it was so sad because she soon died. She had caught her Death of Cold.

So there were the Monks in the Abbey at Culross with a tiny little boy of one day old in their School! They Baptised him Kentigern, but he was such a nice baby that everybody called him Mungo which means Dearest.

When Mungo was old enough he went to the school with the other boys, but they didn't like him because he belonged to the Monks, and the Abbey was his home.

"That Mungo gets all the Tit Bits when we're not looking," they said, "and I expect he Tells Tales about us to Brother Servan." Mungo didn't do any of those things, but the Other Boys used to do every thing that they could to make his life Miserable.

There were no matches in those days, and so the Kitchen Fire had to be kept burning Day In and Day Out, because it was such a bother to relight it. So it was the job of the boys to take turns getting up in the Middle of the Night to make up the fire.

Once, when it was Mungo's turn to get up, he found that the Other Boys had poured some water on it, and that it was dead out. Poor Mungo was Distracted! He wasn't quite sure how to light it again (one of the monks always did it), and if he left it then none of them would be able to have any Breakfast! Now whenever anything happened Mungo used to tell the Holy Spirit, and so, before he thought what he was doing he started to say the Prayer to the Holy Spirit to comfort himself. And what do you suppose happened? When he got to "Enkindle in them the Fire of thy Love," all the wet ashes were gone and there was a lovely Hot Fire! When the Other Boys came down in the morning they were all whispering and Nudging one another while they were waiting for Breakfast. "Now," they said to each other, "that horrid little Mungo will get into trouble, because there won't *be* any Breakfast!"

But when the servery door opened, instead of an Angry Brother Cook, there was their nice Hot Breakfast just the same as usual! So they thought of a worse thing to do and this was the Worse Thing.

Old Brother Servan had a tame Robin that used to come into his room and pick up crumbs and sit on the back of his chair and all that. (I expect that you have often seen Robins in the house. There is one that nearly lives in my Kitchen!) Servan was very fond of his Robin, and he was always hoping that one day it would get tame enough to sit on his finger, but it hadn't yet.

One day, while Brother Servan was teaching in the school, some of the boys caught the Robin and put it in Mungo's pocket with a few feathers sticking out so that it would show. They put the coat in Servan's room so that when he came in and saw the coat he would think that it was Mungo who had done it. But luckily it was Mungo who came in first, and he saw the Robin. "Oh, *poor* little thing!" said Mungo. "What a *shame*! What will poor old Brother Servan do when he knows?" And he began to cry, it was so sad. And he began to say his favorite Prayer to the Holy Spirit. While he was saying, "they shall be Created" the Robin shook out its crumpled little feathers and flew to Brother Servan's desk! There it sat, tidying itself up, and Mungo couldn't thank God enough for saving Brother Servan from being so sad.

But at last Mungo was so Miserable because of the Other Boys that he ran away! Brother Servan followed him.

"Now, Mungo," he said, "never you mind those silly boys! We all know that you are all right, and that you don't do all these Fearful Things," and he patted Mungo's shoulder kindly.

"I know, Brother," said Mungo, sniffing sadly and rubbing his nose, "but I couldn't go back, really I couldn't. Besides, I do want to be a Hermit for a little while, and then I want to be a Priest."

"All right, then," said Servan, "but come and see us whenever you like, we shall always be pleased to see you."

"Yes, I will," said Mungo, "because you are all my Fathers, and the Abbey is my Home."

Mungo found a cave near Glasgow, on the banks of the Clyde, and he did just what he had said. First he was a Hermit, and then he was a Priest, and in time was made the Bishop of Glasgow. He spent a lot of time teaching people about God and once he went to Wales.

Now when Mungo was the Bishop of Glasgow, the King's name was King Roderick, and they were great friends. King Roderick's wife was a Young and Giddy Queen, and once she did a very Young and Giddy thing. She gave her Engagement Ring that King Roderick had given to her before they were married, to a Knight that she liked very much.

"You can wear it as a favor," she said to him. And the Knight put it on his finger and thought that no one would notice.

One day King Roderick and the Knight went hunting together, and they got very hot and tired, so the King said: "Let's stop and have our lunch under these trees by the stream. We can get cool, and we might have Forty Winks."

So they had a lovely Cold Lunch that the Queen had packed for them. They had Chicken Patties and New Bread and New Butter and Cheese and Wild Strawberries and Whisky. Then they put the plates and things back in the basket and settled down for their Forty Winks.

But King Roderick wasn't so sleepy as the Knight, and he lay on his back and stared at the leaves against the sky, and thought about his Young and Giddy Queen. Then he rolled over and looked at the Knight who was asleep, and there, on his finger, he saw the Queen's Engagement Ring!

He was Simply Furious. He leaned over and very carefully pulled off the ring without waking the Knight and Threw it in the stream.

When they got home he asked the Young and Giddy Queen where her Ring was. "You ought to wear it always with your Wedding Ring," he said.

"I've lost it," said the Queen, feeling Rather Nervous.

"Well, why did you take it off, then?" said King Roderick.

"It must have Fallen Off," said the Queen. "I'm thinner than I was," she said in a Pathetic voice.

"Then you must find it," said King Roderick in a Stern voice. "If you don't find it by tomorrow lunch time I shall know that you have been Giddier than usual and you will have to be Executed. Queens can't afford to be Giddy." And he Stamped out of the room.

The poor Queen was very Frightened, and she sent a quick message to her Favorite Knight, and this was the quick message: "Send back my Ring Quickly, because if you don't I will be Executed tomorrow at Lunch Time."

But the Knight sent back a quick message, and this was his quick message: "I can't, because it was lost when I was out hunting with the King."

The Queen was in a Frenzy of Despair, and she sent for the Bishop of Glasgow, who was Mungo, and she went to Confession, and told him all about everything. So Mungo gave her Absolution and a Penance, and he was sorry for her, because she was so Young and Giddy, and so he went to the Church and he prayed and prayed that she wouldn't have to be Executed. "Because, dear Lord," he said, to God, "she really is sorry she was so Silly, and it does seem a shame to Execute her when she is so Young."

When he got back to his Bishop's Palace, in Glasgow, he found a Mysterious Parcel waiting for him. It was Long and Heavy and Rather Damp.

"Well now," said Mungo to himself, "who could be sending me a present at this time of night? I do believe it smells of Fish!"

And he unpacked his Parcel, and there inside it was a fresh-caught Salmon from the River Clyde!

"How very kind of Who-ever-it-is," said Mungo. "I'll invite some Poor-and-Raggy people to dinner tomorrow, and we'll have my Fine Fat Salmon!" And he took it to the kitchen.

Early in the morning, on his way back from Mass, his servant met him. "Look, my Lord," he said. "Look what the cook found inside the Salmon!" And there was the Queen's Ring! Mungo quickly took it to the Queen, and when King Roderick went to see her after breakfast she said:

"Here is my Ring, Roderick. Will you please forgive me?"

And Roderick was so surprised that he said that he would if she promised not to be so Giddy again. And she did.

And what could portray better the seven capital sins than this story of St. Alexander?

Once upon a time there was a forest in Rumania (it is still there, for all I know), but anyway at the time that I am talking about there lived in the forest a man called Alexander, and people sometimes called him Alex for short. Alexander was a Charcoal Burner and he used to collect little twigs and thin branches from the trees in the forest and he made little fires and burned the sticks very slowly so that they turned into black sticks called Charcoal. (If he was in too much of a hurry, they turned into White Ashes instead and he would have to begin all over again.) People use charcoal for quite a lot of things. They draw with it, and make fires with it, and use it for medicine, and make shoe polish with it. So you can see what a useful job Alexander had.

So Alexander looked after his little fires by himself all day and he learned to be very Patient because if he was Impatient his charcoal would turn into ashes. In a quiet job like that the birds and the animals get used to the person who is working and take no notice. Alexander saw baby squirrels playing, and mother foxes taking their cubs to roll in the sun, and all kinds of things that we never see. It made him think how quiet and patient God must be. "Here is this enormous forest," he thought to himself, "and it is full of living things: plants and animals and birds and insects. They all lead busy lives; not one of them is lazy, and yet very few people even know that they are there! There must be hundreds of them that are too shy even for me to see. And yet God knows all about them and what they do all day. He never frightens them however near he is because he is so Still."

While Alexander was quietly living in the forest and burning his charcoal and thinking about God and watching the Birds and Animals there were great Goings On in the town where he sold his charcoal. And this is what was happening: At first there had been very few Christians in the town, but as time went on there were more and more until at last the priest said that they really ought to have a Bishop of their own instead of belonging to a Bishop called Gregory who lived a very long way off and scarcely ever had time to come and see them. So it was decided that Bishop Gregory should come and that everybody should say which priest they wanted to be the new Bishop. Well some wanted This priest and some wanted That priest and some didn't know whom they wanted but they didn't want either of Those. At last they collected seven priests who wanted to be the Bishop and they wrote and told Gregory that they wanted him to come and choose.

The Town Hall was all ready with a Throne at the end of it for Bishop Gregory and chairs and seats for all the people. When everyone was settled the First man who might be the Bishop came in. He was tall and thin with a big nose and a very Grand expression. He looked at the crowds of people as if they were too Common for Words. The people who wanted him to be the Bishop clapped and cheered as he went and stood in front of Gregory. "Do you think that you would be a good Bishop?" asked Gregory. "I am sure I would," said the man. "I think that you are too Proud," said Gregory. "Next please!"

The Second man had silk clothes and a jeweled crucifix, and he had a rosary made of real rubies in his hand. "Would you keep all those lovely things for yourself, if you were the Bishop?" asked Gregory. "Of course I should. They are my own property," said the man, and he held them a little tighter. "You are too Covetous, I think," said Gregory. (Covetous is selfish and miserly.) "Next please!" said Gregory.

The Third man had the gayest colored clothes and a smiling face and beautiful curly hair. He winked at all the people and the ladies clapped their hands because he was so handsome. "Do you want people to go on thinking that you are handsome and clever when you are the Bishop?" asked Gregory. "But of course!" said the man, and he looked quickly at the people to see if they were listening. "Even a Bishop must have his bit of fun." "I think that you are too fond of Pretty Ladies," said Gregory. "Next please!"

The Fourth man had black hair and a frowning face. He stared at the people angrily and then went and stood in front of Gregory. The people who wanted him clapped for him but he shook his head at them and they stopped. "If you were the Bishop, would you be Strict with the people and punish them severely if they broke the rules?" asked Gregory. "I would," said the man. "They are a lazy, sinful lot, but I'd not put up with any of their nonsense!" And he glared at Gregory. "You get Angry too easily," said Gregory. "Next, please!"

The Fifth man was very fat indeed, but he looked kindly at the people and he waved his hand at the ones who wanted him. As he stood in front of Gregory he pulled a buttered bun out of his pocket and began to eat it. "Excuse me!" he said. "Couldn't you have waited until after the Choosing before you ate your bun?" asked Gregory. "Not me!" said the man, "I wouldn't miss my tea for any man on earth. It keeps a man good tempered to be fat." "I think that you are too Greedy," said Gregory. "Next please!"

The Sixth man was thin and mean-looking, he did not look happy. He stared at all the priests who had already seen Gregory. (They were standing at the back of the Throne and waiting to see who would be Chosen.) "Well," said Gregory, "what is the matter? Aren't you happy? Don't you want to be Bishop after all?" "No good me wanting," said the man. "I've no good looks like that man over there, or riches like that one, or a nice house like that one, or a kind family like that one. I never get the things that Other People have." "You are too Envious to be happy," said Gregory. (Envious is being so jealous of other people's things that you haven't time to see what nice things you have yourself.) "Next please!" said Gregory. But no one came.

"Next please!" said Gregory, looking around. "I thought that you said there were seven people who wanted to be Bishop," he whispered to the Mayor who was standing beside him. "I've only seen six." "NEXT PLEASE!!" shouted the Mayor, and all the people laughed. Then the door banged and in came an untidy man with ruffled hair and his shoes undone. He was yawning and rubbing his eyes. "Sorry, my Lord," he said to Gregory. "As I was the last one I thought that I'd have a nap while I was waiting and I didn't hear you call."

"Do you always have naps when you can?" asked Gregory.

"Always, my Lord," said the man solemnly. "A man can't have too much sleep, I always say."

"I think that you are too Lazy," said Gregory. All the people rustled and coughed and sat up and shuffled their feet. They stared at Gregory and waited for him to say which of the seven priests would be the Bishop. "Well," said Gregory, and he looked around at all the people, "I am sorry but I don't think that any of them would do for a Bishop."

The people started talking among themselves and then someone shouted: "But we must have one of them! There isn't any one else!" "No," said Gregory. "They may not be so bad as ordinary people go but they're no good for Bishops. You couldn't have a Bishop who was Proud or Greedy or Lazy or any of the other Seven Deadly Sins, now could you?" "You're too Choosey," said the people. "You can't have a Perfect man." "No," said Gregory, "but he ought to try to be Perfect, and these men don't." All the people started arguing again, and in the noise Gregory said to God: "Please, God, if you really want a Bishop here, will you choose one for yourself? It is very difficult for me with all these seven, and the people are getting so cross." Just then someone shouted: "You'd better have Alexander the Charcoal Burner if you can't think of anyone better!"

All the people laughed because they couldn't imagine having sooty, raggy Alexander for a Bishop! But Gregory knew that this was God's answer to his prayer and so he held up his hand for the people to stop laughing and said: "Who is this Alexander?" "I was only joking," said the man who had shouted. "He is a Charcoal Burner and he lives in the forest." "Will somebody please go and get him?" said Gregory. The people all stared. What was Gregory thinking about? Did he really mean to see if Alexander would do? Yes, he did.

So Alexander was brought along. First he washed the black Marks off his face and hands, then he went to Bishop Gregory and knelt and kissed his ring. Then he stood up and waited to see why the Bishop had sent for him. "Alexander," said Gregory, "do you think that you would be a good Bishop?" "Me, my Lord?" said Alexander. "No, I have no learning. I don't know anything at all." "Would you like a Rosary made of Rubies?" "Why no, thank you, my Lord," said Alexander. "I have a very nice wooden one; it will last me my lifetime." "Do you like Parties and Pretty Ladies?" "I don't know any," said Alexander. "I've never been asked to a Party myself but a bit of fun now and then is good for everybody." He wondered why Gregory was asking him all these questions in front of the townspeople. "Do you think that the Townspeople are a lazy sinful lot?" asked Gregory. "Oh no, my Lord, please don't think that! There's good in everyone if you look for it." Alexander had quite forgotten how mean the people were in paying for their charcoal. "Have you had your Tea yet?" asked Gregory. "I don't have it as a rule," said Alexander, "only when it is raining and I can't burn my charcoal. I eat when I am hungry and that does me nicely." "Are you happy?" asked Gregory. "Have you everything that you want?" "I'm very happy, my Lord," said Alexander. "I love my work, I have enough to eat, I have my own little house, and God is good to me." "Would you change your work for something quite different?" asked Gregory. "I would if God wished it," said Alexander.

Gregory stood up. He walked down the steps of his throne and put his arm round Alexander's shoulders. "Here is your new Bishop," he said to the people. At first they all sat with their mouths open. Surely it could not be true! Surely the

Bishop was having a joke with them! Then, as they began to think, they saw that Alexander was just the opposite to all the other seven, and they looked at Alexander. And looking at him they loved him. So Alexander the Charcoal Burner became a Bishop and he was one for years and years but in the end he was a Martyr. St. Alexander's Special Day is August 11. And people called Alec or Alex or Alastair or Alexandra or even Sandy or Sandra or Zander may belong to him. There are lots of them in Scotland.

So much for the stories about two saints. There are also the tough witness themes such as in "The Legend of St. Genesius."

Long ago in ancient Rome, Emperor Diocletian lounged on an ornately carved chair. Servants brought trays of food to tempt him, dancers twirled to delight him, and musicians played lively tunes to soothe his mood. The emperor yawned in boredom until the actors arrived. Then the emperor sat upright and cried out with delight, "Is Genesius here?"

"Indeed I am!" said a spry young man bounding forward. Genesius was a talented mime and a favorite performer of the emperor's. "Today," announced Genesius, "we will perform the comical play about the Christians." "Begin!" the emperor said, giggling in anticipation, for this was his favorite play. Since Genesius was especially good at doing impersonations, he easily parodied the characters of his day. The early Christians, whose rituals were unfamiliar to the emperor, were a prime target for Genesius' satire.

The emperor howled with delight as Genesius performed a mockery of the Christian rite of baptism. Another actor ceremoniously dunked Genesius in a huge tub of water, seeming to almost drown him. Genesius came sputtering and splashing out of the water. The emperor shouted, "Do it again!" Genesius suddenly stood silent and still. In the midst of the zany mockery, Genesius had in fact been converted to Christianity by the sacredness of the rite he ridiculed. "I cannot do the play again," Genesius said. "But it is the funniest one! I command you to do it again!" the emperor insisted.

"No, I will not perform the play!" said Genesius, defying the emperor. "It would not be true to myself to mock what I now know is sacred."

This was courageous because Genesius knew what would happen. The emperor's face turned crimson with fury. "How dare you disobey me! Guards!" he bellowed. "Take this insolent man away and break his legs!" The guards dragged Genesius away and broke his legs.

In the Christian tradition, Genesius, the mime, became Saint Genesius, the patron saint of performing artists. In modern times people sometimes offer encouragement to an actor who is about to go on stage by saying, "Break a leg!" The expression refers to the story of Saint Genesius and means "only perform that which is true to yourself." No matter what. Have courage.

"How Squirrel Got Its Stripes" has an empowering message for those who may feel or be regarded as weak or non-productive.

Long ago in ancient India, a ten-headed monster called Ravana the Rakshasa kidnapped a king's beloved wife. The king was named Rama and his queen was named Sita. Everyone loved the king and queen because their hearts were pure. King Rama waged war on Ravana and set off to battle. The great king of monkeys, King Hanuman, led the army.

They traveled until they came to a vast sea that they would have to cross to reach Ravana's kingdom. King Rama attempted to calm the raging ocean by shooting his magic arrows into the waves. But the King of the Sea rose up and said, "The seas cannot be overcome by force, but only by building a strong bridge." So King Rama ordered his monkeys to construct a stone bridge that could hold his entire invading army.

Monkey after monkey set to work carrying huge stones and enormous boulders to the seaside. Thousands of monkeys worked ceaselessly and King Rama was pleased. Then the king noticed that a small brown squirrel rushed up and down from the hills to the shore carrying little pebbles in her mouth. "What is that little creature doing?" he wondered.

The monkeys also saw the squirrel and grew angry. "Get out of our way," they screeched. "You are too small. You are not needed." The little squirrel looked up and said, "I am helping to build the bridge to save Queen Sita." All the monkeys began to laugh. They held their sides and roared and hopped and mocked the little squirrel. "We have never heard anything so foolish in our entire lives," they said.

The squirrel answered, "I cannot carry rocks or stones. I can only lift small pebbles, but that is what I can do to help. My heart weeps for Sita and I want to be of assistance."

The monkeys moved the squirrel away, but she continued to carry small pebbles and pile them up nearby. Finally, one monkey grew so irritated that he lifted the little animal and threw her into the air. The squirrel cried out, "Rama!" The king lifted his hand and caught the squirrel safely in his palm.

It was just at that moment that the monkeys realized they needed the little pebbles to place between the larger stones to keep the bridge from falling.

King Rama said to them, "Monkeys, never despise the weak or the deeds of those that are not as strong as you. Each serves according to his strength and capacities and each is needed to make this bridge." With three fingers, King Rama drew three lines down the squirrel's back. "What truly matters is not the strength one has, but how great one's love and devotion is." From that day forth squirrels have had three pale stripes on their rich brown furry backs—marks of the great King Rama. And that is how the strongest bridge across the sea was built.

For both children and adults there is the story of Victor.

A young woman gave birth to her first child just one month after her husband died in a tragic accident. The neighbors, deeply concerned over the plight of the poor young widow, held a shower for the baby. Each person brought a beautiful present to help the mother and child get started in life. When all of the gifts were opened, the mother wept. "Thank you for your wonderful support," she said, brushing back the tears. "You have made a most difficult time easier. Next Sunday my son will be baptized. I have decided to name him Victor after his father." When all of the guests had left, the young widow heard a knock on the door. She opened it to find an old man who lived in the corner house by himself. Everyone called him Doc Burns, though he wasn't a doctor in any normal sense. Few people ever talked to the reclusive old man, though he often waved at the widow as she walked past his home.

"I have come to give you my gift for your young son," he said softly. "Mine is a different kind of gift than the others you have received. I have come to offer you one wish for young Victor. It may be anything that you want. You must make the wish before the child is baptized on Sunday." Having concluded, the little man bowed and walked back to his house on the corner. The young mother was baffled by the words of her strange little friend. Did he really have the power to grant a wish? What should she ask for? All week long she could not make up her mind. Finally, as they walked forward to the baptismal font, she whispered in the infant's ear, "I wish that everyone in the world will love my Victor."

And the wish came true. Victor grew up to be a handsome lad. As a toddler people could not resist hugging and touching him. Even when he was naughty, no one could believe that he had done anything wrong. As he grew older, Victor became known and loved throughout the village. He was always given food and toys by other children. If his mother scolded or punished him, the adults would insist that she was being too harsh to such a wonderful child. But Victor responded to all this attention by treating people with scorn and contempt. Still they seemed to adore him. Only in his occasional talks with Doc Burns did he listen to anyone.

When Victor graduated from high school, he was given a scholarship to a college in the east. At Christmas, when he returned home for a visit for the first time, he drove up in a beautiful, black Cadillac. His trunks were filled with fine clothes, and he had plenty of spending money. He seldom saw his mother during the vacation. He spent his nights out drinking at parties and taverns. After college Victor never worked but continued to live a life of ease. There was no pleasure he did not indulge in and there was no vice he did not practice. Even though women smothered him with attention and friends raved about him, his heart grew empty and his soul sick. He despised people who catered to him. He was disgusted with everything and everyone.

One night Victor decided to commit suicide. He withdrew to his bedroom where he mixed a powerful poison in a glass of wine and lifted it to his lips. Just as he was about to drink it, Doc Burns rushed through the door and took the glass out of his hands. "Good evening, Victor. It has been a long time since we have had a chance to talk," the old man said softly. "You seem to be satiated with your life of frivolity. I am sorry it has been such a meaningless existence for you. I suppose I am the one responsible for your misery. I fulfilled your mother's wish on the day of your baptism, even though it was a foolish one. Suppose I now offer you a new wish? Make it anything you want, and I will fulfill it."

"I don't think you can give me anything that I haven't already had," Victor said sadly. "Think again, my son," Doc Burns said earnestly. "Make another wish for my sake, and for the sake of your dear mother." Victor closed his eyes and thought for several minutes. Finally he spoke through his tears. "Take away the old magic and give me a new wish. Rather than being loved, I ask for the ability to love everyone in the world." "That was good," Doc Burns said embracing the sobbing young man. "Now things will go better for you."

Things did go better for Victor but not immediately. Without his great charm, he began to be abandoned by his friends. Several people retaliated for the past wrongs he had afflicted on them. He was thrown into jail for three months and no one came to visit him. When he was released, he was sick, lonely, and penniless. He returned home to nurse his ailing mother. For the first time in his life he was able to return her great love.

After his mother's recovery, Victor took a job as a janitor in an elementary school. He not only cared for clean floors, but for the children, particularly those who came from poor homes. To all the children he became "Mr. Victor," their friend and companion.

Finally, he met a beautiful young widow who had two small children. They married and he gave all three of them the love that they so desperately needed. Poor in money, Victor was one of the richest men in the world. He discovered that it is in loving, not being loved, that life comes to its fullest expression.

The following stories are related to Chapter Five: Stories for the Second Half of Life. They portray savvy and wise elders, such as Kitta Gray.

Kitta Gray was famous, not for her beauty—she was in fact an ugly old crone—but for the fact that she had outsmarted the Devil.

Here is what happened. One time she made a bet with the Devil that she could beat him in a race by running through a murky swamp. The deal was that if the Devil won, she would give herself to him. If Kitta won, she would gain fame as the one who beat the Devil himself. It was agreed. The race started. They both ran off lickity-split into the swamp. But before long Kitta Gray was falling behind, but the Devil never noticed. He was too busy racing ahead. When, huffing and puffing, he reached the finish line he was shocked to find the old crone already there, peeking out from behind a bush. They immediately lined up again and ran back. Once more Kitta Gray fell behind and the Devil pulled way ahead. But when he arrived at the finish line, there she was again, cool as a cucumber and, not only that, she was thumbing her nose at him! Anyway, they continued on in this way, back and forth, back and forth, until the Devil, totally wiped out, finally gave up.

How did Kitta win? How did she fool the Devil? What happened was that Kitta Gray had a twin sister who looked exactly like her. They dressed alike and she and her sister simply positioned themselves at either end of the swamp! That's how Kitta Gray fooled the Devil.

But it was not to be the last time. There was a merchant in town whose business was doing miserably. One day the Devil sauntered into his store and offered to help him. The merchant complained that even that would do no good. He had no customers, no matter how good his merchandise was. Nothing would work. But the Devil assured him that he'd get him so many customers that he wouldn't be able to meet the demand. The merchant scoffed. He said that if the day ever came that he ran out of goods to sell, the Devil could come for him. Agreed. Perhaps the merchant agreed too soon, for from that day on, business began to pick up until one day the merchant, looking around his store, realized that he had sold almost everything. Now he started to get worried, for he remembered that he had sold his soul to the Devil. What to do?

Then he thought of Kitta Gray. He sent for the old crone and told his sorry tale. She listened intently and, when he was finished, she was silent for a long time. Then she said to the merchant, "Make a glass cabinet and put me inside. Then advertise that I am for sale."

In a few days the Devil arrived. He was humming to himself, thinking that he was to claim his victim. He danced into the store, asking how business was going. Prompted by Kitta Gray, the merchant replied that business was going very well, "Except," he added, "for one item that seems very hard to sell." Curious, the Devil asked to see it. The merchant led him to the back of the store and showed him the cabinet in which Kitta Gray sat laughing. When the Devil saw her, remembering his humiliating defeat at the swamp, his eyes popped and he exclaimed, "Anyone who knows Kitta Gray would never, ever buy her!" And he rushed out the door never to return.

"Grandmother Spider and the Fire" is an empowering story.

There is a legend among the Chickasaw tribes that says that when living things—humans, animals, insects—first came up out of the ground they were encased in cocoons with their eyes closed and their limbs folded tightly to their bodies. The Great Spirit took pity on them and sent an angel to unfold their limbs, dry them off, and open their eyes. But, alas, it made no difference. The opened eyes saw nothing because the world was dark, very dark. There was no sun or moon or stars. All the Living Creatures had to move around by touch, and if they found food they had to eat it raw, for they had no fire to cook it.

Finally one day all the Living Creatures met in a great pow-wow. The Animal and Bird People took charge. They declared that life was not good, but cold and miserable. All agreed and argued that a solution must be found. Then someone spoke from the dark and said, "I have heard that the people in the East have fire."

"Fire? What could fire be?"

There was lots of talk until finally it was decided that if, as rumor had it, fire was warm and gave light, why, then, they should have it too. Just as they were agreed, another voice from the dark said, "But the people of the East, I hear, are self-ish. They won't share with us."

There was silence at first followed by a few whispers until a growing consensus chorused into the decision that the Bird and Animal People should steal what they needed, steal the fire. It was settled. Yes, easily said, but how and by whom? Who should have the honor? It was Grandmother Spider who first volunteered. "I can do it!" she said. "Let me try!"

But she was outshouted by Opossum who, holding his head high, spoke to all. "I, Opossum, am a great chief of the animals. I will go to the East, and since I am a great hunter, I will take the fire and I will hide it in the bushy hair on my tail and sneak away." And it was true. Opossum had the furriest tail of all the animals, so he was quickly selected and off he went.

When Opossum arrived in the East, he soon found it was all true. There was the beautiful glowing red fire and indeed it was jealously guarded by the people of the East. Opossum bided his time, moved closer and closer until swiftly he picked up a small piece of burning wood, and stuck it firmly in the hair of his tail so that he wouldn't lose it. Unfortunately it promptly began to smoke, then burst into flame, arousing the people of the East. They exclaimed, "Look, that Opossum has stolen our fire. After him!" They caught poor Opossum and took the fire and put it back where it came from and mercilessly drove

Opossum away. Poor Opossum! What a sight. Every bit of hair had burned from his tail, and that's why to this day, opossums have no hair at all on their tails.

Once again, the council had to find a volunteer. Once again Grandmother Spider begged, "Let me go! I can do it!" No one paid attention. Instead this time, a bird was elected—Buzzard.

Now Buzzard was a very proud creature. He proclaimed, "I can succeed where Opossum has failed. Yes, I will fly to the East on my great wings, then hide the stolen fire in the beautiful long feathers on my head." So Buzzard flew to the East on his powerful wings, easily swooped past those attending the fire, snatched a small piece of burning ember, and hid it in his head feathers. But, of course, Buzzard's head began to smoke and then burst into flames. (They still did not understand the nature of fire.) The people of the East looked up and said, "Look! Buzzard has stolen the fire!" And they grabbed him and took the fire and put it back where it came from. Poor old Buzzard! His once noble head was now bald, red, and blistered-looking. And that is why to this day, buzzards have naked heads that are bright red and blistered.

The powwow convened again. This time they choose Crow to look the situation over, for, if nothing else, Crow was very clever. Now at that time Crow was pure white and had the sweetest singing voice of all the birds. But when he got to the East he took so long dawdling over the fire trying to find the perfect piece to steal, that his white feathers were smoked black. And he breathed in so much smoke that when he tried to sing, instead of sweet notes, out came a harsh "Caw! Caw!"

The council members were dejected. They said, "Opossum has failed. Buzzard and Crow have failed. Is there anyone else to send?" This time tiny Grandmother Spider shouted with all her might, "Let me try it, please!" Though the startled council members were skeptical and thought Grandmother Spider had little chance of success, it was agreed that she should have her turn. Why not?

Now the first thing Grandmother Spider did was to walk toward a stream where she had found clay and got busy right away. She efficiently made a tiny clay container and a lid that fit perfectly with a tiny notch for air in the corner of the lid. Then she put the container on her back, spun a web all the way to the East, and walked on tip-toe until she came to the fire. She was so small that the people from the East took no notice. She quietly took a tiny piece of fire, put it in the container, and covered it with the lid. Then very slowly she walked back on tip-toe along the web until she came home to the Living Creatures. Since they could not see any fire, they said dejectedly, "Grandmother Spider too has failed." But she quickly responded, "Oh, no. Oh, no. I do have the fire!" She then lifted the pot from her back, and the lid from the pot, and the fire flamed up into its friend, the air.

Now all the Bird and Animal People began to decide who would get this wonderful warmth. Right away Bear spoke up, "I'll take it!" but then he burned his paws on it and decided fire was not for animals. After all, look what happened to Opossum! The birds decided they wanted no part of it. Look what happened to Buzzard and Crow, who were still nursing their wounds. The insects expressed the opinion that indeed it was pretty, but they, too, stayed far away from the fire. Finally a small voice spoke, "We will take it, if Grandmother Spider will help." The others were astounded and looked at who said that. Of all things, the timid humans, whom none of the animals or birds thought much of, were volunteering! So the upshot was that Grandmother Spider taught the Human People how to feed the fire dead leaves, twigs, and wood to keep it from dying and especially how to keep the fire safe in a circle of stone so it couldn't escape and hurt them or their homes. While Grandmother Spider was at it, she taught the humans about pottery made of clay; she was something of an expert. The Chickasaw remember. They made a beautiful design to decorate their homes: a picture of Grandmother Spider with a fire symbol on her back. This is so their children will never forget to honor Grandmother Spider—the one who brought fire.

I once told this story in a mixed group. The women were pleased that a woman had achieved such a feat where men had failed. On the other hand, some men complained that men weren't given enough credit for their efforts and that women never appreciate them and all they do. The women countered that no matter how much they succeed, men tend to denigrate their accomplishments. And so it went back and forth. Everyone read something different into the story. Finally a frail woman (an elder) spoke up and said, "What is important to me is not that she's a woman but that she's old. It's hard to feel valued as an old person in a culture that fixates on youth." In any case, what is clear beyond all of the other interpretations is that the overlooked, the insignificant in the pecking order, the elderly Grandmother Spider refused to be a victim of stereotype.

All these are indeed challenging stories worth pondering. To lighten the soul, let us end this chapter with a sweet chuckle, like a dessert after a heavy meal.

> Once upon a time, a cook named Gretel worked for the town mayor. One day the mayor said, "Prepare two fine hens for dinner, Gretel, as I'm expecting an important guest." Gretel went to the market and bought two fat birds, already plucked. Once home, she stuffed them with raisins and breadcrumbs, basted them with melted butter, and began roasting them over a slow fire.
>
> Before long they were nicely browned and smelled delicious. But she couldn't serve them for the guest hadn't yet arrived. "It's a shame they can't be eaten right now," said Gretel to herself. "They are so hot and tender and juicy. I'll bet they are tasty! But one can't always tell just by looking. I'll have to take a bite, just a little nibble so the mayor won't know." She pulled off one of the wings and quickly devoured it. "Oh my, but that is good! Why, it's one of the best hens I've ever cooked. But the bird looks funny with only one wing sticking out. I'd better eat the other one too, so the mayor won't notice anything wrong."

After she had eaten the second wing, she called to the mayor to see if his guest had arrived. "Not yet," he replied from the other room. "Oh dear, the birds are getting cold. I can't put them back into the oven or they'll burn to a crisp. Maybe his guest isn't coming after all. I suppose it would be all right to eat the rest of the hen while it's still hot."

She devoured the chicken, enjoying each savory bite. Indeed, she thought it so delicious that she pulled a wing from the second bird to see if it tasted equally good. "Oh my, it's even better!" Before Gretel realized it, she had eaten the second hen as well. As she wiped the grease from her chin, the mayor called. "Hurry, Gretel! I can see my guest coming up the path." "Yes...Mister Mayor," she said hesitantly. "I'll serve dinner...in a moment."

The mayor enjoyed the task of carving birds and he began to sharpen his largest butcher knife on a stone. A gentle knock at the kitchen door announced the guest's arrival. He had come to the back door by mistake. Gretel opened it just a crack and said, "Quickly, run for your life! The mayor asked you to dinner, but actually he plans to cut off your ears! Listen, you can hear him sharpening his knife in the outer room." The man was shocked and said, "Thank you for the warning." Then he ran back down the path toward the roadway. Gretel called to the mayor, "Hurry, Your Honor, your guest has just stolen the hens and is running away with them!" "Didn't he leave one for me?" cried the mayor.

"No, he took the pair," she said. Holding the carving knife above his head, the mayor ran after his guest and yelled, "I only want one! Do you hear? It's only one that I want!" The poor mayor only wanted one of the delicious birds, but the guest thought that he wanted one of his ears so he kept on running!

CHAPTER NINE

The Tale of Two Stories

All sorrows can be borne if you put them into a story or tell a story about them. Isak Dineson

Christianity's first self-definition was "The Way." It meant not only that its adherents were dedicated to Jesus, "the way, the truth, and the life," but also that life was a choice. It was a choice to discard the old ways of sin and evil and follow Jesus. The metaphor remained strong and came to indicate that a Christian was one who lived by the Jesus story and rejected the ways of "the world." Christian writings soon were replete with allusions to the two ways, the two stories to live by. From Bunyan's allegory, *The Pilgrim's Progress*, to Robert Frost's "the road less traveled," the choice was brought home to people. Today, the choice of "ways," of stories to live by, still confronts us most urgently as old traditions are dismissed, old stories superseded, and old mythologies forgotten or found irrelevant. A new superficial storyline has been substituted. It is this ever-old, ever-new conflict between two such ways, two such stories, that we want to examine in this chapter.

We begin by repeating that story in all its forms is serious but at this moment in history we have largely lost or forgotten its importance. As we have noted, factuality has replaced stories (even though, as we have seen, *some* stories are factual and *all* stories are true). That has left us without the mega-story, the super story, the mythological story, if you will, the over-arching story that provides the metaphors, symbols, and meanings that shape our lives and interpret our journey. It's a serious vacuum, for we are compulsively meaning-seeking creatures. We possess imagination, the ability to have ideas and experiences that we cannot explain rationally. We almost instinctively embrace mythology, an art form that points beyond history to what is timeless, that helps us see and get beyond the external flux and chaos of daily random events where we can glimpse the core of reality.

A Deeper Look

Myth is difficult to define but it basically deals with the notion of two parallel worlds. (Although there are distinctions, I will use myth, fantasy, fairy tales, and story interchangeably.) Myth says that there is more to life than what we see here. There are hidden spirits and higher plans at work. Unlike secularism, which preaches that we *do* live by bread alone, and that what we see is what we get, and cleverly manipulates atoms and molecules, clones animals and humans, screens out the unwanted, and rearranges faces and bodies (for surface image is everything in a world where there is nothing beneath the surface), the imagination dares to deal in bizarre figures of speech, spectacular events, and powerful magic. All of these support its fundamental assumption that there is always more than meets the eye and that wisdom and truth are to be found where the two worlds interact. (Celtic spirituality calls this point of contact the "thin places.") In short, myth is a more powerful vehicle for truth than language and propositional speech. Or, in a nutshell, myth asks (and answers), as in the song of Emmylou Harris, "If there's no Heaven, what is this hunger for?"

Myth and fairy tales provide the symbols that enable our imagination to make sense out of the world and move beyond what we see. The myths provide the material for working out our moral questions. The enduring Greek myths, for example, are not just stories of gods and heroes and war. They are the stuff that leads to thinking about everything from the nature of the universe to our deepest moral attachments and obligations. The myths use fantastical characters and plots to probe the questions of who we are and how we are related to the gods—and God. Fairy tales speak to us in ways that the language of science cannot. They are repositories of wisdom, if not of knowledge, and they invariably show us that it is better to be wise than to be clever, and it is better to do good to others than to seek mastery over them. They tell us that those who are willing to lay themselves down for others' sake usually wind up gaining much; those who seek to lord it over others usually wind up getting what they deserve. Fairy tales, in short, tell us there is a divine order—a parallel world.

Ursula Le Guin, author of the wonderful fantasy series *EarthSea*, really says it best:

> The great fantasies, myths, and tales...speak from the unconscious to the unconscious, in the language of the unconscious—symbol and archetype. Though they use words, they work the way music does: they short-circuit verbal reasoning and go straight to the thoughts that lie too deep to utter. They cannot be translated fully into the language of reason, but only a Logical Positivist, who also finds Beethoven's *Ninth Symphony* meaningless, would claim that they are therefore meaningless. They are profoundly meaningful, and usable—practical—in terms of ethics, of insight, of growth.

Like poetry and music, mythology invites us to transcendence even in the face of death. The myths of mythology are true in that they give us insights into the deeper meaning of life. It should be noted, by the way, that myths were always inseparable from ritual. Because myths deal with the sacred, they must have rituals that set them apart from ordinary, everyday existence. That's why, even today, in our "rational" world we have Masonic, patriotic, and club rituals. The "loyal orders" of Elk, Moose, Beaver, the swearing in of presidents and the like, must have rituals to indicate that something special is in the making apart from ordinary life. Myth without ritual is incomplete.

But myth has died in the West. Gradually, as modern civilization advanced, mythology declined. Reason, exalted by the Greeks and adopted by Western civilization, triumphed. Truth was gradually narrowed down to what was demonstrated and demonstrable, a devastating diminishment. The genius of technology was that it freed people from dependency and elevated the individual. The direction was always forward. Bigger, better, faster, and more efficient became the watchwords. We dealt with "facts," not stories. Modern heroes would be the technological and scientific geniuses of the day: Edison, Brawn, Ford, Carnegie, Jobs, Gates. Their heroic counterparts would be those who had the ability to conspicuously enjoy the fruits of their genius: celebrities. We were taking control over nature, even over human life to an astonishing degree. The modern rational technology could provide (at least for the developed countries and the wealthy) endless possibilities of comfort, speed, embryonic wonders, cosmetic surgery, gender change. However, what rational and efficient technology has been unable to do is provide human beings with a sense of significance, the very stuff of mythology. And that lack became acutely felt as the events of the twentieth century shook technological confidence: the sinking of the unsinkable Titanic, two world wars, Auschwitz, Bosnia, Hiroshima, 9/11, Iraq, deep corruption in politics, corporate life, sports, church. It turns out that the benefits of travel and global communications have also brought terror. We don't know how to react because we have lost touch with our mystical, spiritual roots.

Filling the Vacuum

Storyless, we have lost our dreams of transformation. As one author put it, we are suffering from a collective depression. In the economic realm, for example, recent surveys show workers sense a deep pessimism because wages have not kept pace with inflation. They work longer hours, and, in a weightless, computer society, company loyalty has disappeared (*New York Times*, August 3, 2006). There is growing violence in our cities, gang warfare, the spread of AIDS, broken homes, ecological deterioration, and terrorism. The drug trade's profits are second only to those of the oil trade. The poor of our planet are sucked into the criminal economy. As Ian Linden writes in *A New Map of the World* (2003, p. 51), "Preyed on by criminal, military, and political elites, the poor supply our world with primary products, oil, minerals, cheap skilled labor, bodies and body parts, narcotics, and the fantasy of the exotic and the frightening. And in turn they are supplied with weapons, cigarettes, alcohol, surplus food, and aid." One-sixth of the world's population lives in extreme poverty. For many, money has become the point of everything, the ultimate goal of human striving. The old story used to warn about injustice to the marginal and about gaining the whole world and losing one's self, but it's a story seldom told in a society where greed is glorified.

The New Narrative

Well, it's not exactly true that we are storyless. We do in fact have a new mythology, a new mega-story that has replaced the old Judeo-Christian classical one. The name of this defining story is called "consumerism," technology's colorful child. It has flowered into global brand names that are the glue and logo of a self-proclaimed society. Today our references, metaphors, and meaningful symbols are those concocted and promoted through the media by the global corporations. Our identities are found no longer in our attachment to the local community but in our levels of ability to master media language and images, consume well, and to be connected to like-minded consumers. What really connects us is our consumption: our Armani suits, Gucci handbags, Gap jeans, mega-mansions, and multiple cosmetic surgeries that announce what we are, who we are, and where we are on the global community's pecking order.

Our mobility has produced communities of the like-minded. We have retreated into shelters of uniformity. We no longer live in neighborhoods where we rub shoulders with all sorts of people and have to negotiate our lives around those we do not like. Now we move into gated communities of like-minded people of the same economic background, people who think like us, dress like us, talk like us. We walk with, associate with, travel with the same people in our class group.

Our consumption identifies our global community. Community in fact has been replaced by identity: "I am a Calvin Kline, BMW, twelve-year-old Scotch, jet-setting kind of a guy. I identify with all others who share my brands." As David Lyons says in his book *Jesus in Disneyland*, "identities are constructed through consuming. Forget the idea that who we are is given by God or achieved through hard work in a calling or a career; we shape our malleable image by what we buy." Indeed, corporate life and consumerism have seamlessly merged. Drugstores sell not only drugs but merchandise. Gas stations have a mini-mall or a McDonald's attached to them. Airports are lined with stores. Movies house fast food chains. There is almost no place where one cannot shop. There is nothing that is not marketable from human eggs to body parts, from baby naming to sports. Comedian Mort Stahl summed it up years ago when he said, "Ask a Californian who he is, and he points to his car."

Brands, the canonization of successful consumption, are like the ubiquitous tattoos marking who's in and who's out. Brands provide both targets and identity. They are the triumphant banners of the capitalist mentality. We have no identity, it appears, other than the brand of clothes we wear. Our bodies have become part of the corporate image of advertising.

Consumption as a way of life and as the messaged measurement of success inevitably produces large inequities. The enormous wealth of the few—we in America pay our CEOs (even those who fail their companies) 475 times the salary of the average worker—is in sharp contrast to the great majority of citizens. Four hundred of the richest Americans have an annual income of $69 billion in comparison with the $59 billion which is the combined income of 161 million inhabitants of Botswana, Nigeria, Senegal, and Uganda. Eight million people a year die of just being poor, while others are unbelievably rich. We live in a new liquid world where people and capital are transferred by a click of a computer key. All you need is a laptop to make money. Companies like Nike do not even own cumbersome factories or employ workers. They let other people do that for them. What they do own are the brand names. Corporations no longer need capital and money. No, they need consumers who have the money. So they strive to cultivate what is called LTV, Lifetime Value, which is a brand relationship with consumers until they are dead. We saw in Chapter Four how corporations strive to train infants to recognize brand names and so ensure loyalty from an early age. For many, in a world of transitory relationships, the brand name often becomes the nearest thing to stability. Note how the sight of a McDonald's in a foreign country gives us a sense of security, of belonging.

Celebrities, whom we idolize, are simply italicized brands, ideals of what we hope to own, what the rest of the world hopes to be. Thus *U.S. News & World Report* featured on its cover for May 1, 2006, "SuperShoppers: How Yuppie Consumers in China and India Are Transforming the World Economy." The article announces: "Spending Spree: They're young. They have money to burn. And the race is on to win them as consumers." They are (or soon will be) branded kin to others of the same brand around the world. Consumerism is the story that defines them. More and more our market economy, not the Bible, provides the filter through which we look at the world.

Consumption as Narrative

The consumer society encourages limitless desire and its typical addiction is shopping. In fact, we do not go shopping as much as take part in a retail drama. Our malls are places of entertainment, fantasy, and virtual reality. Advertising, consumerism's handmaid, has the job of making us go on desiring, never being satisfied, always needing more, always hankering after the "latest," lest we be left behind. We are constantly told of desires we never knew we had. Advertising almost completely breaks the link between goods and their real purpose. So a car is no longer only a means of getting to work, but a means for attracting women or racing across deserts or making your peers envious. It is, as they say, a "statement": "Look how cool and successful I am and (if you are driving the tank-like, gas-guzzling Hummer) how rich and powerful. Out of my way." My $50,000 Rolex watch is not to tell time. It is to announce my status. Thus advertising's success: it has broken the link with reality. We are all consumers. Advertising is our prophet. Brands are our nationality. Consumption is our story.

And that story is often dark. Listen to the misogynist lyrics of rappers. Watch the banality of television. Walk into any art gallery and see images of nihilism and bawdiness incapable of projecting us to a higher meaning. Take note of the names of the most popular rock groups: System of a Down, Dragon Force, Disturbed, Avenged Sevenfold, Bullet for My Valentine, the Dead Kennedys, the New Pornographers. Read the novels that portray our aimlessness and confusion. The depleted media have no stories left to tell except those of violence, recreational sex, and consumption. Two-thirds of the world is struggling to stay alive, and the other third is preoccupied with accumulating and hoarding wealth. (Headline in my morning paper: "Poor Nutrition Kills Millions of Kids Yearly.") We have become a mind without a story soul.

We have opted for "facts" and abandoned the search for the meaning behind them. Indeed, some have declared (especially those in universities) there is no meaning. Creation, the world, life are all absurd. We have abandoned the imagination and become "rational."

This is even true of religion. We wonder why so many are leaving the faith. It's because we no longer tell the story. Religion has become focused on words, propositions, theological precisions, and ideological statements; it has plunged into literalism and generated catechisms, not stories. In the process it has lost sight of the story that sustains and nourishes it. Religion has tried to capture Jesus and define him, all the while forgetting that Jesus told stories that by definition are open-ended, elusive, subversive, and resistant to definition. We have forgotten our very reason for existence: to be at the call of the higher story. In what could be construed as an insightful critique of the sad state of our religious education, Walter Wangerin, Jr., writes:

> Religions do exist without doctrine and theologies; but no religion has ever existed without a story at its core, not as an illustration of some doctrine, but rather as the very truth, the evidence and the testimony of God's action for the sake of the

believers. But a story that goes untold lacks life. It becomes a puzzle to be solved by intellectual analysis alone. And a religion whose story is untold likewise lacks life.

For if we never have, by means of the sacred story (the gospel), experienced the presence, love, activity of our Christ, then we will fall back upon lesser experience; we will fulfill our natural need of religious experience with mere sentimentalities and silly diminishments of God. And so our religion, too, will be diminished. ("Making Disciples by Sacred Story," *Christianity Today*, February 2004)

Do we read or tell cautionary stories anymore, much less pointed Jesus stories? We should. We must remember, embrace, and retell these stories with as much fervor as our consumerist culture seeks to excise, subvert, and compromise them. Reflect on this story, "The Fisherman and His Wife."

Once upon a time, there was a fisherman who lived with his wife in a tiny hut by the sea. Every day he went fishing; and he fished and he fished. Well, one day he sat for a long time catching nothing, until his line suddenly jerked violently. He drew it up and there was a very large fish who said to him,

"Fisherman, I beg you, let me live, for I am an enchanted prince turned into a fish."

The fisherman said, "Why not? Any fish that can talk deserves to be tossed back." And so he did.

Then the fisherman got up and went home empty-handed. His wife said, "You have caught nothing today? What shall we do? We shall starve! Oh, you're a lazy, good-for-nothing lout!"

But the husband replied, "Yes, I did catch one fish who was an enchanted prince, so of course I let him go."

"Let him go!" exclaimed the wife. "Let him go? Why did you not make a wish? You have no sense at all."

But the fisherman said, "But what would I wish for? I am happy."

"What would you wish for?" his wife replied. "I'll tell you what to wish for. I'm sick and tired of living in this rundown shack. You go back and tell the fish we want a cottage. Surely he will do that, since you let him go. Now hurry."

So the fisherman betook himself down to the sea, which was calm and smooth, and called out, "Fish of the sea, listen to me. My wife has a wish to make of thee." And the fish came swimming to him and asked what she wanted, and the fisherman replied, "A cottage."

"All right," said the fish. "Go back home. You live in a cottage."

When the man got back home his wife was no longer in the hut but in a lovely cottage with flowers outside and a bench to sit on. "Oh," said the fisherman, "this is really quite nice. We shall indeed be quite content here the rest of our lives."

"We shall see," replied his wife.

One week later she said, "Husband, this cottage is getting far too small for us. Go back to tell the fish that I want a mansion."

"But," protested her husband, "this cottage is just fine. I can't go back so soon and ask for something else."

"Indeed you can," snapped his wife. "Go, and go right now!"

The fisherman's heart grew heavy and he went back to the sea, which was getting rougher, and he called out again, "Fish of the sea, listen to me. My wife has a wish to make of thee."

The fish came up to shore and said, "What does she want this time?"

"She wants to live in a mansion," the fisherman said.

"All right," said the fish. "Go back home. You live in a mansion."

And the man went back home and he could hardly believe his eyes. There was the loveliest mansion with great fireplaces and gorgeous rugs and splendid furniture. "Oh," he exclaimed to his wife, "this is beautiful. Now we shall be happy."

"We shall see," she said.

Two weeks later his wife said, "Husband, this mansion will not serve any longer. Go back and tell the fish that I want to be queen! And I want to live in a castle!"

"Oh my," said the horrified fisherman, "I couldn't do that. He's already given us so much. He might get angry. I don't really think I can do that."

"But you can and you will," said the wife. "You go back and tell the fish that I want to be queen and live in a castle. And do it now!"

So the poor fisherman betook himself once more to the sea, which was churning with purple and dark green water with heavy clouds overhead, and he called out, "Fish of the sea, listen to me. My wife has a wish to make of thee."

The fish appeared and said, "What does she want now?"

"Alas," said the man, "she wants to be queen and live in a castle."

"All right," said the fish. "Go back home. You live in a castle and she is queen."

The fisherman went back home and there was a giant stone castle with servants and horses. The trumpeters announced his arrival, and he was ushered into the great hall where there was his wife—a queen! She had on a gold crown and a gown of rubies, and a throne made of ivory inlaid with jewels. "Oh," he said, "this is magnificent! This is beyond our wildest dreams. We live in a castle, and you are a queen. Now we will be happy."

"We shall see," said his wife.

Three weeks later his wife said, "Husband, go back and tell the fish that I want to be pope!" The husband was thunderstruck. He was speechless. "What are you standing there for? Go, do as I say."

"But I couldn't do that," he pleaded. "No—this is really quite beyond reason...I mean...."

But she interrupted. "And I mean that you should do as I say. After all, I am the queen, and you must obey."

And so the poor fisherman, bent low, went back to the sea, which by this time was dark and nasty with deep green currents and the winds blowing ominously overhead. He called out over the brewing storm, "Fish of the sea, listen to me. My wife has a wish to make of thee."

The fish came up to the shore and said, "Now what does she want?"

"She wants to be pope!" cried the poor fisherman.

"All right," said the fish. "Go back home. She is pope."

And he went back home and he saw that the castle had been turned into a huge cathedral. He entered and saw prelates of all kinds filling the place. There were hundreds and thousands of candles lit, and kings and emperors were on their knees kissing the hem of his wife's robe, for now she was the pope! He approached, bowed, and said, "Oh wife, now you are the pope. You cannot become anything greater now. Now we will be happy."

"We shall see," she said.

Four weeks later she said to her husband, "Husband, go back to tell the fish that I want to be ruler of the earth and the sun and moon and the stars. I want to be empress of the universe!"

The fisherman said, "No, I cannot and will not do this. It's impossible. I just can't!"

But his wife badgered him day and night, screamed at him, and drove him to such distraction that he gave in.

Once more he went down to the sea, which by this time was a cauldron of wild waves. Thunder and lightning were sounding overhead, and the rain was pelting the sea and the ground mercilessly. He called out, "Fish of the sea, listen to me. My wife has a wish to make of thee."

And the fish came up and said, "Well, what does she want now?"

The poor fisherman shouted over the storm, "She wants to be ruler of the heavens and the sun and the moon and the stars. She wants to be empress of the whole universe!"

"No!" shouted the fish. "And you go back home and you will find your wife in your tiny hut by the sea and there you shall live hand-to-mouth until you die."

So he went back home. And there was the hut as the fish said. And there they lived until they died.

Giving a nod to the striking metaphor of an increasingly angry sea and setting aside the stereotype of the wife as shrew, see the story as a parable of the essence of advertising: the perfect product will bring you perfect happiness—until the next new and improved product. The cycle endlessly escalates and ultimately goes nowhere. Only at the end does one realize that living by bread alone has left one eternally hungry.

This is pretty heavy stuff, but story is serious and that seriousness is the hidden subtext of this book, the subliminal plea to use and stretch the imagination, to break free of the consumer story and embrace the Jesus story as a truth that will make us free.

Telling Our Story

By definition, Christians are supposed to be countercultural—not better than others but rather being a kind of mild irritation, an annoying dissonance to society because they insist on living by another story. They are called, as Saint Paul would remind them (Phil 3:20–21), to belong to a holy commonwealth that is distinct from the consumerist regime of this age. They are to be church, a communion of saints for preaching, teaching, sacrament, prayer, and service. Alas, the truth is that Christians today are indistinguishable from the culture. Every poll shows that we live, marry, divorce, abort, watch television, consume, and social climb like everyone else in the country. We are part of the suburban sprawl that celebrates individual autonomy, choice, entertainment, and efficiency. We're captivated by the same obsessions as everyone else: individualism, therapy, and sentimentalism.

Still, Christians are those people who see, or should see, differently. As Robert Barron declares:

> Christianity is, above all, a way of seeing. Everything else in Christian life flows from and circles around the transformation of vision. Christians see differently, and that is why their prayer, their worship, their action, their whole way of being in the world, has a distinctive accent and flavor. What unites figures as diverse as James Joyce, Caravaggio, John Milton, the architect of Chartres, Dorothy Day, Dietrich Bonhoffer, and the later Bob Dylan is a peculiar and distinctive take on things, a style, a way which flows finally from Jesus of Nazareth.

Rabbi Harold Kushner also reminds us, "Religion is not primarily a set of beliefs, a collection of prayers, or a series of rituals. Religion is first and foremost a way of seeing." Religion is, in our context, a way of living out a peculiar story, one different from the glitzy and attractive story of consumerism.

Holy Unease

Fortunately there are always people who keenly feel a "holy unease" in a one-dimensional culture. One such person was Francis of Assisi. Another was Thomas Merton, and countless others have identified with his experience. They have felt the insufficiency of "what most people take for granted" and have heard the call to fullness of life, a call beyond the agenda of a world out of kilter. And they have reacted as Augustine did to the story of Saint Anthony: with astonishment "to hear of the wonders God had worked so recently, almost in our own times."

One of these modern people is James Martin, a young American Jesuit priest, whose memoir, *In Good Company*, describes his own "fast track" from the corporate world to a life rooted in the traditional monastic vows of poverty, chastity, and obedience. Although he was raised as a somewhat nominal Catholic, his youthful ambitions were unaffected by any religious concerns. He was seeking success, which meant a high-powered job and tons of money. So he enrolled in the prestigious Wharton School of Business. By the time he was in his mid-twenties he was well on his way to success: a junior executive at General Electric, he was rapidly climbing the corporate ladder. Yet eventually he found himself confused and unhappy. As he wrote, "Simply put, I couldn't figure out the point of what I was doing with my life. Something basic was missing....Is this life?"

Martin was disturbed by the cold and impersonal atmosphere of the corporate workplace. He was upset by the callous "downsizing," the constant pressure to make the quarterly "numbers." Was this what life was all about? He began to increasingly feel that his life had "no real order, no real purpose, and no real meaning." At Mass one Sunday he heard the same gospel story that had once struck Saint Anthony: Jesus' invitation to the rich young man to sell all that he had and "come, follow me." Inevitably Martin identified with the young man in the story. "That was me," he reflected, "a rich, young (and depressed) man."

A turning point came one day when he happened to see a documentary on public television about the life of Thomas Merton. He had never heard of Merton. Yet something in this story, some sense of a greater reality, a more abundant life, captured his imagination. So the next day he bought a copy of Merton's autobiography, *The Seven Storey Mountain*. What he read corresponded powerfully with his own experience. "Thomas Merton seemed to have struggled with the same problems I did: vanity, false ambition, careerism. The more he confessed his shortcomings, the more I felt the urge to listen to what he had to say and the more resonance I felt."

A strange impulse, at first mysterious, but increasingly irresistible, began sounding within him: the thought that he would like to become a priest. He tried pushing this thought away. But underneath there was a growing certainty: "I wanted to live the kind of life that Thomas Merton lived—even though I didn't much understand it. I wanted to feel the calm that he felt when he entered the monastery."

In the end he found that calm not by living the life that Merton lived, or Saint Augustine, or Saint Anthony, but in his own way, as a Jesuit, living in a world that was "charged with the presence and reality of God." Robert Ellsberg, another example, was moved by the example of Dorothy Day, became a Catholic, married, is the father of three children, and finds his spiritual fulfillment in his work as a writer. These people recognized the false promises of a false story. They tapped into a different story, the story of the one who emptied himself and took on the form of a slave.

The Challenge to the Young

Still, we must sympathize with the young of today who have it tough. Today's prominent cultural voices tell them at every turn that religion—its story and rituals—is a private, subjective matter. These voices preach to them that, apart from science, there is no objective truth. Moreover, the young are reminded that for society to work we must be tolerant, and so one religion is as good as another. Any exclusive conviction, any claim to truth, is shameful.

Second, it is a well-known sociological fact that religion, like so much else, is socially transmitted, especially from the family and the significant persons of one's life. But with so many broken homes and high mobility, any convictions ingested have no time to take root before they are battered by diversity and political correctness. Besides, if you are born into a religion, it's considered a random accident. You could just as well have been born into another religion.

Third, there is the popular "I am spiritual but not religious" mantra. Needless to say, the young are impervious to any warning that any unmoored spirituality runs the risk of insufficient institutional challenge or direction. You don't have to rub shoulders with people you don't like. You can make up your own mind. There are no outer demands, checks, or balances. The recent Army recruiting slogan catches it well, "I am an Army of One." A perfect mantra for the vaunted individualism and "self-actualization" that dominate society. That can be dangerous.

The young, as we have noted, are brought up without an appreciation of story. They do not see the complex connection between story and truth, between faith and truth. They are raised on unchallenged presumptions; religion, though helpful for some, is purely a subjective matter. Its truths cannot be proved scientifically. Religion belongs to the private sphere. And so on. On the other hand, science is objectively demonstrable and based on universal principles.

These are really questionable presuppositions. Truth is not confined to science, and the young must learn what we have tried to point out in this book: that truth also resides in other modes. Water is made up of hydrogen and oxygen and a Samaritan rightly helping a Jew are truth claims of a very different order, but that does not diminish the validity of either. The laws of gravity and the story of Tanzan and Ekido in Chapter One are truth-telling of a different order.

Truth comes in different ways, in different dress. The prejudice of the modern world has hoodwinked many by imposing on story, especially the religious story, a scientific burden of proof it was never meant to carry.

One plus one is two is true. So is "The Stolen Skin."

We have now, dear readers, come to the end of this book. We will sign off as we began: with an appreciation not only of the value and power of story but also of our instinctive status as "storytelling creatures." To remind us once more of that truth, here is the tale of "Joseph the Tailor."

Joseph was such a good tailor. He was always busy. He always had work to do. And he never had time to work on his own clothes. Now he wore an overcoat every day to work. His wife, she hated the coat. Now one day, while Joseph was working, he looked down and he noticed that at the edge of his coat, it was frayed. There were holes at the bottom. He said, "Sarah, look, my favorite coat is ruined."

She thought to herself, "Now is my chance." And very quietly she said to him, "Joseph, why don't you take the coat and THROW IT OUT."

"Why should I throw it out? After all, I am a tailor." And he took it off and he cut and he snipped, he stitched and he sewed, and he made himself a little jacket to wear on cool evenings.

But time went on and suddenly there was a rip in the sleeve of the jacket, and he said, "Oh, Sarah, look, my favorite jacket is ruined."

She thought again, "Now is my chance." And very quietly she said, "Joseph, why don't you take the jacket and THROW IT OUT."

"Why should I throw it out? After all, I am a tailor." And he took it off and he cut and snipped, he stitched and he sewed, and he made himself a fine vest.

But time went on and suddenly there was a rip in the pocket of the vest. "Oh, Sarah, look, my favorite vest is ruined."

"Joseph, please take the vest and THROW IT OUT."

"Throw it out? Why should I throw it out? After all, I am a tailor." And he took it off and he cut and he snipped, he stitched and he sewed and made himself a long scarf he wore to the synagogue on Friday nights.

But, you know, time went on and suddenly that frayed as well. There were holes in it, and he said, "Sarah, look, my favorite scarf is ruined."

"Joseph, please, take the scarf and THROW IT OUT."

"Throw it out? Why should I throw it out? After all, I am a tailor." And he took it off and he cut and he snipped and he stitched and he sewed, and he made himself a fine necktie.

He wore it to a wedding, but he was a sloppy eater. He got spots all over it. When he came home, he looked at the tie and said, "Ooo, Oooo, my new tie is ruined."

"Joseph, if it's ruined, please take the tie and THROW IT OUT."

"Throw it out? Throw it out? Why should I throw it out? After all, I am a tailor."

He took it off and he cut and he snipped and he stitched and he sewed and made himself a fine handkerchief. He wore it around his neck when he would eat, but I told you he was a sloppy eater. One day he looked at the handkerchief and said, "Oooo, Oooo, this is disgusting. I can't use this handkerchief anymore. Sarah, it's ruined."

"Joseph, please, take the handkerchief and THROW IT OUT."

"Throw it out? Why should I throw it out? I told you, I'm a tailor." And so he took it and he cut and he snipped, he stitched and he sewed and made himself a fine button. He wore it on his trousers to hold his suspenders.

But one day he lost the button. He couldn't find it anywhere. He went looking through the whole house. It wasn't there. "Oh, Sarah, I lost my favorite button."

She smiled at him. "Ah, Joseph, today I'm a happy woman because there is one thing I'm sure of in this world and that one thing is that you can't make something out of nothing."

"What? Not only am I a tailor, but I'm also a storyteller." And he took a pencil and he wrote down this story I'm telling you, proving that you can make something out of nothing!

Credits and Notes

Though some stories are factual, all stories are true.
<small>STORYTELLING AXIOM</small>

Every attempt has been made to give proper credit to the marvelous authors of some material in this book. The sources for the quotes from books and magazines are straightforward and easy. The sources for the stories, however, are considerably less so. The problem is that the stories have gone through so many mutations over so many years, if not centuries, and through so many hands, that it is difficult to know whose versions they are.

Perhaps, unsurprisingly, I can illustrate the problem with a delightful story.

> There was once a king who considered himself a great and clever king. He would proudly stroke his long beard and proclaim, "Ah! I am a clever king! To demonstrate my cleverness, I invite anyone to challenge me with a riddle or puzzle to solve."
>
> One day, this king received a package containing three dolls and a challenge that read: "O King, if you are as great and clever as you maintain, please be so wise as to tell the difference between these three dolls." The king announced: "Aha! I am a great king and a clever king, and I shall easily solve this

little riddle." So the king stroked upon his beard and hummed to himself as he studied the three dolls: "Hum-hum-hum, hum-hum-hum, hum hum-agh!" He pulled upon his beard in frustration, for he could see no difference between the dolls. The three dolls were exactly alike, in every form and feature, down to the minutest detail. "Aha!" thought the king. "I am a great king and a clever king. And it is said that a great king will keep a wise man nearby to help him solve his problems. I have such a wise man."

Then he called for the wise man. The wizened old wise man hobbled into the court. Leaning upon his staff, he bowed before the king. "Majesty, in what wise matter may I be of service?" "Wise Man," said the king, "I have before me three dolls, exactly alike. What is the difference between them?" The wise man bent to examine the dolls. After a great deal of consideration, the wise man thought to tell the king this matter was not worth his time. He thought to tell the king many other things, too, but finally he wisely said nothing. For it is wise to keep your thoughts to yourself, especially in the presence of a powerful monarch. The king sent the wise man away.

"This wise man is of no use to me," thought the king. "He is too shrewd. But I am a great king and a clever king, and it is said that a great king will sometimes listen to the counsel of a fool. For a fool will rush in where wise men fear to tread. I have such a fool."

Then he called for the fool. The fool indeed rushed in, slapped the king merrily upon the back and said, "Hiya, King! How ya doin'?"

"Fool," said the king, "I have three dolls exactly alike. What is the difference between them?"

The fool did not listen. He saw the three dolls and only thought to play with them. "Whee! Dollies! Let's play pretend! Let's pretend we're going on a picnic!"

But before the fool could have much fun, the king sent him away. "This fool is of no use to me," thought the king, "for this fool is a fool! But, I am a great king and a clever king, and it is said that a great king will retain a storyteller. For the tellers of tales carry in their stories many words of wisdom." He called for the storyteller.

Into the court came the storyteller, bowing low with a great flourish. The storyteller began to speak at once. "Majesty, how may I serve you? A fable, perhaps? Or a recitation of the glorious deeds of your greatness in verse and song? Or perhaps..."

"Enough," commanded the king. "Storyteller, don't get started. Today I have a riddle."

"Ah! Such as the riddle of the Sphinx?" the storyteller interjected. "Or the riddle of the little man who spun straw?"

"Precisely!" The king held up his hand to keep the storyteller from speaking further. "Now listen: I have three dolls exactly alike. You are a teller, can you tell the difference between them?"

The storyteller studied the three dolls briefly and exclaimed, "Majesty, you cannot see any difference between these dolls!"

"I have already determined that myself," groaned the king.

"Majesty," said the storyteller, "if you cannot see a difference between these dolls, the answer must be much like the story of the three caskets: their outward show is greatly different from that which they contain. Likewise, the differences between these three dolls must be within."

"Ah, very good," said the king. "But how can you show these differences?"

"Majesty, there must be many ways to reach inside a person. However, the one way with which I am most acquainted is through the ears. If you will permit me." The storyteller reached up and plucked a hair from the king's beard.

"Ow!" exclaimed the king. "How dare you?"

"Forgive me," begged the storyteller. "But as you shall see, it was most necessary."

He then lifted the first of the three dolls and began to thread the king's hair into the doll's ear. The hair went in and in and in the doll's ear until it was gone. "Majesty," said the storyteller, "this doll must be a wise one. What it hears, it keeps to itself!"

"Very good," said the king. "And what of these others?"

"If you will permit me," said the storyteller, and again he plucked a hair from the king's beard.

"Ow!" winced the king.

Now the storyteller lifted the second doll and began to thread the hair into its ear. The hair went in and in and in. But as he was threading the hair in one ear, it came out the other.

"Majesty, this doll is obviously a fool: what goes in one ear comes out the other."

"Very good," said the king. "And this last one?"

"If you will permit me."

"Ow!"

Once more the storyteller plucked a hair. Lifting the third doll, he began to thread the hair into its ear.

The hair went in and in and in. It did not come out the other side, but it did not stay altogether in either. For as he was threading the hair into the doll's ear, it came slowly out the doll's mouth.

"Majesty, this doll is a storyteller: what it hears, eventually it tells."

The king looked at the three dolls. "Storyteller, you have solved this riddle. But I see you have given me a new riddle to consider. For when you put the hair in the doll's ear, it is a straight hair. Yet, when the hair comes out the doll's mouth, it is all curled. Why?"

"Majesty," said the teller, "no storyteller worth his salt will ever tell a tale exactly as he heard it. We must always add a special curl of our own devising in the retelling of the tale!"

That's a story from India and is David Holt's and Bill Mooney's version found in a book they edited, *Ready to Tell Tales* (August House, 1995). But not all sources are that clear or certain. There are so many "curls!" And so, if I have used someone's version without attribution, it is quite by accident and a notice to the publisher will ensure proper credit in future reprints.

With that said, we proceed to each of the chapters.

Chapter One: The Seven Basic Plots

This first chapter and half of the second, plus a few scattered parts in the rest of the book, are dependent on Christopher Booker's book *The Seven Basic Plots* (Continuum, 2004). It is his topical outline and some of his words that I gratefully use and freely acknowledge. His is a big book of over 700 pages.

The excerpt from Lenny Bruce at the beginning of the chapter has been censored. (I said he was crude: I changed his phrase "whacking the shit out of us" to "whacking the crap out of us" and his "breaking our balls" to "busting our chops.")

"The Soul-Taker," like so many stories in this book, is an old story of many versions in many different parts of the world. One often sees the same basic story in local or national idioms, so reworked and upgraded that it's hard to tell its real source. I think this particular telling might be from Megan McKenna. The same may be said of "The Beggar."

For the persistence of the combat myth, see Walter Wink's fascinating *Engaging the Power* (Augsburg Fortress Press, 1992), where he analyzes its presence in modern literature and pop culture.

"The Green Cap" version comes from Pleasant DeSpain in his collection, *Thirty-Three Multicultural Tales to Tell* (August House, 1999).

Chapter Two: Tellers, Types, and Techniques

The metaphor samples used in this lecture are culled from *Metaphors We Live By* by George Lakoff and Mark Johnson (University of Chicago Press, 2003).

In July 8–11, 2006, there was an international meeting in Padua, Italy, of more than 400 Catholic ethicists. John Allen interviewed Rev. John Mary Waliggo of Uganda, a widely influential theologian. Rev. Waliggo remarked that Western theology has lost some of its creativity and he spoke of the African theology of remembering as akin to the Exodus story and then went on to say this:

> Our theological style is very concerned with narrative, express-
> ing teaching in story. Our people listen better when you give
> them a story. This means using local expressions and rituals,
> linking the gospel to their story. Everything is brought into

story, the animals, the plants, the whole environment. It's a way of doing theology that's almost dead in the West, but it's very biblical.

When will the church in the West learn: "Story first, catechism second"?

Chapter Three: The Healing Power of Stories

"The Baal Shem Tov" story is retold by Belden C. Lane on his tapes, *Storytelling: The Enchantment of Theology.*

"Am I a Man Yet?" is from a story by Don Doyle that appeared in *Storytelling Magazine* (March/April 2001).

The retellings of "The Stolen Skin" and "The Lady of the Lake Waters" are by Allison Cox who specializes in storytelling and healing. She is a storyteller, therapist, editor, and an author in *The Healing Heart* books and in the Healing Story Alliance's journal, *Diving in the Moon: Honoring Story and Facilitating Healing.*

The Ananias story is John Shea's inimitable version.

The half story about the Jews can be found in *Because God Loves Stories* by Rabbi Tsvi Blanchard, edited by Steve Zeitlin (Touchstone, 1997).

The Tommy story is the now classic tale authored by Rev. John Powell, S.J., from his book *Unconditional Love* (Tabor Publishing, 1978).

In this chapter I didn't mention forcefully that stories can give us redirection in our crosses, losses, and sicknesses, and that stories effectively show us the significant difference between curing and healing. Ram Dass, an American spiritual teacher in the Hindu tradition who suffered a debilitating stroke in 1997, makes the distinction well:

> While cures aim at returning our bodies to what they were in the past, healing uses what is present to move us more deeply to soul awareness....Although I have not been cured of the effects of my stroke, I have certainly undergone profound healings of mind and heart. In other words, healing, which refers to the soul, can happen without cure, which refers to the body. In fact, it is often in the uncured sickness that the healing begins.

In his poem, "Fever," John Updike, in an almost playful way, repeats this wisdom:

I have brought back a good message
from the land of 102 degrees:
God exists. I had seriously doubted it before;
but the bedposts spoke of it with utmost confidence,
the threads in my blanket took it for granted,
the tree outside the window dismissed all complaints,
and I have not slept so justly for years.
[Yes] it is truth long known, that some secrets are hidden from
health.

He's right. Some patients report a greater sense of being alive and in communion with others when they were sick. When they were cured, they returned to normal life, a life often characterized by numbness and rote obligation. Cure of the body actually threatened healing of the soul. This was the case with a man by the name of Fred. He was diagnosed with terminal cancer. After an initial period of distress, he says, "Something amazing happened. I simply stopped doing everything that wasn't essential, that didn't matter." His terminally ill life became vital and peaceful. But the doctors changed their mind. He was not terminally ill. He had a rare but curable disease. "When I heard this over the telephone," he said, "I cried like a baby—because I was afraid my life would go back to the way it used to be."

Chapter Four: Stories and the Moral Lives of Children

The quote from Joseph A. Califano, Jr., is found in "A Weapon in the War on Drugs: Dining In" (*The Washington Post*, October 19, 1998).

A good book worth looking into in this whole area of consumerism and media is Tom Beaudoin's *Consuming Faith: Integrating Who We Are with What We Buy* (Sheed & Ward, 2007).

Concerning parents and their kids, I add these statistics without prejudice: seventy-three percent of mothers with school-age children work outside the home. Nearly one-fourth of all children under age eighteen live with a single parent, and only seven percent of school-age children live in a household where there is only one wage earner. Almost all public elementary schools teach drug and sex education, with more than half starting in kindergarten. (It is significant to recall that public education is a monopoly.) Teachers have reluctantly taken over parental roles and report that parents most driven professionally can be the least helpful at school and readily pull their kids out of school for ski trips and the like. An educator named Peter Buttenheim calls some of these "Designer Parents" who are obsessed with the end product of education rather than the process. Within our context, all this means that most of the formative stories are not coming from parents but from surrogates who may or may not share their values.

In slightly more than two years, the Internet site MySpace has gone from zero users to tens of millions. Here kids and teens "express themselves" to countless known and unknown people in cyberspace. They express their thoughts, communicate with strangers, and visually display themselves in various stages of dress and undress. They are basically advertising themselves. Police are alarmed, calling MySpace a "predator's buffet," and warn parents to monitor their kids' online activity. Whether it's good or bad remains to be seen. But MySpace and sites like it are basically self-generating stories. An eye-opening book on pornography is Pamela Paul's *Pornified: How Pornography Is Transforming Our Lives, Our Relationships, and Our Families* (Times Books, 2005).

The reader might be interested in the work of Sr. Rose Pacatte, FSP, the director of the Pauline Center for Media Studies in Culver City, California, and film columnist for *St. Anthony Messenger Magazine*. With Peter Malone, MCS, she is the co-author of the series *Lights, Camera...Faith! A Movie Lover's Guide to Scripture*. They are helpful in discerning the hype from the solid, in discerning the question behind the question. Check also Jesuit Richard Leonard's book *Movies That Matter: Reading Film through the Lens of Faith* (Loyola Press, 2006). Yes, Hollywood produces movies and television shows that dismiss human dignity and exploit the body, movies of mindless violence and vengeance, because it is a business and will make anything that sells. On the other hand, Hollywood does make movies that matter, such as those mentioned in the text. More recently, *The Constant Gardner* makes us aware of social teaching and globalization. *Hotel Rwanda* gives a searing portrayal of human suffering and heroism. Nor should we dismiss significant movies like *Erin Brockovich* simply because the heroine dresses indecently.

An account of scientists working to change behavior through story rather than commands or directives can be found in Alan Deutschman's article "Making Change" (*Fast Company*, May 2005).

The précis of "The Velveteen Rabbit" has been aided by the work of Vigen Guroian's book *Tending the Heart of Virtue: How Classic Stories Awaken a Child's Moral Imagination* (Oxford University Press, 1988).

Chapter Five: Stories for the Second Half of Life

"The Magic Towel" and "Fortune and the Woodcutter" are from Allan B. Chinen's *In the Ever After: Fairy Tales and the Second Half of Life* (Chiron, 1989).

The versions of "Edith and Bessie" and "The Bribe" probably come from Megan McKenna.

The leader of the futurists and trans-humanists is the genius Raymond Kurzweil, recipient of many awards, inventor of technological marvels, and author of many books on technology as a way of achieving immortality. He claims that our biological evolution is about to be made obsolete by our fast-moving technological revolution.

The quote from Wendell Berry is from his essay, "Quantity vs. Form" in his book *The Way of Ignorance and Other Essays* (Shoemaker and Hoard, 2006).

"How Death Became Life" is from Catherine de Hueck's *Not Without Parables* (Ave Maria Press, 1977).

"Death Comes for the Aunt" is from Arthur Gordon, *A Touch of Wonder* (Fleming H. Revell/Baker Book House, 1974).

A good book for this section is *Growing Old in Christ*, eds., Stanley Hauerwas, et al. (Eerdmans, 2003).

The reflection from Sr. Margaret Dorgan, DCM, can be found in *The Living Pulpit* (April–June, 2006).

Chapter Six: Stories for the Spiritual Journey

The remarks from William Willimon are from his homily notes, "Pulpit Resources," April 10, 2005.

The source for Nicholas Leman's remark is *Time Magazine* (March 6, 2006). The source for the size of Harvard's paychecks is from Mortimer Zuckerman's editorial in *U.S. News & World Report* (April 10, 2006).

In my remarks in no way do I imply a return to "the good old days." The sharing of worship and ministry are too valuable a development to be either denied or suppressed. I argue, rather, for a marriage between the best of the Catholic imagination and the best of an open church. Our empty pews and failure to capture the next generation are daily evidence that a less sensuous Catholicism in the twenty-first century has not yet become that compelling to a generation awash in imagery.

The Bruce Springsteen accolade comes from Jim Cullen, who is the author of *Born in the USA: Bruce Springsteen and the American Tradition* (Wesleyan University Press, 2005).

"The Christopher" version is John Shea's.

"The Very Pretty Lady" is from *The Devil's Storybook* by Natalie Babbitt (Farrar, Straus & Giroux, 1984).

"Maum Jean" is from Arthur Gordon's book *A Touch of Wonder* (Revell, 1996).

"The Tin Box" is from the always engaging Ed Hayes from his book *Twelve and One Half Keys* (Forest of Peace Books, 1981).

Chapter Eight: Stories That Challenge

"The Sacrifice Flower" is from Sr. Jose Hobday's book *Stories of Awe and Abundance* (Sheed & Ward, 1999).

"St. Mungo" and "St. Alexander" are from Joan Windham's marvelous collections, *Sixty Saints for Boys* and *Sixty Saints for Girls* (Continuum International Book Publishing, Ltd., 1999.)

Bibliography

Saints exist in and through their stories.

KENNETH WOODWARD

Concerning children's literature in modern times, there have been three revolutions. The first, instigated by John Locke, demanded that children's education be reformed by getting it out of the hands of dominating clergy. Scripture was out, for it was not suited to the child's capacity. Forget the denominational jingles the kids had to learn. Stories should be more humanistic, secular, and rational, and kids would learn their morals from that.

In the late nineteenth century, the second revolution occurred as the emphasis moved away from moralizing toward entertaining fantasy. Lewis Carroll was prominent in this school of thought. Fantasy celebrated the innocence and the playfulness of children. They were to be free of the worry and grief of adults.

Then came the third revolution, beginning in the 1970s, for by then kids had much to worry about. The envelope was pushed further and further until, for example, the publication of the painfully politically correct *The Norton Anthology of Children's Literature: The Traditions in English* (W.W. Norton, 2005), which, as the editors say, "can deal with sex, violence, disease, and death—in particular because many of them believe that the innocence of childhood has been destroyed by the media and the commodification of childhood." Since the lines between adulthood and childhood have been blurred, the editors continue, children's literature must use "frank and provocative language to depict and discuss social problems such as homelessness, drug addiction, abuse, terrorism, and expanding notions of family to include nontraditional families led by single parents, stepparents, and gay and lesbian parents."

Thus appeared the much endorsed *The Facts of Life* by Jonathan Miller with its "pop-up penis," *Heather Has Two Mommies* by Leslea Newman, and Lia Block's *Wolf,* a take-off on Little Red Riding Hood. Here the heroine is the victim of a rape by her mother's boyfriend, whom she kills with a shotgun at Granny's house. (We can't get more current than that.) The editors comment that this "story shows how a young girl can take charge of her life, while at the same time exposing the sadomasochistic ties that exist in many dysfunctional families."

Then, too, there's the racy teenage market such as the *The Gossip Girl* and *The A-List* series (on bestseller lists), whose characters go clubbing, drinking, smoking marijuana, and, of course, having lots of sex. As one of the Gossip Girl books has it, "As they kissed, she couldn't help but think that sex with Dan might be a whole lot more meaningful than it had been with Clark." As the owner of a bookstore in Greenwich said, "I had a thirteen year old in here yesterday with her mother, and she didn't want anything but sex, drugs, and rock 'n roll." The series mentioned is intended for fourteen-year-old girls and up, but it's hard to keep them from the fourth and fifth graders. As another bookseller commented, "Reading *The Princess Dairies* is passé; it's not racy enough." (The sources for these commentaries are from Dorothea Israel Wolfson's review in the *Claremont Review of Books,* Summer, 2006, and *The New York Times,* August 20, 2006.)

We've come a long way from Nancy Drew and the Hardy Boys! Like all literature, today's racier books assume and promote a value system and offer symbols and metaphors for believing and living. Parents need to be alert. Don't worry too much about that Norton anthology by the way. It weighs a couple of pounds, is nearly 2,500 pages long, and costs a hefty $76.70. Besides its deeply secular bias, these are reasons enough to shun it.

Here are sounder suggestions. Besides the works listed in this text, these suggestions are hardly exhaustive. There is so much material available, including a very good overview of the importance of storytelling in Amy E. Spaulding's *The Wisdom of Storytelling in an Information Age* (Scarecrow Press, 2004). Also worth getting is *Telling Tales: Storytelling in the Family* by Cecila Barker Lottridgre, Gail De Vos, and Merle Harris (University of Alberta Press, 2003).

In addition to the books listed in Credits and Notes, here are other valuable resources:

Dancing with Wonder: Self-Discovery through Stories by Nancy King

Gently Grieving: Taking Care of Yourself by Telling Your Story by Constance M. Mucha

Feeling Good: The New Mood Therapy by David Burns (on depression)

You Just Don't Understand: Women and Men in Conversation by Deborah Tanner

Relationship Rescue: A Seven-Step Strategy for Reconnecting with Your Partner by Phillip C. McGraw, Ph.D.

Spirit to Heal: A Journey to Spiritual Healing with Cancer by Michael Torosian and Veruschka Biddle (on forgiveness)

Healing Wounded Emotions: Overcoming Life's Hurts by Martin H. Padovani

The Yellow Brick Road: A Storyteller's Approach to the Spiritual Journey by William J. Bausch (stories that heal)

The gospels

Bible Stories That Speak to Our Heart by Charles M. Wible

Story Resources for Children

First confer with the librarian in your Catholic school or public library for suggestions. Also seek out publishers like August House, which publishes wonderful folktale books for children of all ages (PO Box 32233, Little Rock, AR 72203). Get on their mailing list.

Also seek out Joan Windham, whose books are truly delightful, for example, *Sixty Saints for Boys* and *Sixty Saints for Girls*. They are out of print, but you can get them on the Internet.

Other suggestions:

Children's Bible, edited by Thomas J. Donaghy. Lots of stories and good illustrations.

A Child's Bible by Shirley Steen and Anne Edwards

Great Men and Women of the Bible by Marlee Alex, Anne de Graaf, and Ben Alex

The Children's Book of Virtues, edited by William Bennett

The Moral Compass: Stories for a Life's Journey, edited by William Bennett

The Boy Who Ran with the Gazelles by Marianna Mayer

Zen Shorts by Jon J. Muth

Haunted Halls of Ivy: Ghosts of Southern Colleges and Universities by Daniel W. Barefoot (for adolescents)

Astonishing Tales of Spiritual Truth: Gripping Stories Based on the Sayings of Jesus by Steven James (for adolescents)

The Ugly Ducking by Hans Christian Andersen

The Velveteen Rabbit by Margery Williams

Where the Wild Things Are by Maurice Sendak

Rocking-Horse Land by Laurence Housman

Little Daylight: A Fairy Story by George MacDonald

The Selfish Giant by Oscar Wilde

The Reluctant Dragon by Kenneth Grahame

The Trumpet of the Swan by E.B. White

Charlotte's Web by E.B. White

The King of the Golden River by John Ruskin

The Wonderful Wizard of Oz by L. Frank Baum

A Wrinkle in Time by Madeleine L'Engle

The Chronicles of Narnia by C.S. Lewis

The Little Prince by Antoine de Saint-Exupéry

Alexander and the Terrible, Horrible, No Good, Very Bad Day by Judith Viorst

The Children's Book of Saints by Louis Savory

Loyola Kids Book of Saints by Amy Welborn

Saints and Angels by Claire Llewellyn

Saintly Tales and Legends by Lois Rock

Mischief and Mercy: Tales of the Saints by Jean McClung (older children)

Saints Alive: Stories and Activities for Young Children by Gayle Schreiber

Echo Stories for Children: Celebrating Saints and Seasons in Word and Action by Page McKean Zyromski

Saints for Kids by Kids by Robert Charlebois, et al.

Bedtime Stories of the Saints: for Little Ones by Frank Lee

Little Book of Saints (Vol. I) by Kathleen M. Muldoon

Midlife and Death

Once Upon a Midlife by Allan B. Chinen

Lament for a Son by Nicholas Wolterstorff

This Incomplete One: Words Occasioned by the Death of a Young Person, edited by Michael D. Bush

Death and the Rest of Our Life by John Garvey

General Collections

The Complete Grimm's Fairy Tales

The Oxford Book of Modern Fairy Tales

The Classic Fairy Tales, edited by Maria Tater

Favorite Folktales from around the World, edited by Jane Yolen

Best Stories from the Texas Storytelling Festival from August House

An Indian grandfather shared this wisdom with his grandson. He told his grandson that we have two wolves inside us who struggle with each other. One is the wolf of peace, love, and kindness. The other is the wolf of fear, greed, and hatred.

"Which wolf will win, Grandfather?"

The wise man replied, "Whichever one you feed."